CARL E. BRAATEN is pastor of Lutheran Church of the Messiah, Minneapolis, Minnesota, and instructor of theology, Luther Theological Seminary, St. Paul.

Born of missionary parents in 1929, Dr. Braaten spent the first sixteen years of his life in Madagascar. A graduate of St. Olaf College, Northfield, Minnesota (B.A.), Luther Theological Seminary (B.Th.), and Harvard Divinity School (Th.D.), he has also studied at the University of Paris (Fulbright Scholarship), the University of Minnesota, and the University of Heidelberg, Germany (Sinclair Kennedy Traveling Fellowship from Harvard).

ROY A. HARRISVILLE is associate professor, Department of New Testament, Luther Theological Seminary, St. Paul.

A graduate of Concordia College (B.A., *magna cum laude*), Luther Theological Seminary (B.Th.), and Princeton Theological Seminary (Th.D.), Dr. Harrisville did post doctoral work in the University of Tübingen, Germany, under a fellowship from the Lutheran World Federation.

Dr. Braaten is editor and Dr. Harrisville associate editor of the new theological journal *Dialog*, a co-operative effort of younger Lutheran theologians.

*Kerygma
and History*

KERYGMA
and HISTORY

A SYMPOSIUM ON
THE THEOLOGY OF RUDOLF BULTMANN

Selected, Translated, and Edited by

CARL E. BRAATEN
and
ROY A. HARRISVILLE

New York   ABINGDON PRESS   Nashville

KERYGMA AND HISTORY

Copyright © 1962 by Abingdon Press

Library of Congress Catalog Card Number: 62-9383

SET UP, PRINTED, AND BOUND BY THE
PARTHENON PRESS, AT NASHVILLE,
TENNESSEE, UNITED STATES OF AMERICA

ACKNOWLEDGMENTS

Special acknowledgment is made to the following who have granted permission for the translation of copyrighted materials listed below: "Rudolf Bultmann's Interpretation of the Kerygma" by Eduard Ellwein, "Historical Criticism and Demythologizing" by Ernst Kinder, and "Bultmann's Philosophy and the Reality of Salvation" by Walther Künneth. Translated from *Zur Entmythologisierung, Ein Wort Lutherischer Theologie,* edited by Ernst Kinder and first published by Evangelischer Presseverband für Bayern, by permission of the authors.

"Myth and Gospel" by Regin Prenter. Translated from "Mythe et Evangile," *Revue de Theologie et de Philosophie,* by permission of the author.

"The Problem of the Historical Jesus" by Nils Alstrup Dahl. Translated from *Kerygma und Dogma,* by permission of the author and Vandenhoeck & Ruprecht Verlagsbuchhandlung.

"Myth and Gospel: A Discussion of the Problem of Demythologizing the New Testament Message" by Günther Bornkamm. Translated from *Theologische Existenz Heute,* edited by K. G. Steck and G. Eichholz, by permission of Chr. Kaiser Verlag.

"The Earthly Jesus and the Christ of Faith" by Hermann Diem. Translated from *Sammlung Gemeinverständlicher Vorträge und Schriften aus dem Gebiet der Theologie und Religionsgeschichte* by permission of J. C. B. Mohr (Paul Siebeck).

CONTENTS

7

ONE

CARL E. BRAATEN

A Critical Introduction

Dr. Hans-Werner Bartsch[1] in his supplement to the third
edition of *Kerygma und Mythos* (Vol. I) bitterly complains that the
debate on demythologizing which began as a fruitful conversation has
ended in a heated controversy. The earliest phase of the conversation
grew out of the context of the *Bekennende Kirche* through whose crises
Rudolf Bultmann had been a leading and courageous participant.
Among the earliest voices opposing Bultmann were those of Julius
Schniewind and Helmut Thielicke. Both of these theologians, however, acknowledged the theological legitimacy of the issues which
Bultmann raised in his essay "New Testament and Mythology" and
concurred with Bultmann that no serious preacher of the gospel or
theologian of the Church could afford to ignore them. Furthermore,
they carried on their discussions with Bultmann as a conversation taking place within the Church, recognizing that both sides had the same
goal in mind, despite whatever differences there might be in approach.
Bartsch feels that the conversational mood dominating the early phase
yielded, unfortunately, to a polemical temperament. Bartsch refers to
a number of statements circulated by bishops and synod officials to
pastors and congregations warning them against a new liberalism, but
omitting any specific mention of Bultmann's name. But what was intended was clear to everybody. They had Bultmann's theological position clearly in mind. Bartsch feels that progress in the debate was

[1] Dr. Hans-Werner Bartsch is the editor of *Kerygma und Mythos*, appearing in
five volumes of essays on the demythologizing debate. He has also written numerous
articles in Church periodicals and theological journals on kerygma and history, not
only moderating the discussions but on the whole aligning himself on the Bultmannian side of the controversy. His sermons, *Die Anrede Gottes*, have manifested a

arrested when an "official" Lutheran voice was raised against Bultmann in the debate, with the deplorable effect of pronouncing Bultmann's position *extra ecclesiam*. Bultmann was now no longer regarded as a venerable teacher and theologian *of* the Church, but as an outsider advocating a modern *Weltanschauung*. Theologians of the Church could still carry on the demythologizing debate—only not *with* Bultmann as a co-participant but *against* Bultmann as an outsider. This is what Bartsch bemoans, for what theologian wishes to be in such an unenviable position? The consequence, then, is that genuine concerns are suppressed and driven underground, rather than brought into the free atmosphere of discussion. While the latter method may keep the Church in constant tension and acute anxiety, the former can only shore up dishonesty and guilt feelings later to erupt in perhaps worse form—"and the last state of that man becomes worse than the first" (Luke 11:26).

I believe that Hans-Werner Bartsch takes an overly pessimistic view of the actual situation. While the intervention of ecclesiastical officialdom cannot solve the problem for theologians on a theological level, it is the responsibility of the elected leaders to take notice of the effects of theological tendencies upon the pastors and teachers of the Church. Bartsch is perhaps right in quarreling with the particular way in which they reacted to the situation, but he over-evaluates the effect which the official statements had upon the theological levels of discussion. The debate has gone on, and that not only in the form of sheer opposition to Bultmann. No circular could by official fiat arrest the development of an issue which is coextensive with the history of Protestant theology since the Enlightenment. As the Tübingen theological faculty made explicitly clear in its brochure entitled *Für Und Wider Die Theologie Bultmanns*, "Bultmann is not the *cause* but rather the *symptom* of a crisis." Bultmann's theology has opened up a wound in a painful way, but he did not create the wound, nor did he ever claim to be able to cure it by himself. Rather, he appealed to our whole generation, and even generations to come, to face up squarely to a complex of problems, all of which are united in their bearing upon the mission of the Church to preach the authentic kerygma in a manner which our modern age can understand.

---

consistent application of the principles of Bultmann's interpretation and exegesis of the New Testament.

10

The demythologizing debate has not been confined to German universities. The English edition of the symposium on *Kerygma and Myth* in its earliest phase was received in 1953. Since that time a broader foundation for understanding the debate has been laid for English readers through the translation of many writings by Bultmann and on Bultmann. Especially noteworthy is the edition of Bultmann's earlier writings, *Existence and Faith*, edited by Schubert Ogden. The editors of this new symposium, *Kerygma and History*, have felt the need for a companion volume to the early symposium, one that takes cognizance of the shift in the focus of the debate from myth to history. Those who have followed the demythologizing debate in German know that the problem of the relation of kerygma to history has superseded, to a large extent, the earlier discussion of the mythological elements in primitive Christian preaching. From the perspective of a later stage in the debate, it can now be more clearly seen that what caused such alarming offence in theological circles was not the discovery of mythical deposits in the New Testament—for Bultmann was not the first to point this out, nor did he himself wait until 1941 to make it known—but rather the negative implications which Bultmann drew from his research regarding the historical basis of the kerygma. Therefore, it was not so much the demythologizing of the New Testament as such, but rather the dehistoricizing of the kerygma which implicitly was impelling the debate all along. Of course the categories of kerygma, myth, and history cannot be separated, though they can be differentiated, and the focus can shift from myth to history.

The question of how the concepts of kerygma, myth, and history relate to each other has met with the most varied responses. The immediate conservative reaction to Bultmann's suggestions argued that myth and history are mutually exclusive concepts, that there are no mythical elements in the Bible, and that the framework of the New Testament kerygma, the picture of the world (*Weltbild*), is not mythological in any sense. H. Sasse and E. Stauffer took this position. The biblical records are historical in the strictest, shall we say positivistic, sense of the word. Other conservative theologians, however, took quite the opposite view. The concept of myth, properly defined, is not alien to the New Testament, Christian faith, and theology. With Regin Prenter they would find it necessary to speak of a "Christian mythology" as inherent in the Christian manner of speaking about God and

God's acts in history. For them myth and history do not erase each other; both may and must be maintained in speaking of the specifically Christian view of God's saving revelation. In this sense we may speak of God acting in history, but the communication of this act and of its intrinsic meaning requires myth as a genre of linguistic discourse. To eliminate myth is to eliminate God from our language. Yet, while such different approaches in the evaluation of myth could take place, both would insist on retaining the full force of a *historical* revelation, and thus from different approaches they meet in their criticism of Bultmann's concept of history. To reduce history from the New Testament kerygma is to minimize the significance of Jesus for our faith. Does Bultmann do this? That is the question which all the theologians writing in this volume are concerned to discuss.

Three of the essays in this volume originally appeared together in *Ein Wort Lutherischer Theologie Zur Entmythologisierung,* edited by Ernst Kinder. These are the essays by Eduard Ellwein, Ernst Kinder, and Walter Künneth. All three are systematic theologians in Neuendettelsau, Münster, and Erlangen respectively. The title of this book had the unfortunate, and certainly unintended, consequence of giving the impression that here we might find the definitive judgment of Lutheran theology on Bultmann's demythologizing program. Hence, the position presented in this book played into the hands of Church administrators who were eager for a prompt settlement of the issues, and also provided the occasion for Friedrich Gogarten's spirited attack against the official theology of the Lutheran Church in *Demythologizing and History.* Kinder and company thus found themselves caught in an unhappy squeeze. Certainly, a fair reading of these essays will discredit the impression created by Gogarten's book that these theologians are blind stooges of an official theology. As Kinder said in a rebuttal of Gogarten's treatise, they simply spoke their piece, as they had to, without being responsible for whatever any Church official might wish to do with it.

However, if it was ever hoped that a united Lutheran front could be formed against Bultmann by the position taken in *Ein Wort Lutherischer Theologie,* a big disappointment was soon forthcoming. From various quarters came the insistence that Bultmann's main concerns are germane to Lutheran theology and, in fact, are only conceivable on that basis. An impressive array of witnesses came forth to remind the Lutheran theologians that they cannot so easily come to terms with Bultmann, but must recognize that Bultmann's program has its roots deep in Lutheran soil. Even Bultmann's impulse to radicalism in theology—e.g. his use of biblical criticism (literary, historical, and form criticism), his definition of faith and of the *pro me* orientation of the kerygma, his *theologia crucis,* his christocentricism, the law and gospel dialectic, justification by faith alone, his preference for John's Gospel over the Synoptic Gospels, and his preference for the Pauline epistles over the others, also his interest in hermeneutics, can be understood out of his Lutheran heritage.[2]

To extend this line of discussion a bit further, we might call attention to a few of those who interpret Bultmann as a consistent, or better, a radical Lutheran. The strongest case has been made by Gerhard Gloege, systematic theologian at Jena, in *Mythologie und Luthertum,* where he views the problem of demythologizing in the light of Lutheran theology. He argues that the basic hermeneutical principle guiding Bultmann's biblical exegesis is Lutheran in origin and advises those critics who summarily reject Bultmann's approach to reconsider whether their own theology still remains within the Lutheran structure of thought. Gloege proposes the idea that Bultmann's basic motif is rooted in Luther's distinction between law and gospel. Bultmann's distinction between mythology and kerygma is completely commensurate with the Lutheran distinction between law and gospel, in the sense that in both instances the intention of the former—i.e. mythology and law—is interpreted as a servant of the latter—i.e. kerygma and gospel. Bultmann inquires into the intention of the mythology to discover the kerygma just as Luther inquired into the meaning of the law to set off the gospel. Both of them were thoroughly governed by the criterion of *"was Christum treibt."* Gloege is far from accepting Bultmann's theology as such. He proceeds to discuss many issues with Bultmann, but his criticisms are kept within

[2] How Schubert Ogden in his introduction to *Existence and Faith* could overlook these basic motifs in Bultmann's thought is to be wondered at. Rather, he makes out of Bultmann a kind of existentialist deist, chiding Bultmann for having, inconsistently and unnecessarily, retained the claim "that it is *only* in this event (*viz.* Jesus Christ) that God's final judgment and redemption are so revealed as to make an authentic human existence factually possible." This stress of Bultmann on the *sola* is allegedly contrary to his "intended meaning" and "is inconsistent with most of the content of his theology as well." A more complete misunderstanding of Bultmann could not be imagined. If Bultmann's real intention and chief concern

the framework of the basically Lutheran dialectic between law and gospel.

The statement issued by the theological faculty of the University of Tübingen, *Für Und Wider Die Theologie Bultmanns,* asserts that Bultmann narrows down his exegesis to the central theme of the New Testament, which without doubt is the doctrine of justification through faith alone. Bultmann's interpretation of Paul is in many respects a faithful representation of the deepest intentions of Lutheran theology, only in a completely different language. That this is felt to result in a tremendous reduction of the biblical contents should be no cause for alarm. It was felt to be so by the Roman Church of the sixteenth century, when Luther made the doctrine of justification through faith alone the whole summary of the gospel. The Tübingen faculty suggests that Bultmann stands in a similar position today. The basic insights of the Reformation come to provocative expression in Bultmann's insistence on the closest correlation between saving event and faith, and only in this way can we speak of justification through faith alone, apart from the works of historical science and apart from a *sacrificium intellectus.*

It is significant that Bultmann understands his own theological endeavors in the light of the justification principle. He says:

> Our radical attempt to demythologize the New Testament is in fact a perfect parallel to St. Paul's and Luther's doctrine of justification by faith alone apart from the works of the law. Or rather, it carries this doctrine to its logical conclusion in the field of epistemology. Like the doctrine of justification it destroys every false security and every false demand for it on the part of man, whether he sees it in his good works or in his ascertainable knowledge. The man who wishes to believe in God as his God must realize that he has nothing in his hand on which to base his faith. He is suspended in mid-air, and cannot demand a proof of the Word which addresses him. For the ground and object of faith are identical. Security can be found only by abandoning all security, by being ready, as Luther put it, to plunge into the inner darkness. Faith in God means faith in justification.[3]

is over a dialectical theory of God and the world, and Christology enters in as a misplaced afterthought, no serious theologian would have to waste two minutes on Bultmann *qua* theologian. Though as a philosopher of religion he might possibly still be of interest to theologians as a Jaspers or a Whitehead. But theologians have been taking Bultmann seriously now for several decades because of his clear intention to explicate the meaning of the New Testament kerygma that Jesus is Christ and Lord, and the goal of his interpretation is homiletically oriented.

[3] *Kerygma and Myth,* ed. H. W. Bartsch, tr. Reginald H. Fuller, pp. 210-11.

14

The Roman Catholic reaction to this intramural Protestant controversy also views Bultmann as a consistent disciple of Luther. Bultmann's ultimate theological principles are derived from the standpoint of the Reformation. (The fifth volume of *Kerygma und Mythos* reports the discussions taking place within Roman Catholic theology on Bultmann's demythologizing project.) One of the curious developments in the debate is this: Those who without any question pass muster in the public view as spokesmen of Lutheran theology take little or no notice of these referrals of Bultmann's deepest theological intentions to the Reformation heritage. They do not meet squarely the argument that Bultmann's program is on principle legitimate from the standpoint of the inner theological dialectic of law and gospel. They begin their case against Bultmann from particular negative details in his theology—e.g., Bultmann doesn't believe in miracles, virgin birth, empty tomb, second coming, et cetera—failing to distinguish therefore the programmatic principles of theology from incidental doctrinal decisions. In Bultmann's theology, it would seem, the latter are not always necessarily deduced from the former. The offence which the details have caused has apparently prevented many theologians from taking Bultmann's formal proposals seriously and has obscured the real connection of Bultmann's theology with the central principle of justification in Reformation theology.

This does not mean that the first three essayists, Ellwein, Kinder, and Künneth, who contributed to *Ein Wort Lutherischer Theologie,* have not touched on some salient deficiencies in Bultmann's theology. They share the common conviction that the threefold dimension of history in the kerygma—past, present, and future—has been collapsed to the unidimensional present tense realized in the act of proclaiming the kerygma here and now. They fear lest the kerygma which Bultmann has in mind become self-grounded and self-perpetuating without real continuity with the historical facts upon which the New Testament kerygma is founded. They discern a divorce between fact and act, substance and meaning, *extra nos* and *pro nobis,* in Bultmann's definition of the kerygma. Here they rest their case upon a real incarnation, which does not first happen spiritually or verbally in the kerygma, but *corporeally,* even physically and sarkically, in history in the objective sense of the term. That is their basic concern and, I think, the basic concern of evangelical theology as such. Their critical

15

inquiries into other areas of Bultmann's theology, such as Bultmann's appropriation of an existentialist system of categories, his radical form-critical research, and his view of the modern man, are relatively subsidiary to their argument that Bultmann dehistoricizes the kerygma. A kerygma which does not proclaim redemptive events which happened in history, and especially in the history of Jesus Christ, is no longer the authentic kerygma of the New Testament. It becomes a vacuous form without materially saving content.

How does the contemporary believer gain access to the historical content of the kerygma? How is the objective historicity of the redemptive events proclaimed in the kerygma to be guaranteed unto faith? On this issue the authors of *Ein Wort Lutherischer Theologie* (Ellwein, Kinder, and Künneth) seem to waver to and fro on the methodological question of how faith gains access to the historical basis and content of the kerygma. On the one hand the historical facts in question are said to be objective in the sense that they may be ascertained and established by scientific historical methods, while on the other hand the redemptive occurrences are supposedly accessible as such only to faith. Now, which is it? Friedrich Gogarten singled out these methodological ambiguities as the basis of his attack upon what he called "the official theology of the Church." This attack set off a series of polemical exchanges between Kinder and Gogarten.[4]

Gogarten's main thesis is that the whole demythologizing debate concerns a new concept of history, historicity, historical thought and method, which not only is to be found in variant forms in Troeltsch, Dilthey, Heidegger, and Bultmann, but is also the one which stems originally from the Scriptures and, of course, also from Luther. It presents a totally different way of conceiving of revelation, history, and faith from that of the metaphysical tradition of theology in the old Church, dominated as it was by Hellenistic categories. Kinder's response argues that the modern idea of history may find a place within theology, but it cannot assume the exclusive role of pontificating to theology what it may or may not say in its own way. Theology cannot

---

[4] Ernst Kinder made three replies to Gogarten's book *Demythologizing and History*. (1) "Die Verbindlichkeit des neuzeitlichen Geschichtsdenken für die Theologie," *Evangelisch-Lutherische Kirchenzeitung*, No. 24, 1953. (2) "Das neuzeitliche Geschichtsdenken und die Theologie," *Luthertum*, vol. 12, 1954. (3) "Die 'Geschichtlichkeit' des christlichen Glaubens," *Evangelisch-Lutherische Kirchenzeitung*, No. 15, 1955.

bind itself to a uniform method, however modern it may be, since theology is primarily guided in its interpretation of the Scriptures by the needs and experiences of the Church. Nor does the so-called modern idea of history solve the problem of kerygma and historical facts; it merely circumvents it. The upshot of this discussion, it seems to me, is that Gogarten has not eased the restiveness of theologians on the question of kerygma and history, of the history which the New Testament has elevated into the kerygma, while his opponents have not attained a clear concept of theological reality, and a consistent methodology calculated to grasp that reality. Furthermore, they were led aside by Gogarten down a blind alley, where the focus of the debate was shifted from the inner theological dialectic of law and gospel, which they consequently never confronted, to a modern concept of history, which no one yet seems to understand.[5]

Besides the essays by Ellwein, Kinder, and Künneth we present five others by Lutheran theologians who approach Bultmann's theology from quite different angles. In fact, none of them would fit precisely into the scheme of argumentation presented in *Ein Wort Lutherischer Theologie,* especially in respect to two issues: (1) They give a higher evaluation to the role of the historical-critical method in theology, and (2) they do not recoil from the recognition of myth in the New Testament, though they do not unambiguously accept Bultmann's definitions.

In respect to the latter issue Dr. Regin Prenter [6] points out inconsistencies in Bultmann's attempt to demythologize, caused by Bultmann's striving for a third point of view between orthodoxy and liberalism. Prenter does not feel that Bultmann can succeed in demythologizing, for a real demythologizing would entail the elimination of myth. Even Bultmann must hold on to a residuum of myth when he speaks of God's act in Christ. When Bultmann responds that he does not intend

[5] James Robinson in *A New Quest of the Historical Jesus* proposes that the new quest has to its advantage a new concept of history, but how this new concept helps the historian discover or establish historical facts, or solve a strictly historical problem, e.g. the messianic self-consciousness of Jesus, we are never told. Now, it seems, we have additional problems: What is the new concept of history, and what do we do with it?

[6] Dr. Regin Prenter, systematic theologian at the University of Aarhus, Denmark, is already well known to English readers for his *Spiritus Creator,* a study of Luther's doctrine of the Holy Spirit.

to eliminate the myth, but merely to interpret it, Prenter answers that he does not carry out his intention.

Next, Prenter disapproves of the implied anthropocentricism of an existentialist interpretation of mythology. The picture of God in Christian mythology cannot be accommodated to the categories of existentialist philosophy. In this way Prenter calls for a full acceptance of the biblical mythology, for mythology is the house of religion. Only by retaining mythology can religion be prevented from being transmuted into philosophy, psychology, or metaphysics. Prenter realizes that he has not solved the problem of a quest for a third point of view between liberalism and orthodoxy—but neither has Bultmann. Prenter resigns himself to a dualistic epistemology, leaving philosophy and theology to go their separate ways. We would ask two questions about Prenter's essay: (1) If we accept the idea of a Christian mythology, is it still not necessary to make clear distinctions between myth as the appropriate expression of faith's concerns and myth as a primitive view of the world and spiritual phenomena, and therefore between a literal and a symbolic interpretation of Christian mythology? Would not the undifferentiated acceptance of biblical mythology lead possibly to an uncritical biblicism, which simply believes without understanding? (2) Can we dispense with existentialist categories so easily since Bultmann at least has demonstrated their applicability in the interpretation of the New Testament? Perhaps we should be reminded again that *abusus non tollit usum*. We would be better advised not to allow the *existential* mode of interpretation to acquire a monopoly on the presuppositions and categories to be used in theology. They do however help us in understanding the biblical view of man and history—simply because the first-century man is not so utterly different in his *existentiell* self-understanding from the twentieth-century man.

Günther Bornkamm's [7] and Nils Dahl's [8] essays may be viewed to-

---

[7] Dr. Günther Bornkamm is professor of New Testament at the University of Heidelberg. He is the first among the disciples of Bultmann to have written a book on Jesus of Nazareth, now available in English translation. His essay *Myth and Gospel* has enjoyed three printings and has been widely quoted by other critics, generally in an approving manner. He speaks with the authority of one who knows Bultmann's thought from within, and therefore his criticisms of Bultmann are felt to be fair and soundly based on firsthand knowledge.

[8] Dr. Nils Dahl is professor of New Testament at the University of Oslo.

18

together. As New Testament scholars it is not surprising that these theologians evaluate more positively the function of the historical-critical methods for theological work. Recognizing that these methods were born in the era of liberalism and were refined especially by liberal scholars, they do not thereby confuse the methods themselves with a liberal Christianity. One of the weaknesses in the essays by the dogmaticians (Ellwein, Kinder, and Künneth) is apparent in their reluctant acceptance of the profane methods of historical research and their confusion of the historical-critical school with liberalism as such. The critical method has nothing in principle to do with liberalism, since some conservative scholars accept it as readily as any. Bornkamm and Dahl are both committed as scholars to the most scientifically developed techniques of research and, in general, carry on the line of criticism which runs from Wrede and Wellhausen to Dibelius and Bultmann. They see no hope of returning to the pre-critical evaluation of the Gospels as historical source documents, but rather accept the insight of Martin Kähler and the Form Critics that the Gospels are primarily the documents of the preaching which established the Church. They represent the theology of the Church, rather than a historical record of objectively certifiable events. Furthermore, they advocate a completely profane historical method of research, rather than a religious historical method based on the presuppositions of faith. They would not understand what kind of method that would be. This does not rule out a dogmatic-exegetical approach, but the latter cannot determine beforehand the results of the former. On this point there is a noticeable cleavage between the approaches of the systematic and biblical theologians today, a situation which in the opinion of Ernst Käsemann has reached the critical point. Each discipline carries on its own labors in relative isolation from the other.

A good example of the New Testament and systematic disciplines riding on two separate rails is the present-day renewal of the quest of the historical Jesus. The need for a new quest originated among New Testament theologians in Germany, and paradoxically, under the aegis of Bultmann's leading disciples, Günther Bornkamm, Ernst Käsemann, and Ernst Fuchs. Nils Dahl also believes that the new quest is both theologically permissible and relevant, not absolutely but relatively. It is not essential to the being of faith, but to the well-

19

being of theology. This conviction that we need to resume the quest, and that it is historically possible and theologically relevant, has not been shared to the same extent by the systematic theologians. Karl Barth has for his part expressed himself as hopelessly indifferent to it. None of the systematic theologians to my knowledge has demonstrated any great enthusiasm for the new "Jesus of history" movement.

It is by no means accidental that the appeal for a new quest of the historical Jesus has arisen within the Bultmann school. First, it has never been overlooked that Bultmann himself wrote a monograph on Jesus, despite his continual insistence that there is no good theological reason why we should need to penetrate behind the kerygma. Secondly, Bultmann's disciples have begun to be uneasy about the possibility of a docetic kerygma, one which emerges out of a shadowy historical background.

Ernst Käsemann has been the most articulate in calling for a re-examination of the problem of the historical Jesus. For him the new quest is a matter of "inescapable theological necessity" in order to become assured of a basic continuity between the kerygmatic Christ and the historical Jesus. No longer is he satisfied with the formula that we do not need to penetrate behind the kerygma for its foundation in history. Käsemann justifies his demand by two observations: The earliest evangelists at least believed that the Christ they preached was none other than the earthly Jesus, and our own faith itself requires confidence in the identity of the earthly Jesus with the exalted Lord. Günther Bornkamm holds the same viewpoint. Faith permits and historical science requires an independent putting of the historical question (*historische Fragestellung*).

This new research will undoubtedly force systematic theologians to take another look at the problem of revelation and history, and no doubt dialectical theology with its solution will come in for more careful scrutiny. Yet, when all this is done, where will we have been brought by the new quest? Will we not be methodologically in the same kind of situation which prompted Martin Kähler to turn against the old quest with passionate vigor? [9] The same reasons which directed Kähler to oppose the old quest can be revived and restated with equal

[9] We refer to Martin Kähler's attack on the "Life of Jesus" movement of the nineteenth century in *Der sogenannte historische Jesus und der geschichtliche biblische Christus* (1896).

relevance a propos the new quest. While the methods of research have undergone a critical evolution and the summary of assured historical results has become, if anything, more meagre, the issues as regards the faith and preaching of the Christian Church remain the same. While the meaning of the new quest requires an exhaustive treatment,[10] we would like to raise several questions by way of suggesting its inherent limitations. Can the historian *qua* historian establish the continuity of the kerygma with antecedent history on purely historical grounds? Can the threat of a docetic, mythological kerygma be overcome in the fires of historical criticism? Kähler thought it nothing less than naïve or preposterous for the historian to establish the ground and the content of faith. Is this not precisely what the modern historians are attempting, however, when they set out to establish a continuity or identity between the earthly Jesus and the post-Easter Christ of the kerygma? What more do we get for all the effort than a highly problematic *fides historica,* a fluctuating magnitude upon which the historians themselves cannot agree, and therefore an unsure foundation for faith's point of departure? These questions radicalize the present-day cleavage between New Testament and systematic theology, for the leading systematic theologians are neither asking nor expecting the New Testament theologians to establish the essential point of continuity between Jesus and the kerygma. Käsemann is right to this extent: The question of the continuity he has in mind is an "inescapable *theological* necessity." Every Christian knows this, but in the nature of the case the historian will not be able to make good on his promise to penetrate behind the kerygma to guarantee its continuity with history and thereby to legitimize objectively faith in Jesus Christ.

A careful reading of Bornkamm's book *Jesus of Nazareth* in the light of his essay "Myth and Gospel" will illustrate, I believe, how a historian changes over to theological categories when he is at the end

---

[10] Cf. a Harvard University dissertation on this subject: Carl E. Braaten, *Christ, Faith, and History: An Inquiry into the Meaning of Martin Kähler's Distinction Between the Historical Jesus and the Biblical Christ Developed in its Past and Present Contexts* (Harvard University, 1959). The running dialogue in this essay, with its immanent criticisms, is based upon a systematic position unfolded in the dissertation. Unfortunately, space does not permit an exposition of the theological basis from which this critical introduction proceeds. Perhaps, by implication a good measure of that might also have been disclosed en route.

of his historical rope. Even so critical a researcher as Günther Bornkamm becomes so involved in his subject that at times he trespasses
the boundaries of a method which requires him to forget that he is
a believer. This becomes especially clear in his treatment of the resurrection. Bornkamm knows that the only accessible datum to the historian is the Easter faith of the early Church, but in his story of Jesus
he nevertheless includes a section on the resurrection, in which he
affirms not only the Easter faith, but also the Easter event. Bornkamm's
essay makes clear that for him the Easter faith is not the Easter event,
as Bultmann sometimes seems to suggest. Therefore, he tries to develop
a theological concept of reality, free from the limitations of positivism
within which both Bultmann and his critics are confined. The thrust
of his argument recapitulates the position of Martin Kähler in his
attack on psychologism and historicism. This position holds that faith
alone can penetrate the kerygma to grasp its reference to the reality
of Jesus Christ and that faith cannot be satisfied with the mere
existential significance of the kerygma apart from history, when the
very meaning of the kerygma involves history. The reality of the
saving events cannot be grasped by historical science, however, but
by faith alone. Bornkamm acknowledges this well enough, but what
is he then doing with a book on Jesus? What kind of literature is
this? Is this a portrait of Jesus drawn by a believer in the kerygma?
Or is it a purely historical-critical treatment, relating those things
which an unbeliever can also know and see in Jesus? Actually, it
would seem that his book on Jesus is a mixture of both, for when he
can no longer deal with a question in his capacity as historian, he
draws upon a theological appeal to *das Wesen des Glaubens*. His difference with Bultmann hinges upon a larger use of this appeal to the
nature of faith, which in turn drives him to enlarge upon a theological
concept of reality irreducible to the minimal perceptions of historical
reason. From this standpoint Bornkamm's book on Jesus must become
an enigma even to himself.

The significance of Hermann Diem's [11] article is that it shows his
attempt to bridge the gap between the theological and historical ap-

---

[11] Hermann Diem is a dogmatic theologian at the University of Tübingen. He
is usually referred to as a Barthian, but that he is much more than a Barthian is
evident from his *Dogmatics*, where his concessions to Bultmann and his criticisms
of Barth's monological style of solving problems are set forth.

proaches to the earthly Jesus. This interest in mediating between left- and right-wing tendencies in theology has been carried out to a greater extent in his *Dogmatics*. Diem is looking for that third point of view beyond Barth and Bultmann, and, as he puts it, "between historicism and existentialism." In his essay on "the earthly Jesus and the Christ of faith" he tries to break new ground by putting the historical and theological questions in a novel confrontation with each other. In this way he intends to suggest a solution to the methodological dichotomy which hampers theology today. He believes this can be done out of the context of a genuinely Reformation theology.

The last essay is an American entry into the discussion by Roy Harrisville,[12] who carries on what the Germans call a *Sachkritik*—i.e. a criticism of the subject from an inner material standpoint. He sees as particularly vulnerable Bultmann's concept of that new life which emerges out of the transition from inauthentic existence. The "newness" which grace effects in man does not seem to be radically immanent in the structures of human existence. No *real* change takes place in the transition. Here, then, from another perspective Bultmann is linked up with a radically objective Lutheran doctrine of justification—a purely forensic view of what takes place in justification. Harrisville brings his concern for a dynamic view of justification from his research into *The Concept of Newness in the New Testament*.

Arguing from a biblical basis he examines the effect which Bultmann's existentialist analysis and hermeneutical method have upon his view of the new righteousness and the new life of faith. The element of continuity between the old and the new is stressed by Bultmann to the suppression of the element of contrast, of radical newness and real change in man. Bultmann seems to be pressed to hold such a view on account of his desire to make room for a "natural theology" in the forecourt of theology—a *preambula theologiae*. The philosophical preunderstanding (*Vorverständnis*) of human existence thus forms the Procrustean bed into which theology must place its concept of the new man in Christ. Harrisville has here developed in detail a point which Bornkamm and Künneth also found to criticize in Bult-

[12] Dr. Roy A. Harrisville is New Testament theologian at Luther Theological Seminary, St. Paul, Minnesota. His book *The Concept of Newness in the New Testament* (Minneapolis: Augsburg Publishing House, 1960), forms the background for this discussion.

mann, *viz.*, the anthropological orientation is so severe in Bultmann that the new things in history and human existence revealed by grace, transmitted in the Scriptures, and experienced through faith in the context of the Church suffer an enormous reduction—and at times seem to evaporate altogether. Harrisville sees, however, that this criticism of Bultmann only raises but does not solve the perennial question of the relation between philosophy and theology. It would not follow that Bultmann's failure to grasp the biblical view of newness with "its attendant features of continuity, contrast, finality and dynamic" [13] must necessarily result in a total abandonment of his program. The correlation of existentialist analysis of human existence with a biblical theology of revelation is possible without loss to either side. I think that Harrisville would agree in principle with this view, else he would scarcely conclude his essay by saying that "the theology of Bultmann might well become the source and spring of a healthy tradition to follow." If this happens, not the least of the reasons will be that other Protestant scholars will discover that Rudolf Bultmann in some important respects has served the best interests of theology by radicalizing the Reformation understanding of justification by faith alone—in a new conceptuality, to be sure, and in the context of a fresh encounter of Reformation theology with modern problems.

[13] *Ibid.*, pp. 106-7.

TWO

EDUARD ELLWEIN

Rudolf Bultmann's Interpretation of the Kerygma

In *Verkündigung und Forschung* Herbert Braun writes a review of Bultmann's *Theology of the New Testament*, Volume I., under the title: "Die Überwindung des Liberalismus auf der Ebene des Kritizismus." [1] We wish to make this title our theme and ask: To what extent is liberalism really overcome in Bultmann's theology? To what extent is liberalism overcome on the level of criticism? What does the interpretation of the apostolic witness to Christ look like on this level of criticism? And what questions does it present to us?

I

In seeking to answer the first question, we must first of all realize the nature of Bultmann's concern in his interpretation of the New Testament message. From this perspective it will become clear whether and to what extent liberalism is overcome in his exegesis. Now there is no doubt that Bultmann does not intend to dissolve the kerygma of the early Church. Rather, he would like to understand it in that basic sense in which the New Testament intends it, and he would like to make it accessible to the modern man of our time. We must take Bultmann's concern here in utter seriousness—otherwise we would be improperly simplifying our task. Bultmann wants to translate the language and the world of concepts and ideas in the New Testament, which have been largely determined by the presuppositions of the ancient picture of the world, into our own language, which means into a language that is shaped—indeed irrevocably shaped—by the

[1] *Theologischer Jahresbericht,* 1949-50, fascicle 1/2, 1951.

modern picture of the world and by modern scientific thought. In doing this he does not simply wish to lay aside, throw out, remove, or eliminate the mythological ideas of the New Testament, but to interpret them "existentially." This means that he wants to discover the understanding of existence which these mythological ideas possess and strive to express, and to discover their real intentions. In precisely this way he wants to confront the modern man, for whom the mythical picture of the world is irrevocably past, with the authentic message of the New Testament and to place him inescapably before the actual scandal of the New Testament message. It does not help to present him with a mere reproduction and repetition of the ideas and words of the Bible. These must rather be transposed into our modern conceptual forms of thought. The interpreter must understand the art of ἀλλάξαι φωνήν (Gal. 4:20).[2] But that does not mean ἀλλάξαι τὸ κήρυγμα. Rather it means the following: To state in the terms of a totally different—and indeed entirely secular and demythologized—language[3] the same thing which the New Testament witnesses preached in the terms of their own time. Bultmann's concern is to have the old eternal gospel ring out in all its purity in our modern language and conceptuality. He wants to set off in bold relief the message of God's saving and redemptive action in Christ and to preach the salvation contained in Christ. By stripping the New Testament of its mythological dress, and with the aid of his existentialist interpretation, Bultmann merely wants to let the paradox of the New Testament message come fully into its own: "That is, the paradox that the eschatological emissary of God is a concrete figure of a particular historical past, that his eschatological activity was wrought out in a human fate."[4] "The transcendence of God is not as in a myth reduced to immanence. Instead, we have the paradox of a transcendent God present and active in history: 'The Word became flesh.' "[5] When Julius Schniewind says in his reply to Bultmann's decisive essay "New Testament and Mythology," that the scandal con-

[2] Julius Schniewind, "A Reply to Bultmann," *Kerygma and Myth,* ed. H. W. Bartsch, tr. R. H. Fuller (London: S. P. C. K., 1954), p. 47.

[3] Götz Harbsmeier, "Mythos und Offenbarung," *Kerygma und Mythos,* ed. H. W. Bartsch (3rd ed.; Hamburg: Herbert Reich, 1954), p. 71.

[4] Bultmann, "New Testament and Mythology," *Kerygma and Myth,* pp. 43-44.

[5] *Ibid.,* p. 44.

26

cerning the person of Jesus is what "the Christian Church has always asserted, that our salvation is One who was involved in all the relativity of history," Bultmann answers that he is in definite agreement with him. He wishes to say exactly the same thing.[6]

In this way Bultmann has in fact abandoned the field of liberalism according to the traditional sense of the term. A book such as his *Theology of the New Testament*, or better, his *Commentary on the Gospel of John* which occupies a totally unique position in the chorus of interpretations would have been unthinkable by the conventional type of liberalism. Bultmann himself characterizes this kind of liberalism in the following way: The older liberal theology distinguished between the husk and the kernel, between the mythological conceptions, conditioned and limited by the period, and the great moral and religious principles in the preaching of Jesus. "The kerygma is here reduced to a few basic principles of religion and ethics, to an idealistic ethic motivated by religion." [7] According to Harnack also the whole gospel can be expressed within the framework of God the Father, providence, sonship, and the infinite value of the human soul. The basic elements of the gospel are timeless and can be separated from the husk of Jesus' picture of the world and history. "Unfortunately this means that the kerygma has ceased to be kerygma: it is no longer the proclamation of the decisive act of God in Christ." [8] While liberalism is concerned with a self-unfolding of religious ideas, Bultmann definitely wants to adhere to the person of Jesus as the decisive event of salvation by means of a rigorous criticism of liberalism.

After the older liberal school there arose the school of comparative religions which recognized the full range of myths in the New Testament. It did not find the essence of the New Testament in its great religious and moral principles, however, but in the development of piety, of a religion culminating in mysticism. Whatever the mythological conceptions in which such a mystical piety expressed itself— that was of no basic importance. Here as well the kerygma is abandoned as kerygma because there is no recognition of God's decisive and unique eschatological act in Christ.[9] Bultmann's one and only desire

---

[6] Schniewind, *op. cit.*, p. 69.
[7] Bultmann, *op. cit.*, p. 13, (Editors' translation.)
[8] *Ibid.*
[9] *Ibid.*, p. 15.

27

is to preach this final eschatological act of God in Christ in the language of today, and in this respect we can only declare ourselves to be in complete agreement with him.

The overcoming of liberalism! Anyone who wishes to observe this needs only to read Bultmann's interpretation of the Gospel of John, in which one finds not only a mastery of the subject matter and an erudition before which one can only bow, but above all a theological exegesis which vigorously and persistently confronts the reader with the actual scandal of the message of salvation. The same must also be said on the whole for the *Theology of the New Testament*. Here, to cite one instance, the reader will discover a presentation of the Pauline theology which in form and content could scarcely be more masterfully conceived. Worthy of admiration also is the mastery of language and presentation. We are thinking for example of how the basic anthropological concepts of the Pauline theology are developed and how the understanding of existence expressed in them is discovered! How the great themes of the Reformation theology come alive: The law and its meaning; life under the law; the righteousness of God and its revelation apart from the works of the law, and through faith alone; reconciliation as the complete reversal of the relation between God and man; grace as God's deed, present, and gift; the death and resurrection of Christ as the occurrence of salvation κατ' ἐξοχήν, becoming present for us in the word of preaching which addresses, demands, promises, and calls the hearer to decision; faith as the answer to preaching and as the radical abandonment of the καυχᾶσθαι, the arbitrary effort to gain salvation out of oneself, faith as ὑπακοὴ πίστεως; and the new life which originates from faith, the eschatological existence—freedom from sin, freedom from the law, freedom from death, life in the Spirit! Thus, by the one event of salvation in Christ the horizons are illuminated in a wide circumference. To be sure, one also frequently comes upon places which, so to speak, take one's breath away, and a contradiction becomes evident. But what does that matter? The wealth exhibited here is so great that one cannot help wanting to profit greatly from this pioneering venture into the depths of Pauline theology.

Besides the presentation of Pauline theology there is the Johannine kerygma dealt with in the second volume of the *Theology of the New Testament*. With unequalled force the royal theme is made central that in the Son the revelation of the reality of God—the ἀλήθεια—takes place; that in the Son this transcendent reality of God becomes audible, visible, and palpable in the sphere of this earthly world. Jesus, the revealer, is a specific historical man and, as such, the revelation of the divine *doxa*. His authority is the authority of a man who speaks the word of *God*, so that his word possesses final and absolute meaning. His words are ultimately self-expressions, for his word is he himself. All revelation is concentrated in the great statements of the ἐγώ εἰμι. Jesus as the holy one of God is the absolutely transcendent One, who stands on the side of God and confronts the world as the representative of God. Thus he shatters all human self-assertiveness, disrupts all human standards, and fulfills all human longings for genuine life and reality. Accordingly, faith overcomes the offence of the cross and encounters Jesus himself in the word of preaching. This faith is defined as "desecularization (*Entweltlichung*), transition into eschatological existence."[10] In short, we find here words, sentences, insights, and views which are simply not mentioned in any type of liberal theology. It is easy to understand why Bultmann defends himself against the reproach that he is abbreviating the witness of the New Testament and dissolving theology into anthropology, into the pure stuff of consciousness. Should we not then completely revise our position towards Bultmann and abandon all worry that such an interpretation of the New Testament could harm the Church and theology? Let us see further.

II

Overcoming liberalism on the level of criticism! What does this mean? It is characteristic of Bultmann that his concept of revelation and of the occurrence of salvation in Christ is connected with a radically critical kind of historical research. His research is so critical that the synoptic witness, for example, is practically dissolved as a testimony to the life of Christ. We want to attempt to show the kind of results to which the criticism of Bultmann and his disciples leads.

Bultmann is the terminal point of a line which began at the turn of the century with Wilhelm Wrede. In his book *Das Messiasgeheimnis in den Evangelien*, 1901, Wrede argued that the messianic secret in

---

[10] Bultmann, *Theology of the New Testament*, tr., Kendrick Grobel, II (London: S. C. M. Press, 1952), 78.

Mark is a theory in no way corresponding to historical reality. According to Wrede, Mark threw the net of his messianic dogma over the primitive traditions, so that Mark actually belongs in the history of dogma. Mark has no value as a source for the life of Jesus. Throughout, the faith of the primitive Church has been dated back or retrojected into the narrative of the historical Jesus. There can be no talk about the messiahship of the historical Jesus. In fact, this theory of the messianic secret has completely falsified and distorted the gospel record of Jesus. It is useless as a historical source. Wrede's thesis was then taken up and further developed in the continuing course of critical research. Martin Dibelius also taught that all the fragments of the traditional materials were joined together by one golden thread, that is, by this theory of the messianic secret. Thus the Gospel of Mark becomes a "book of secret epiphanies." It is a mythical book and receives its mythical interpretation from Mark or from the primitive Church, even though the original figure of Jesus may still be recognized —at least to a certain degree—despite all of its mythical covering, but there is no doubt that the christological contexts have been inserted by the evangelists and reflect the faith of the early Church.

Now Bultmann gives the most critical expression to date regarding the previous results of historical research in his *Die Geschichte der synoptischen Tradition*, 1921. Wrede's thesis is fully endorsed by Bultmann. The faith and confession of the primitive Church are dated back into the narrative material of the historical Jesus of Nazareth. The primitive Church had only one single desire, to magnify Christ. The material was shaped by this concern of the Church. What we find in Mark is for the most part a reflection of the later faith of the Church, "a productive formation of the Church," or the work of creative imagination. This not only accounts for the framework of the life of Jesus, but also to a large extent for the picture of Jesus within this framework. The historical reality of Jesus is very much covered over by myth and legend. The schema of the Christ myth has distorted the actual historical tradition. Out of this peculiar process the "gospel" originated as a type of literature such as took shape, for example, in the Gospel of Mark. This "gospel" is an original creation of the Hellenistic Church, but the inner law at work in this productive formation of the Church can be recognized when we discover the *Sitz im Leben*

30

(life situation), that is, the need of the Church, which at any given time has determined the selection and form of the materials.

It is therefore not the historical content, not "the history of Christ" (Schlatter) which makes the gospel record significant for us. We have already seen that we no longer have any direct access to that because the original picture of Jesus has been painted over by the Christ myth. Thus, for example, most of the words of Jesus have been placed in his mouth by the primitive Church, such as the words in which he speaks of his having come or of his having been sent. Here the Church has retrospectively interpreted the mission of Jesus. That is true also of the commissioning of the twelve (Matt. 10) and of the Savior's call (Matt. 11:28). The Church's faith consciousness created new words of the Lord. The myth of the "Son of Man" was superimposed upon the life of a mere man who possessed no messianic glory. Likewise, the presentation of Jesus as a θεῖος ἀνήρ is the creation of the primitive Church. All of the historical material from the birth to the passion and Easter narratives is legendary through and through. High points in the gospel presentation, such as Peter's confession at Caesarea Philippi and the pericope of the transfiguration of Jesus, as well as Peter's draught of fish, are Easter stories which reflect the Church's Easter faith. The passion prophecies are *vaticinia ex eventu,* creations of the Hellenistic Church. The narrative of the Lord's Supper was shaped into an etiological account of a cult in which the later eucharistic liturgy was inserted into an older report of Jesus' Last Supper. In form the report of Jesus' entry into Jerusalem is as legendary as the passion narrative. That Jesus was crucified *as the Messiah* is legendary embellishment. The ideas of sacrifice, the theory of satisfaction, et cetera, are mythological interpretations of the death of Jesus—no longer tenable for us in such a form. The way in which the Easter faith of the disciples arose is likewise obscured by legend. The empty tomb is a legend. The resurrection of Jesus is nothing else than faith in the saving event of the cross; it is therefore a specific spiritual interpretation of the cross as an event or as *the* event of salvation—and so forth.[11]

Thus the status of the Synoptic Gospels as sources of history in the usual sense of the term is almost completely demolished under the

[11] *Ibid.,* I, 45-46, 84, *passim;* Bultmann, "New Testament and Mythology," pp. 35, 41.

blows of a bold and fearless criticism that does not recoil from any consequence. Despite this, the Gospels possess great value for us, for in this mythological clothing of the original tradition about Jesus an ultimate decision of faith is appropriately expressed in the symbol of the messianic dogma. This decision of faith knows of the eschatological significance and the absolute character of the person of Jesus as the Lord. That and only that is the motive which effectively drove the primitive Church to create those formations which do not represent real history but rather interpret a fact. It is not strange that these constructions of the Church move within the world of ideas and concepts of primitive man. If we want to get a view of the original figure of Jesus we must strip away these mythological wrappings, for they are nothing else than a certain mode of understanding which attempts to grasp Jesus as the eschatological event of salvation. Naturally this mode of understanding cannot be our own. We should not simply eliminate these mythological ideas, but should rather inquire into their specific intentions and thus apply an existentialist (*existential*) and existential (*existentiell*) interpretation to them. Negatively this means to "demythologize." Today we have the task of accomplishing in our language, in our way, with our conceptuality, and with our methods exactly the same thing which the first witnesses accomplished in their own way, namely, magnifying Christ. This means to witness to him as God's eschatological deed of salvation, as the event of salvation which decides concerning life and death.

We shall refrain from showing in detail how this criticism does not even check itself in the face of the Pauline and Johannine kerygma. Only a few things will be mentioned. Bultmann points out that neither the human personality of Jesus nor his teaching plays any role in Paul. The "Christ after the flesh" does not enter into consideration. The only significant thing is *that* he existed—not the questions of *what* and *how*. The Pauline theology is also impregnated with pictures, ideas, and conceptions of a mythological nature—for example, when it attempts to illustrate the saving significance of the death of Christ. All of these require a relevant, that is to say, an existentialist interpretation. The same holds true of the witness to the resurrection in I Cor. 15. Here Paul wants to secure the resurrection of Christ as an objective fact by enumerating the witnesses who have seen the resurrected Christ. "But is such a proof convincing?" Bultmann asks.

32

In reality the resurrection faith is faith in the significance of the cross. When Paul in I Cor. 15 and elsewhere uses the old realistic eschatology he falls somewhat into contradiction with his own ultimate intentions. More about this later.[12]

Let us take a brief look at the critical evaluation of the Johannine witness. We shall limit ourselves to the statements about the death and resurrection of Christ. The common Christian view of Jesus' death as an expiatory sacrifice which is found in I John 1:7 plays no role in John's Gospel. It is an alien element taken over from the tradition of the Church and in the process of later editing has been interpolated as a gloss by the Church.[13] "If Jesus' death on the cross is already His exaltation and glorification, His resurrection cannot be an event of special significance. No resurrection is needed to destroy the triumph which death might be supposed to have gained in the crucifixion. For the cross itself was already triumph over the world and its ruler."[14] "It is not surprising that the evangelist, following the tradition, narrates some Easter-stories. The question is, what do they mean to him?"[15] The resurrection appearances are evidently conceived as signs just as the miracles. They represent Jesus' triumph over the world. "So far as they are actual occurrences—and the evangelist need not have doubted their reality—they resemble the miracles in that ultimately they are not indispensable; in fact, there ought to be no need for them, but they were granted as a concession to man's weakness."[16] In the story of Thomas there lies "a criticism of the small faith which asks for tangible demonstrations of the Revealer. It also contains a warning against taking the Easter-stories for more than they are able to be: Signs and pictures of the Easter faith—or, perhaps still better, confessions of faith in it."[17] Easter, Pentecost, and the Parousia are not three separate events, but one and the same. "But the one event that is meant by all these is not an external occurrence, but an inner one: The victory which Jesus wins when faith arises in man by the overcoming of the offense that Jesus is to him."[18] The "facts of salva-

---

[12] Bultmann, *Theology of the New Testament*, I, 77, 292-313, *passim;* "New Testament and Mythology," pp. 41-42.
[13] Bultmann, *Theology of the New Testament*, II, 54.
[14] *Ibid.*, p. 56.
[15] *Ibid.*
[16] *Ibid.*
[17] *Ibid.*, p. 57.
[18] *Ibid.*

tion" in the traditional sense play no important role in John "and the entire salvation drama—incarnation, death, resurrection, Pentecost, the Parousia—is concentrated into a single event: The Revelation of God's reality (ἀλήθεια) in the earthly activity of the man Jesus combined with the overcoming of the 'offense' in it by man's accepting it in faith." [19] The passage about the Paraclete is a mythologically formulated statement, and the description of Jesus as a person who intercedes is also a mythological idea.[20] If these ideas are mythological it does not mean that they are to be eliminated, but by being stripped of their mythological dress, they are to be interpreted in terms of an existentialist dialectic.

III

The result is that we see a reduction ruthlessly carried out in the name of demythologization, or more positively, in the name of an interpretation of the New Testament message on the basis of an existentialist analysis. Now does this nullify everything that we have already said about Bultmann's overcoming of liberalism? Not at all, from Bultmann's point of view. Rather, on the foundation he has laid Bultmann constructs a Christology which in its own way is impressively concise. We would like to call attention to some of its basic elements. (1) The Χριστὸς κατὰ σάρκα does not concern us. He has no special meaning for Christology. Who is the man Jesus? He is a man like ourselves, not a mythical figure; he is without messianic radiance, a real man—but merely a man, a teacher and a prophet, who worked for a brief time, who prophesied the imminent end of the world and the breaking in of the rule of God, who renewed and radicalized the protest of the great Old Testament prophets against legalism and cultic worship of God, and who was delivered up by the Jews to the Romans and was crucified. Everything else is uncertain and legendary. Only the cross and perhaps a few words of Jesus can be historically established. To attempt to say anything more would actually mean to say something less, for it would devaluate the paradox of revelation that an "earthly phenomenon," a "relative X," scarcely historically evident, is as such the place where the absolutely authoritative word

[19] *Ibid.*, p. 58.
[20] *Ibid.*, pp. 87-88.

34

of God, the living reality of the living God, encounters us. The authority of Jesus is the paradoxical authority of a man who, while possessing none of the glory of God in any evident sense, is nevertheless as such the Word of God absolutely.[21] If, as the synoptists describe him, Jesus is depicted as a "divine man" (θεῖος ἀνήρ), then the fact is not understood "that from the world's standpoint the Revelation must always be a 'hidden thing' and that it nevertheless occurs 'openly' —not, however, with demonstrative obtrusiveness but with the unobtrusiveness of everyday events." [22]

2. The cross as a brute fact corresponds to the naked humanity of the earthly Jesus. It is the crucifixion of the Isenheimer Altar, picturing a man completely "finished off" by the world, totally abandoned, with no assurance, and in the eyes of the world swallowed up in defeat. But it is just this cross—the only objectively tangible event —which is now preached as the eschatological event of salvation. God has made this Jesus of Nazareth to be Lord and Christ. That is to say, God sees to it that the One who is crucified becomes preached as the Lord, as our Lord. Now we no longer know Christ after the flesh, the "historical" Jesus, but only the Christ preached in the kerygma. We do not know the historical reality of Jesus but only the Christ of preaching.

3. The resurrection also is not a fact which can be objectively established. Only the Easter faith of the disciples can be historically grasped. This Easter faith is the Easter event and is only present for us in the word of preaching. He who is resurrected has arisen in the word. Only in that way is he living and present for us.

4. When the word is proclaimed the cross and resurrection become present for us. Then the eschatological "now" occurs. Good Friday, Easter, Pentecost, and the Second Coming are all comprehended in one moment. The historical has entered into the event of preaching in such a way that its only reality is contained within the preaching, and not at all outside of it. Every guarantee based upon an event outside of faith is resolutely abandoned.

5. Faith is the answer to preaching. In the naked humanity of Jesus and in the naked factuality of the cross faith apprehends God's deci-

[21] *Ibid.*, pp. 51-52.
[22] *Ibid.*, p. 45.

sive act of salvation. It sees the revelation of God in this brute fact. It overcomes the inner offence which the cross presents. Faith understood as this inner event is the triumph of Christ. It is Easter. Any recourse to an unambiguous situation lying outside of faith, such as "facts of salvation," in which a person could believe would be nothing less than a denial of faith.[23]

6. In this faith the intentions of the "realistic eschatology" come into their own when they are "demythologized," that is to say, when they are historicized. As radical surrender to God, faith is radical "openness" to the future, the truly eschatological existence, the life that comes from the future, that is, from the God who is always turning toward us.[24] An eschatology that speaks of the salvation drama in terms of an end sometime in the future or of Christ as the future judge of the world is mythological. The intention of the New Testament eschatology is to place me in the state of openness to the God who is ever coming to me in the here and now. This openness of Christian existence knows of no end.[25]

7. There is yet one more point worth mentioning: The personal relation to Christ is really not a relation to him as a person. Rather it consists of being determined by the event of salvation in Christ; it is a new relation to God. To believe in Christ means to place oneself under this event of salvation and from it to obtain a new understanding of oneself. Thus we have indeed a personal relation to the eschatological event contained in Christ, to God's deed of salvation in Christ. We do not, however, have a personal relation to Christ as a heavenly figure who, as in the gnostic myth, has laid aside his earthly garment.[26] There is no direct relation of faith to Jesus. The *Christus pro me* is my self-understanding under grace.[27] The language about a direct personal relation to Christ is mythological.[28]

[23] *Ibid.*, I, 318-19.
[24] Bultmann, *Primitive Christianity*, tr. R. N. Fuller (New York: Meridian Books, 1958), p. 184.
[25] *Ibid.*, p. 208.
[26] Bultmann, *Theology of the New Testament*, II, 85.
[27] *Verkündigung und Forschung*, p. 65.
[28] Bultmann, "A Reply to the Theses of J. Schniewind," *Kerygma and Myth*, p. 109.

IV

Thus Bultmann showers us with an abundance of questions and at the same time knows how to meet all objections with a brilliant and ingenious dialectic. What is the total impression that remains for us? What kind of help are we offered here for our ministry on the frontier, that is, for preaching, teaching, and pastoral work; for the ministry of the Church in the midst of so much sinfulness, misery, and suffering on earth; for the ministry to those on sick- or death-beds, at funerals, or at grave sides? Is it true that the old and "eternal gospel" is merely being preached here in a new tongue? Or does this attempt to transpose the old gospel into modern language, into a conceptuality coined by modern existentialist philosophy, touch the substance of the apostolic witness to Christ? We would like to raise and consider a few questions in this regard.

1. Bultmann asserts with the greatest possible emphasis that we can only speak about God in the most existential manner. All theological statements have a reference to existence. They can therefore only be expressed in the context of existence, and hence only existentially. They concern me; they refer to me; they touch me; they grasp me and decide about me. Every statement about God is always at the same time a statement about ourselves. To know God is to acknowledge him, to acknowledge him in obedience and at the same moment to understand oneself anew from the standpoint of God, thereby becoming transparent to oneself. Every statement about Christ has validity for us only in so far as we realize: *Mea res agitur.* Faith is therefore not concerned with the acknowledgment of objectively reasonable facts. Rather, the *pro me* vertically penetrates all statements. We can only speak of the gift of Christ in such a way that thereby we also understand ourselves as being given by him. We can only witness to the cross of Christ in such a way that we let ourselves be questioned whether we will be crucified with Christ and bear the cross with him.[29] Thus all theological statements require an existentialist and an existential interpretation.[30] To that extent theological and anthropological statements belong most closely and inseparably together. On the

---

[29] Bultmann, "New Testament and Mythology," pp. 35-38.

[30] An "existentialist" interpretation which refers to existence inquires into the human understanding of existence as expressed in a text, while an "existential" interpretation refers to the *mea res agitur.*

one hand we will agree with Bultmann in the sense of Melanchthon's sentence: *Hoc est Christum cognoscere beneficia eius cognoscere.* On the other hand, however, we reject the idea that the theological realities are exhausted in the *pro me* so that all of a sudden the accent is falsely shifted from the theonomous thinking of Holy Scriptures to an anthroponomous thinking which proceeds from and revolves around man's existence.

As certain as it is that all the theological and christological statements of the Bible are oriented to the *pro me,* it is equally certain that this *pro me* rests upon the rock of the *extra me.* But what does this mean? What is meant by the *extra me?* Nothing other than the Word of God itself which has happened—"And it happened by the Word of the Lord"—and which as the creative Word of God has become history and has entered into history. "He spake and it was done." This *extra me* is the "history of Christ" in its perfect tense, "this thing that has happened, which the Lord has made known to us" (Luke 2:15), the perfect tense of the history which God enacted in Christ. This *extra me* is the Word which became flesh (John 1:14). In this connection we cannot for a moment forget that with this history of God the ultimate end of history, τὰ ἔσχατα, meaning the eschatological boundary of all history, breaks in. To be sure this history of God is "an event which can be fixed in history, although in its true essence this event cannot be historically grasped." [31] It is that chain of the μεγαλεῖα τοῦ θεοῦ in which the eschatological activity of God occurs right within so-called world history, is secretly at work in it, and is only brought to light through the word of revelation. The New Testament speaks in the aorist, present, and future tenses of this "history" of God, of this Word of God which has become flesh. God has acted on our behalf, *extra nos,* "while we were yet sinners" (Rom. 5:8). He *has* acted for us and *will* act for us when all flesh is wilted and withered as grass.

We ask: Does not the paradox of the New Testament proclamation consist in the fact that in the event of the ongoing proclamation and in the concrete moment of faith's decision which answers this proclamation the perfect tense—*ubi et quando visum est Deo*—becomes the present perfect in a marvellous way, becomes an event which refers

---

[31] Hans Lietzmann, *An die Korinther I-II, Handbuch zum Neuen Testament,* IX, ed. W. G. Kümmel (4th ed.; Tübingen: J. C. B. Mohr, 1949), 192.

to me and takes hold of me? Does not the paradox consist in the fact that the aorist becomes the "today" and the "now" of the time of salvation, but in such a way that this perfect tense does not cease to remain a strictly perfect tense completely transcending the possibilities of my existence, namely, the decision of God which has been made, the work of God which has been accomplished, and the Logos which has become flesh? Does not that which is present in the living act of preaching and in the occurrence of faith's decision derive its life from what God has done to Christ and in Christ for us? Is it not true that from the perspective of such a present occurrence God's act of salvation in the perfect tense becomes visible as such in all its glory, as the boundary of all history which in its eschatological significance impinges upon all history? Should the incarnation of the Logos in the Word and sacrament, in the here and now of preaching, make us forget that the Logos of God first became flesh in history and that all preaching refers to the "mighty deeds of God" which have occurred, to the "works of God" which form the basis upon which we stand and which at the same time are wholly orientated to the *telos?* "History does not run toward an end which can be one way or another . . . it runs toward a decision which has already been made." [32]

Just as we speak in the perfect tense, at the same time we also speak in the future tense. This future of God, the future of the resurrection, which happens when the ways of God are brought to an end and God will be all in all (I Cor. 15:28), certainly becomes present in the witness which calls us to decision in a unique way. Again in a marvellous way—baffling to all human reason—it becomes the future present, is anticipated by faith in a certain sense, and becomes an event which breaks into our existence, overpowering and illuminating it (e.g., John 5:24 ff.). Does it mean, however, that this future thereby ceases to be the future of the resurrection, the "divine horizon," absolutely transcending all of the possibilities of our existence—transcending, because something has appeared which no eye has seen and no ear has heard and which has not entered into the heart of man? Does our existence cease to be drawn from the temporality of this world just because it has confronted the light of the divine horizon? Does not this faith, in which the things of the future are anticipated,

[32] G. Eichholz, "Erwählung und Eschatologie im 1 Johannesbrief," *Evangelische Theologie,* I (1938), 12.

see and witness to and long for this future as a real future in all its glory? In this faith, which anticipates the future, the end of all things has come into view and has ignited the flame of the Maran-atha. "It is characteristic of John and of primitive Christianity in general that both statements are kept side by side. Primitive Christian thought is abandoned in the moment when this paradox is felt to be intolerable." [33]

Is it not a matter for concern when the past and future references of the biblical proclamation are so nullified, emptied, and dissolved by an existential-dialectical interpretation of the aorist and future tenses that they coincide to the point of virtual identity with the event of preaching and with the decision of faith, and only exist in that manner and place? To be sure, this history of God, which as God's history is the eschatological event, the crisis and end of our history, can be grasped only in faith and encounters us in the preaching and the decision of faith awakened by it. Does that mean that this history of God, this Word of God which has become flesh, has become so diminished in the act of faith, so incorporated or drawn into the event of preaching, so located and enclosed in the hearing and believing subject, that it disappears into it, so to speak—or better, only in that way and in that place exists at all? Is it not rather the case that this history of God, τὰ μεγαλεῖα τοῦ θεοῦ, stands as the mountains of God, indissoluble, in eternal validity, *pro nobis,* but also *sine nobis* and *contra nobis,* despite the unbelief of the world? It is as Luther says of the saving reality of baptism, that it is not invalid even though one "has fallen from it," that it "continues and remains," for which reason there is a "return and approach" in baptism for the man who has fallen from faith.[34]

As surely as in preaching the perfect tense becomes the present perfect, namely, an event which occurs now, just as surely, absolutely everything depends upon the identity of the Christ encountering us in the present—namely, the preached Christ, with the Logos which became flesh. In the present moment that "high mountain-chain" of God, that work of God which has taken place, becomes visible. The

---

[33] E. Gaugler, "Das Christuszeugnis des Johannesevangeliums," *Jesus Christus im Zeugnis der Heiligen Schrift und der Kirche* (1936), p. 58.

[34] Martin Luther, *The Large Catechism, Triglot Concordia* (St. Louis: Concordia Publishing House, 1921), p. 751.

whole history of the tradition is an impressive witness to the interest which primitive Christianity had in this work of God which occurred. "Their whole religious possession was grounded upon what God had wrought in the presence of eye-witnesses." [35] Indeed the perfect tense is directed toward nothing else than the present, that is to say, to me and to my existence in order to involve me fully in this history of God. Thus existential history (*Geschichte*) is created out of the mere historical past (*Historie*), but the present is what it is by being caught and overwhelmed by that past which has occurred *extra nos,* and with which we become contemporaneous through believing perception of the message of salvation. Has not Bultmann so overstated the indisputably correct proposition that faith is a matter of existential hearing and obedience in face of the preached word (to be sure under pressure applied by modern critical thought) that what has occurred historically in the past fades away, disappears, is dissolved, and every reference to it is suspected of being an uncritical acceptance of the "facts of salvation" or of the elements of tradition—all of this being a denial of what faith really is?

2. According to Bultmann the acknowledgment of Jesus as the Revealer in whom God speaks the decisive word and who for that reason is the "Messiah," the "Son of Man," the "Lord," is a pure act of faith. It is born out of an inner triumph over the offence of faith, and it is an event which is completely independent of the question of whether Jesus regarded himself as the Messiah. Only the historian is supposed to be able to answer this question, but the result of his work has no relevance for our decision of faith. We ask: Is this act of faith really so completely independent of the historical appearance of Jesus as Bultmann asserts, or is faith not rather an answer to that history which has occurred, an effect of the reality of Jesus in his bodily form, a reflection of the light which proceeds from him as the evangelists have depicted him for us? It is true that he is the Bearer of the decisive Word of God, but surely not just because he spoke the Word or because he speaks it now, but because he speaks it *as the Christ of God.*[36] The decision is made for him because it is a decision

[35] Gerhard Kittel, "The Jesus of History," *Mysterium Christi,* ed. G. K. A. Bell and A. Deissmann (New York: Longmans, Green and Company, 1930), p. 41.
[36] Cf. Gerhard Kittel, *Die Religionsgeschichte und das Urchristentum* (Gütersloh: C. Bertelsmann, 1931), p. 155.

in favor of the Christ of God, the bearer of the Spirit κατ' ἐξοχήν, "who has been crowned with the royal crown of the Holy Spirit," [37] of whom it has been made known: ὁ θεὸς ἦν μετ' ἀυτοῦ (Acts 10:38 ff.). "If the question whether or not Jesus ever lived has absolutely decisive significance in sharpest possible opposition to all more or less clear or veiled docetic tendencies, then of equal significance is the question as to precisely what and who this Jesus of Nazareth actually is." [38] Is it not also the theme of John's gospel to show not only that the Revealer has now appeared, the One and Only, and that the revelation which occurred and occurs in him is absolute, but also to show *who Jesus is?* Is Jesus for the primitive Church only a more or less depersonalized "event," or does he not possess for the Church quite a definite appearance?

Is it not a disturbing feature of Bultmann's interpretation of the New Testament message when the historical reality of the historical Jesus of Nazareth becomes a "relative X"? This means that the occurrence of God's revelation which has assumed bodily and historical form in Jesus evaporates and is, so to speak, placed within parentheses. What has taken place in the past is weakened for the sake of the future proclamation and of the act of faith which continually results from it. The real connection between the history of Jesus and the preaching of the apostles is broken. All that remains is the punctual event of preaching, a kind of "mathematical point" which lacks any extension just because this very extension would illicitly render the "other-worldly" into something "this-worldly." All that remains is the naked "thatness" of revelation interpreted by the Synoptists in the mythological form of their Gospels or by John in a form of witness which sovereignly transformed the whole tradition. In both cases we have to do with an interpreted history, with a witness which has been transposed into the gospel tradition and which has creatively shaped it. What happens is that the history of revelation has been largely transformed into "significant ideas" *(Bedeutsamkeiten)*. The New Testament speech, that of the Synoptics for example, is no longer understood as authentic. "It is changed into a network of significant

---

[37] Weimar edition of Luther's works, Vol. 46, p. 612, 1. 32.

[38] K. L. Schmidt, "Das Christuszeugnis der synoptischen Evangelien," *Jesus Christus im Zeugnis der Heiligen Schrift und der Kirche*, p. 28.

ideas; it is dissolved into a mere *significat* and has lost the force of the *est*." [39] When the gospel is only understood as a *significat*, however, as referring to Jesus' eschatological significance and, moreover, in the language, categories, and mythology of the time, or as a statement in which a final decision of faith is expressed in face of the word and claim of Jesus—but which is obviously unacceptable to us literally— then the reality attested by the evangelists enters completely into the contemporary event of preaching. It exists only in the form of preaching and has relinquished its own being to this event of preaching. According to Schniewind, Bultmann's statements remain "strictly limited to our human existence. Of a unique event wrought out in the personal relationship between God and men on the stage of history, of a story of the dealings of God with man, of a unique and final revelation of God in Christ crucified, there is never so much as a word." [40] There is so little said of this that the Christ after the flesh, the historical personality of Jesus is, so to speak, left out of consideration. Not the historical Jesus, but only the preached Christ is of any concern to us; only the latter is really the Lord. The Christ after the flesh remains in an impenetrable darkness when observed from the historical point of view. Therefore the synoptic gospel is not valid as a historical witness. Only its "significance" is important for us when taken as an expression of the decision of faith made by believers, as the reflection of the later faith of the Church. The bridge between the historical Jesus and the preached Christ has, so to speak, collapsed.

Is it really true that for primitive Christianity the kerygma of the earthly Jesus was ultimately insignificant? Did it not have a very fundamental meaning for the primitive Church? Did not the Church pay close attention to him who was in person the Word of God which became flesh, and did not this incarnate Word possess very definite and indispensable features for the primitive Church? Is not all Christology based upon this "history of Christ," including its past and future points of reference? Therefore, does not the testimony of the eyewitnesses have the greatest significance for Paul as well as for John (I Cor. 15:6 ff.; John 19:35)?

In a review of Bultmann's *Urchristentum im Rahmen der antiken*

---

[39] Günther Bornkamm, "Myth and Gospel," *infra*, p. 187.
[40] J. Schniewind, *op. cit.*, p. 66.

Religion, Erich Dinkler states: "In many respects one may judge that Bultmann is scarcely interested in knowing what particular historical event actually kindled the faith of primitive Christianity. Rather, he throws into relief the primitive Christian faith as an event. The question whether this event has an historical basis or whether Jesus as the end of history is, with his death and resurrection, really historical appears irrelevant to Bultmann as a scientific theologian." [41] In view of this undoubtedly apt characterization of Bultmann's New Testament interpretation we may ask where we really stand if the question is unessential as to what event ignites faith over against the act of preaching and the decision of faith which answers it—that is, if the question seems irrelevant whether the event of faith has any basis. Do we do Bultmann an injustice when we ask whether a legitimate interpretation of the apostolic witness or the preaching of the Christ event for our time must assume such a form, or whether the real connection between the historical Jesus of Nazareth and the witness of the primitive Church has not been severed, so that the kerygma is suspended, so to speak, in a vacuum?

3. What has happened to the "earthly Jesus" happens also to the "resurrected Christ." Just as the crucifixion has been collapsed into a naked "that" divorced from the reality of the "history of Christ," from the prehistory to the passion story, so also the event of the preaching of the resurrection of Christ is divorced from what the Lord God did to his Son "early in the morning of the third day." According to Bultmann the resurrection witness of the primitive Church did not originate because the resurrected Christ appeared to his disciples in person—of course we have in mind a supra-earthly form of personal reality, giving them a new personal encounter, a new personal word, and appointing them anew to their apostolic office. [42] Bultmann does not inquire at all into the origin of this assurance that Jesus lives. The origin of the Easter faith and of the Easter message is concealed from us, and according to Bultmann it is not even a matter of theological interest for us. All that can be said historically is that the resurrection witness in the primitive Church arose with an enigmatic and mighty force. One should not make any further inquiry behind this witness of faith for something "external to faith," for that would abolish

[41] *Verkündigung und Forschung,* p. 74.
[42] Cf. Paul Althaus, *Die Wahrheit des Kirchlichen Osterglaubens,* pp. 42 ff., 58, 69.

faith as faith. The Easter witness is basically a report about a purely inner process. The offence of the cross is overcome, a radiant assurance comes over the disciples, and the "divine depths" of the cross light up within them.[43] Only in such fashion does Jesus encounter the disciples in living form. Only in such a way is he that living One. Easter is the present power of the cross for us, for you and me. As a fact which happened to the entombed body, the resurrection is a mythological idea and is therefore as such to be rejected. Christ has arisen in the Word, in the kerygma. The meaning of this, however, is not simply that the resurrection of Christ is something that had to become immediately proclaimed as a message, immediately made known. If that were the meaning we would have to underscore most forcefully the statement that Christ has arisen in the Word. The meaning of this statement is rather that the faith of the disciples is identical with the fact that God raised Christ from the dead. Thus everything that God has done in the past coincides with our Easter faith and is completely identical with it. Easter is the new possibility of understanding one's own existence anew in the light of the Easter message and also of becoming transparent to oneself in a new way. We do not know how the apostles attained to this new self-understanding or what actually helped them to overcome the offence of the cross and to recognize its divine depths. That is not even supposed to interest us. Only the Easter witness of the disciples in which the resurrected Christ encounters us should lay claim to our interest. Therefore the Easter stories are essentially dispensable; they are only concessions to our weakness and at best they are only signs and pictures which show us how the new spiritual interpretation of the crucifixion is represented.[44] They are forms of the break-through of the Easter assurance—not the very basis of this assurance. They are modes of thought and speech—not the very beginning and foundation of preaching. Even the question of whether faith is an answer to a reality wrought *ab extra* is not supposed to be raised, for the history and the historical foundation of the truth exist in the message itself, in the event of preaching, and not outside it. The history of revelation and the event of faith are therefore like a single chord that is struck and sounded upon one instrument, blending to-

---

[43] *Ibid.*, pp. 57-58.
[44] Bultmann, *Theology of the New Testament*, II, 56-57.

gether into a complete unity so that the first is raised to the second, or should we say drowned in it. For that reason I Cor. 15 operates as a vexatious alien body within Bultmann's interpretation. There is no doubt that Paul at this point stands firmly upon the foundation of the apostolic *paradosis,* which he himself received and transmitted in his preaching, and which, as the story of what God has done in Christ, always precedes all specific personal decisions of faith and all theological reflection.

What becomes of the Easter kerygma, however, if it is not the *solemnis promulgatio* (Calvin) of the mighty deeds of God, the solemn proclamation of the event that God has raised Christ from the dead? "The actual Easter message of the New Testament does not merely state that Jesus lives, but that Jesus is arisen. Something has happened, and God has done something unheard of and unique. This unheard of something is a fact which can only be designated by the word resurrection. It is not an inference from the Easter experience, not something derived, not something which one can disregard as unessential in favor of the truth that Jesus lives, but this must be the content, the core of the Easter experience." [45] What is the Easter message if it is not the witness of the majestic self-revelation of Christ, the witness of the miracle of a new encounter of the Lord with his disciples, which, according to Kähler, lifted them over the abyss by showing himself to them as the living Lord? Does the ὤφθη really deal only with a new spiritual interpretation of the cross or is it not an event with its own significance and its own majesty as the supreme self-manifestation of the resurrected Lord? Does not the act of the living God—who has raised the great Shepherd of the sheep from the dead—become manifest in the ὤφθη, an act which precedes the Easter event and which reaches and unites everybody in their individualities? Is not the uniqueness of the apostolate a sign of the fact that something has happened which has absolutely no analogy and cannot be grasped by human thought? This fact is simply a suprahistorical event which breaks into history and portrays itself within it. The event happened when God raised Jesus from the dead and thereby brought the "new creation" into being. In brief, the statement that Christ has risen is "in a certain sense an undialectical statement which calls all dialectical

---

[45] Cf. Hermann Sasse, "Jesus Christ the Lord," *Mysterium Christi,* pp. 98 ff.

46

theology to a halt. Here revelation is history." This history is not to be dissolved in the kerygma. "It is absolutely essential to recognize that the Easter story is not telling primarily about the origin of faith and of the kerygma, but about the history of God." [46]

The disciples drew the picture of the Lord from the perspective of the reality of Easter. How else could they have done it? How else could they regard this picture than from the standpoint of the confession which the Lord God himself made at Easter by raising his Son? Thus they view the picture of the "earthly Jesus" and the picture of the "glorified Christ" as inseparable. Every word, every deed, his journey to the cross, the cross itself, indeed everything now stands in the light of the "Yes" which God spoke at Easter. *Omnia spirant resurrectionem.*" Only then did the picture of the historical Jesus acquire its ultimate divine depth and this can never be grasped by a merely historical critical method. Does this mean that the original picture of Jesus has been embellished, or does it not rather mean that the ultimate depths in the life of the earthly Lord have been disclosed? To see the earthly Jesus in the light of Easter as the early Church did—does this mean to veil the picture of the earthly Jesus or does it not rather mean to unveil it totally? The primitive Church sees in it a hidden secret—the messianic secret—which is now declared with power to it (Rom. 1:4). Therefore, the Church sees the following joined together in a living unity: The picture of the earthly Lord and the person who was exalted and raised by God from the dead. Now every page of the Gospels, every word, and every single story acquires that transparency, that lucidity which is not concealed from any reader of the Bible whose eyes have once been opened to see it.

4. The way in which Bultmann speaks about eschatology corresponds to the way in which the history of revelation, marked by the aorist in the New Testament, is dissolved into the existential mode of preaching and into the decision of faith. He describes faith as eschatological existence, as radical openness to the future, as a perpetual pilgrimage which never achieves an end. Radical openness to the future is openness to "that which is ever approaching me now," to the God who is always approaching us. It is an ever constant abandonment of ourselves to God. What makes our existence a specifically Christian

[46] Karl Barth, *Unterwegs*, II, 1951, 106.

existence is just this—our experience of God as he who continually
approaches us "together with our knowledge of our own fulfillment
as always imminent." But now Bultmann shows that the unfolding
of this fundamental idea in the New Testament is at the outset
shackled by the fact that the expectation of the end of the world and
the creation of a definitive state of salvation derived from Jewish
tradition, is encumbered by the idea of a cosmic catastrophe. If faith
is a state of being open to the future, "being directed to the grace of
God as continually imminent," then such a completed state of salvation is not "conceivable." Rather, it is just in this openness that the
eschatological future becomes present. It is a basic feature of Pauline
theology and especially of Johannine theology that eschatology is conceived as radically realized in the present. "With all this, Paul still
combines the apocalyptic picture of the Parousia, the resurrection of
the dead, and the judgment. But for the Fourth Gospel, the redemption is exclusively a present process." [47] The apocalyptic pictures of
the future in the New Testament, which are in essence an unnecessary
encumbrance, can of course no longer be accepted by us in such
fashion. The future "can only be understood in the light of God's
grace as the permanent futurity of God which is always there before
man arrives, wherever it be, even in the darkness of death." [48] A con-
summation in which the other-worldly becomes a simple possession is
unthinkable. "The openness of Christian existence never comes to an
end." [49]

We must make one thing clear: If the primitive Christian eschatology is interpreted as continual openness to "that which is ever approaching me," as an openness which never comes to an end, then
any reference to a real future event of salvation is eliminated. Eschatology becomes something "existential," that is, a description of the
structures of Christian existence.[50] Bultmann does not acknowledge
an eschatology in the biblical sense; rather, he attaches to the word
"eschatology" a meaning different from that of the New Testament.
For Bultmann eschatological existence is always a state of being thrown
into a crisis or of standing on the most extreme frontiers where the

[47] Bultmann, *Primitive Christianity*, p. 199.
[48] *Ibid.*, p. 208.
[49] *Ibid.*
[50] Erich Dinkler, *Verkündigung und Forschung*, p. 74.

"this-worldly" is divorced from the "other-worldly" and where the "other-worldly" is experienced as that which is always approaching us. All concrete eschatology is given an existentialist interpretation, and in reality thereby eliminated. Eschatology is not interpreted as that future of God which is anticipated in the experience of faith. Rather, it is completely dissolved in the existential act of preaching and of faith. Just as the perfect tense in the revelation of the history of God is so incorporated into the eschatological event of faith that it possesses reality only within that event, so also the future element in the history of God which points to an end is lost as the *history* of God, and becomes identical with the decision of faith. Whatever the New Testament says about eschatology beyond its existential meaning is unimaginable and unthinkable. It is therefore mythology, which unfortunately still encumbers Paul's theology.

Now it is evident that a basic characteristic of the apostolic preaching is that in the word and work, cross and resurrection of Jesus the *eschata* become present in an incomprehensible, blessed, saving, and judging way. Here the royal sovereignty of God breaks in. In the encounter with Jesus the last things are determined. "In Jesus the world is confronted by the end." [51] In his word and work God's own word and work encounter us, unto life or unto judgment. There is no doubt that in Paul and especially in John the eschatological event is represented as realized. The way in which this has been developed in Bultmann's commentary on John or in his New Testament theology is exceedingly impressive and can only be accepted with complete gratitude. Just as the past becomes present in the living proclamation, so also the future is drawn into the present time of salvation, in the here and now. Here, however, we must repeat the question which we already tried to elucidate: Does not the living dialectic within the New Testament message consist precisely in the fact that God's past activity in history becomes a present event in the *viva vox evangelii*, but without ceasing to remain also that high mountain chain which indestructibly, indissolubly, and immovably towers above all human existence and is prior and superior to it? Is it not likewise true that the last things inflame our existence by the living word of preaching, but without ceasing to be the end of the ways of God and

---

[51] E. C. Hoskyns and F. N. Davey, *The Fourth Gospel* (London: Faber and Faber Ltd., 1947), p. 268.

the fulfillment of the promises toward which God is directing history in a way surpassing all reason? What happens in the νῦν according to Calvin (on John 5:28) is *quoddam ultimae resurrectionis praeludium.* But what happens to this paradox of the New Testament when on the one hand the divine reality of the perfect tense and the future on the other are so interpreted that they are practically eliminated? Moreover, can that thesis be a valid principle of scriptural exegesis which states that what is unthinkable or unimaginable for one's own self-understanding is not true?

5. Luther once defined the situation of the Church as a standing and living in the twilight of the early morning at the break of day. This picture of the early twilight inseparably joins both aspects in a paradoxical way: In the epiphany of the Son of God in the flesh and in the apostolic witness of the Church, which is the body of Christ, "daybreak" has appeared. In the reflection of this early light Christianity lives "between the times" and awaits the day of Jesus Christ which brings the end of the ways of God. We have received the adoption of sons and we eagerly long for it (Rom. 8:15, 19 ff.). We are children of God, but it has not yet appeared what we shall be (I John 3:2 ff.). This *simul* constitutes the mysterious tension in New Testament eschatology. What happens to this *simul* when eschatology is reduced to the possibility of a new understanding of existence and is interpreted as continual openness to the grace which approaches us, when everything that exceeds this existential understanding is regarded as an encumbrance with which eschatology is still burdened? Does this not mean that our self-understanding is about to become a decisive hermeneutical principle?

6. According to the New Testament witness Christ is ὁ αὐτός yesterday, today, and to all eternity. Yesterday he was the One who called sinners, helped the weary and heavy laden, brought the good word of forgiveness, and blessed the children; the One who crossed the Mount of Olives and entered into the Holy City, suffered and died under Pontius Pilate, and appeared again to his disciples as the living Lord. Today he is the One who encounters us in Word and sacrament as the living Lord and who through his suffering and cross was exalted to the majesty of God. At the same time he is the Lord-to-be who will fulfill the promises of God and consummate the *telos* of the history of God. But in all this he is ὁ αὐτός. This also means that he himself is

the One who brings us personally into his saving fellowship and encounters us personally. Can we write off this New Testament witness of our assurance of Christ's wholly personal fellowship with us and of our personal union with him—an idea which Bultmann sees as a "pietistic misunderstanding of the Revealer"?[52] Is there not the danger here that the living person of Christ becomes more or less an event practically deprived of any personal features? In Bultmann there is only a union with Christ as the eschatological event of salvation. To believe in Christ means to let oneself be determined by this event, to gain a new understanding from it, and to let one's existence be illuminated by it. Hence the formula πιστεύειν εἰς χριστόν does not mean our personal union with Jesus as our Lord, but is a shortened phrase for faith in God's saving act in Christ.[53] What happens to such key words in the New Testament as δικαιοσύνη, ἀγάπη, εἰρήνη, χαρά, ἐν Χριστῷ εἶναι, et cetera, when we may no longer see in them the personal living reality of Christ as the evangelists portrayed him for us? Has the whole wealth, the fullness of the New Testament message really been declared if our fellowship with Christ as a personal union with the exalted Lord or as personal safety in him has been left out, and if the phrase πιστεύειν εἰς Χριστόν must be understood as a figurative, abridged mode of speech?

7. Karl Barth views Bultmann's exegetical method as dominated by a systematic "Axiomatik,"[54] executed in a threefold way. Faith as obedient decision answers the *viva vox evangelii*. This creates the possibility of a new qualification of human existence. In this way full accent is laid upon the actuality of the message of Christ, upon the real presence of the saving word and of the saving event in preaching and faith. Just as sunlight caught in a glass is concentrated at one single point, which has the power to ignite a flame, so also in Bultmann's systematic "Axiomatik" everything is concentrated upon that

---

[52] Bultmann, *Das Evangelium des Johannes, Kritisch-exegetischer Kommentar über das Neue Testament,* ed. H. A. W. Meyer (11th ed; Göttingen: Vandenhoeck and Ruprecht, 1950), p. 43.

[53] Bultmann, *Theology of the New Testament,* I, 91 ff.

[54] Barth, *Die Kirchliche Dogmatik,* III/2 (Zollikon-Zürich: Evangelischer Verlag, 1948), pp. 531 ff. Cf. W. Klaas, "Der systematische Sinn der Exegese Rudolf Bultmanns," *Theologische Existenz Heute,* 26 (Munich: Christian Kaiser Verlag, 1953), pp. 26, 29 f., 45 f.

one point where the proclamation of the saving event in Christ occurs and where the obedience of faith is born. We are greatly indebted to Bultmann for having reminded us in a penetrating way of the marvellous actuality of the proclamation of Christ. The kerygma is in fact an address which places us before an ultimate decision. We are all too familiar with the art of falsifying the message of salvation into pious speculation and of allowing it to bypass us as a theologico-natural event without our really becoming involved in the "now" of the proclaimed message and without permitting ourselves to be called by it from death into life. For Luther God was a *vis rapiens,* and his word no less so. Luther said in his commentary on the epistle to the Galatians: "Paul is impassioned. He speaks from the abundance of his heart. He wants to enter into the *iustitiam, quae est resurrectio mortuorum.*" [55]

Therefore when Bultmann makes most emphatically clear that God's saving act in Christ is a direct message of comfort and claim, an address which saves and demands, when in this sense Christ rises into the word, then we will agree without any objection. The question which troubles us is: Can the salvation occurrence, "this thing that has happened, which the Lord has made known to us," be transmuted into something that is only an interpreted history, into a witness of faith which only wraps itself in the garment of a gospel narrative, but which of course cannot be understood in *propria sua sententia?* Can the *actum est,* the *perfectum est* of God's unique historical act in Christ as well as the *futurum resurrectionem,* the end of God's dealings with the world and us, be so set in brackets that they are dissolved in the proclamation and the faith responding to it? Is not the kerygma primarily *solemnis promulgatio,* a preaching which established the Church concerning the "mighty deeds of God" which have happened and will happen, without which the kerygma becomes a hypostasis floating in a vacuum? When this happens the past, the present, the future, the resurrection, the last day, and eternal life are all collapsed into one and merged into one single timelessly simultaneous occurrence. What if something similar to the Corinthian Gnosis should happen here? The kerygma as a message of God's act in Christ is in danger of being dissolved into assurance of a present fulfillment, of a Gnostic enthusiasm—except that now the existential-dialectical in-

[55] W. A., 40, I, 64, 3 ff.

terpretation of the kerygma replaces that enthusiastic Gnosis. Are we then faced merely with a question of a reinterpretation of the message of Christ in terms of a modern conceptuality which portrays to the contemporary Church the actual source and basis of its life? Or are not the biblical statements so abbreviated in Bultmann that the Church can no longer recognize in this interpretation the fullness of the apostolic witness?

8. Evangelical theology is continually being reproached from the Catholic side for having not yet learned that theology is only possible as theology of the Church.

> The Church is the condition for the very possibility of theology. . . . Theology is a function of the Church. The Church is not the product of theology or of theologians. The Church does not depend upon theology, but theology depends upon the Church. . . . A theology fundamentally emancipated from the Church overlooks what is essential—whatever else it may prove. The great theologians are saints and teachers of the Church. It is significant that the formula of the Mass begins: *In medio ecclesiae aperuit os eius et implevit eum dominus spiritu sapientiae et intellectus.*[56]

Is it entirely irrelevant for us to consider what such a phrase within the formula of the Mass might mean for a Church and a theology based on the Reformation? Must we not first understand what the Church is in its very depths as described by the New Testament and what the meaning of theological work is which takes this Church seriously and which does its thinking within its context and is directed only to its service? What service, what help, and what edification can the people of God here on earth receive from a theology which is developed *"in medio ecclesiae"*?

We raise this question also with a view to the mission field. What form must the interpretation of the New Testament kerygma take if it should stand the test of the mission field? We should listen for once to the men who work on these crucial frontiers of the Church. Is it not true that God himself gives us the interpretation of his message—that is, wherever the mighty deeds of God occur also today? On the one hand this occurs when the Church has become the "Church of God in action," and on the other, when the kerygma really builds the Church and drives men to their knees so that they must confess, "My Lord and my God." (John 20:28.)

[56] Herrmann Volk, *Das Neue Marien-Dogma*, p. 85.

In conclusion a statement from Luther: *"Sacrae literae volunt habere humilem lectorem, qui reverenter habet et tremit sermones Dei; qui semper dicit: Doce me, doce me, doce me! Superbis resistit Spiritus."* [57]

If this debate with Bultmann and the careful and grateful attention we pay his interpretation of the saving message lead us to approach the Scriptures with the petition, *"Doce me, doce me, doce me,"* in order to let ourselves and our own wisdom be radically questioned by them, then this struggle for the true knowledge of the saving message, broken out anew among us, will bring rich blessing for us and for our Church.

[57] Tischreden, *Luthers Werke in Auswahl*, ed. Otto Clemen, VIII (Berlin: Walter de Gruyter & Co., 1950) , 5017, 256.

THREE

ERNST KINDER

Historical Criticism and Demythologizing

If we take seriously "the Holy Scriptures as living witness" [1] in the sense that they express the Word of God to men through
real human words, then by the very nature of the case, we are compelled to apply historical and literary critical method as well as an
existentialist interpretation to the biblical witnesses. In this way we
are simply taking seriously the *true humanity* of the Bible. We must
take seriously the true humanity of the Bible just as we must take
seriously the true humanity of Jesus Christ against all Docetism. In
both instances the Word of God has really become flesh, first by
entering into the world and then by becoming the word of man.
Therefore, in neither case may we disregard the secular and human
approach. Hence the question is not whether we as theologians should
deal with the Bible from historical and literary critical points of view
or interpret it existentially. This is simply required in order to take
seriously and to illuminate the nature of the Bible as reality. The
question is rather how this is to be done and what place and dignity
one grants the Bible. The question is whether the human and secular
approaches can provide the standard and norm by which the actual
material content of the Bible should be defined and judged. The
question is whether primary axioms and ultimate standards for the
proper exposition of Holy Scripture can be gained from the requirements of historical and literary criticism and of existentialist interpretation.

[1] This was the theme of the conference at which this lecture was delivered.

We will not be dealing here with specific questions of historical and literary criticism or of existentialist interpretation of the Bible. Rather we will be carrying on a discussion with the theological program which we suspect stands behind them. We can hardly deal in any exhaustive way with the very complex and multifaceted modern theological movement which we call "the theology of demythologizing"—certainly an inadequate term. We will only attempt to understand something of its basic approach and method in the light of four critical observations and to say some fundamental things about it.

I

AN OBSERVATION FROM THE HISTORY OF THEOLOGY

The modern theological movement characterized by the term "demythologizing" is mainly a revival of the old "historical-critical school," the course of which was for some time interrupted. Yet it has allied itself with characteristic motifs which in the meantime have resulted from recent theological reflection.

a) The motifs and tendencies of the old historical-critical school were revived in German Protestant theology after the Second World War—in a new way, to be sure—and now seem to have an increasing fascination for the younger theological generation.[2] Toward the end of the twenties and the beginning of the thirties we imagined that "liberalism" in Protestant theology had been basically overcome in Germany and disposed of, especially as a result of the new theological consciousness awakened by Karl Barth. Other things also contributed to this, however, such as the former "theologies of crisis," the rediscovery of Luther's theology, the reawakening of a Church consciousness in theology, the Church's struggle, renewed reflection on the Lutheran confessions, et cetera. Now we see that we were deceived; the old liberalism was not actually overcome, but, when it seemed to have come to a dead stop or to a deadlock it was dialectically circumvented by a daring leap. It was argued down and reasoned away by theological rhetoric. Instead of going through it theologians bypassed it, and we are still suffering from its effects. Now it is evident

[2] Cf. Georg Merz, "Harnack redivivus," *Evangelische-Lutherische Kirchenzeitung,* (1951), p. 10.

that our new theological movement possessed more radical critical than constructive power. And to the extent the positive impulses of the Barthian theology for various reasons lost their impetus and no longer sustained themselves after the Second World War, with the result that a certain theological vacuum arose, once more the old liberalism reared its head. Yet it was no longer the old liberalism, for it had assumed a new form and a new face. The "theology of demythologizing" may be called the old liberalism in the dress of existentialist philosophy and dialectical theology.

Basically there was nothing new in the program of the theology of demythologizing. The questions and tendencies are identical with those which two-hundred years ago were introduced into Protestant theology by the "neology" of the Enlightenment. Ever since, they have been virulent and are still alive today because we have not succeeded in disposing of them. For that reason they keep returning to disturb us and cause us anxiety, and because their particular outward forms were usually "overcome" only partially or by a short circuit—that is, only apparently overcome by dealing with terms and posing false alternatives—as a consequence the specific person who challenges and "overcomes" them is in reality the one who perpetuates them. Thus these motifs and tendencies reappear in a new dress, whether it be the religious a priori of Schleiermacher and the theology of experience, the Kantian transcendentalism and ethicism, the Hegelian ideological speculation of the type of David Friedrich Strauss or of historicism and psychologism, or at present the philosophy of existence.

The actual entelechy of the theology of demythologizing is to a great extent more than its advocates and opponents realize the old rationalism of the Enlightenment. It is well for us first to view it honestly in terms of this lineage—and then of course we must see the other side too. While it is true that the theology of demythologizing picks up and extends the questions and methods of the old historical-critical school, which for a time were interrupted, it is not a simple repristination of them. It is markedly different since it unites certain motifs from recent theological reflection with tendencies which continued to survive from the old schema. Such motifs as the following could be mentioned: For example, the Christocentric approach (which, however, can already be found in Schleiermacher), or the

57

emphasis on the kerygmatic character of the Bible (which is already present in Kähler), or the existential focus of the biblical message in the sense of justification as found in Ritschl and Holl. (Together with all recent movements of Protestant theology since the Enlightenment the theology of demythologizing intends to be in its own way the actual fulfillment of the Reformation concern and approach!) Still other motifs are the radicalization of the Protestant *sola,* the use of ecclesiastical and theological language such as "Word of God," "revelation," "preaching," "eschatological," et cetera, and also the one-sided emphasis on the transcendence of God which wholly abandons this world to a pessimistic relativistic outlook, and above all, the dialectical method!

If we wish to recognize the nature of this theological movement we must keep in mind both the difference between the theology of demythologizing and the old historical-critical school characterized by such slogans as well as the distinctive connection between them. This constitutes its peculiar attraction. It also explains why it is so difficult and usually so frustrating to carry on any discussion with it.

b) The difference between these two parallel schools is that the historical-critical school was single-mindedly historical or so to speak, dogmatically historical. Whatever could not withstand the test of the historical approach had to be eliminated from theology. In contrast to it the theology of demythologizing is dialectical. With a peculiar flexibility it has a passionate interest in the *Wissenschaftlichkeit*— i.e., universal rationality and verifiability—of theology (a term used since rationalism) as well as an interest in the strict, irremovable historicity, and clearly with a predominantly negative effect. Here is also, however, the dialectic which says that our ultimate concern is not with historical factuality [3] but with kerygmatic efficacy and existential significance. In the one instance, therefore, we meet a critical decomposition of the objectively real character of the great and decisive facts of salvation demanded by the universally human concept of science and reality, and in the other the translation of their content into their existential significance. It is clear that the latter is done in order to solve the problem created by the former, but in such a way

[3] The concept "historical" itself is ambiguous here. Does Bultmann mean by it that which is *verifiable* by general historical means or that which has actually *happened?* Usually he makes a short circuit from one to the other without mentioning it.

that it makes a virtue out of a necessity. The theology of demythologizing shares the former tendency in common with the old historical-critical school in so far as those facts of salvation which are unverifiable in terms of the categories of our natural experience of reality are considered to be "myths." The result is different, however. Whereas the historical-critical school sought to eliminate these myths from the New Testament message simply because they were myths in order to discover in what remained the valid content of the New Testament, the theology of demythologizing, by attempting to interpret the "myths" existentially, ventures to retranslate their content into the understanding of existence inherent in them and in this form to retain their relevance for us today and to make them theologically fruitful.

On the one hand, therefore, we have here the continuation of the critical work of the old liberalism, though perhaps more radical and in its effect more negative, because one can afford to be less concerned, or in any case more emphatic and more *weltanschaulich*. The supernatural facts of salvation are not "historical." On the other hand we have a relativizing of these discoveries when it is said that no harm is done, that it is actually better that way, for by opening up the dimension of sheer validity the way becomes clear for a truly theological explication. Now in this area and in this form are applied the aforementioned motifs which have arisen with the recent theological movement. Thus, the two-hundred-year-old line of rationalism is perpetuated by the fact that the old rationalistic concept of science and the picture of the world of classical physics prevail. At the same time, however, the new theological pathos is taken up with emphasis. By and large the psychological effect and the triumphant mood of this theological movement are based upon the union of both the old and the new elements. Because of dialectics it is possible to do justice to both, but the price is high! In order to understand the second rightly it must be seen on the basis of and in connection with the first. The kerygmatic efficacy and the theological and existential significance are gained essentially at the cost of the objective facts which have been abandoned by means of historical criticism. Banned from the dimension of being, these theological statements have their essence only in the "flattened" form of sheer validity.

59

c) By virtue of its connection with these modern theological motifs the whole pathos of the theology of demythologizing is different from that of the old historical-critical school. Besides the dreary demand for exact *Wissenschaftlichkeit* which emerges here with its aversion to pietism, orthodoxy, ecclesiastical tradition, and clericalism, one can also sense here a certain theological—or pseudotheological?—passion, a feeling, and an impelling interest in what concerns our world view. It seems as if the theology of demythologizing is effective not so much because of its critical results or its theological interpretations, but more because of the dialectic which unites them, the rhetoric of existentialist philosophy, and because of its modern character as such. The powerful influence of this program, which, though in existence for some time, did not give rise to a movement until after the Second World War, seems to be more psychological than explicitly theological in nature. So the actual problem here is not so much theological, but, properly understood, more pedagogical—that is, in terms of the history of theology. In principle one could pronounce this program with its presuppositions and methods as having been for some time theologically obsolete. But what good does that do? The movement and its powerful influences do exist and will surely continue yet for a while. There are minds that are fascinated and troubled by it now. Why this should be so, and what else of greater quality could replace that which is obviously theologically deficient—that is the problem!

It seems that here we clearly and plainly see what has afflicted the whole of Protestant theology for the last two centuries and from which we all suffer. It seems that the seeds of a certain *als ob* theology are virulent within all of us, and that for this reason the theology of demythologizing greatly disturbs and troubles us. Therefore, we cannot and should not try to defame anybody personally in a pharisaic way, but we must still ask with responsible seriousness where this leads us and how we may avoid it—perhaps by means of a thorough reflection regarding our theological method. More important and promising than mere protests and proclamations is a positive solution which, instead of compensating for the Protestant feeling of uncertainty in some novel way, is not ashamed to think devoutly and resolutely from the perspective of the substance itself, and which thus fills up the vacuum in a much more positive way.

II

AN OBSERVATION FROM HERMENEUTICS

As in the case of the historical-critical school, the theology of demythologizing in principle disregards the phenomenon of the "Church" when evaluating and handling the Bible. The heuristic principles which should issue from the Church for the understanding of the content of the New Testament are replaced by those dictated by a modern world view.

a) In our discussion with the theology of demythologizing a viewpoint should be discussed which appears of secondary importance, unscientific, contrary to the Reformation, but which in reality plays a considerable role; a viewpoint which, in reference to the matter at hand, leads to a genuine scientific approach and which is in complete conformity with a genuine Lutheranism untainted by subjectivism and spiritualism. Just like the old historical-critical school, the theology of demythologizing does not take and handle the Bible essentially as a *Book of the Church*. Its whole approach as well as the particular methods which it uses when evaluating and dealing with the Bible in a fundamental and practical way indicate its definite disregard for the fact that the Bible must be considered primarily as the Book of the Church if we are not at the very outset to go astray when it comes to grasping its true content. On the contrary, it is almost one of its axioms and guiding principles that from the start the tradition and the confession of the Church concerning the New Testament are suspect,[4] essentially to be mistrusted, and had better be negatively evaluated.

By accepting this more or less negative presupposition for *Wissenschaftlichkeit* the theology of demythologizing is in agreement with the historical-critical school, and to that extent it is "liberal," despite the numerous assertions to the contrary on the part of its spokesmen. From the beginning it eliminates and ignores the fact that if one wishes to grasp correctly the true content of the Bible it must be taken

---

[4] In line with the theology of demythologizing we limit ourselves in what follows to the New Testament and to the great saving facts concerning the person of Christ to which it bears witness.

first and foremost as the Book of the Church. Such an approach as a heuristic a priori is rejected here as unscientific because it is prejudiced from the start. By "scientific" the theology of demythologizing means that we must a priori and in principle place more weight upon the insight and judgment of a neutral, disinterested, and impartial witness regarding the definition of the character of the reality in question than upon the testimony of one who is interested and partial in the matter. Therefore, to grasp the substance of reality behind the New Testament we must be guided more by universally human criteria of reality than by such as stem from the Church's experience of faith in connection with the Holy Scriptures.

When we postulate a regard for the experiences of the Church in connection with the testimonies of the New Testament as an essential point of departure for correctly grasping the content of the New Testament, we do not mean thereby subjection to an infallible teaching office of the Church or anything of the kind. Rather we have in mind the inner living connection with the actual content of the New Testament which cannot be had except by being brought into the Church's fellowship of faith. Then this means that we must accept and not deny the methodological implications of this living connection if we wish to interpret rightly the testimonies of the New Testament. Here we could mention, for example, the sacraments, without which we do not acquire such a living connection with the New Testament content. Can and ought we disregard the sacraments altogether as does the theology of demythologizing when we define the content and interpret the original testimonies of the New Testament? Further, we must take into consideration all the genuine experiences which the Church has ever enjoyed existentially in connection with the Holy Scriptures, including all that pertains to the faith of the Church today. Can and ought we disregard its methodological implications in the very first act of our theological inquiry into the Scriptures, or, what is even worse, depreciate it? Must this not rather act as a signpost and compass required by and appropriate to the subject matter when entering into the Holy Scriptures? Finally, we must mention also the requirements of ministering to the Church today as witness and pastor, requirements which arise directly out of the New Testament, the requirements of preaching, of gathering, of nurturing, and of edifying, as well as pastoral care. Are not these categories much more appropriate as heuristic principles in approaching the New Testament than those of the so-called "modern man," this symbolical figure in whom for the most part are concentrated only certain prejudices of some world view?

By these references we merely suggest in what sense we understand the whole complex of the Church, namely, as the pneumatic living connection which we possess with the living and personal substance of the New Testament—of course out of its own power! Here we must ask with all earnestness whether and to what degree this complex belongs methodologically to the presuppositions and the goals of theological study of the New Testament, so that this approach may be truly scientific—that is, pre-eminently appropriate!

b) Our question is whether we can altogether disregard this involvement in the Church and the directives inherent in it when we attempt to get a better grasp of the New Testament content, or whether any treatment of the New Testament and any attempt to discover its actual content apart from the complex of the Church is not an impossible and inappropriate, that is to say, an unscientific abstraction. The term "scientific" surely suggests what is appropriate, what is required by the matter itself, rather than something of one's own choosing. Is not theology as science only possible as a function related to the life of the Church? Only because there is a real Church which has certain needs is there such a science as theology, just as there is dental science only because there are teeth which need to be repaired. Hence, if theology really wants to be scientific—that is, appropriate to the substance in virtue of which it exists and for the sake of which it exists—it must derive its basic categories and heuristic principles from the actual life of the Church, and not from some place or feeling for life outside the Church. Is it not true that theology has been upset by an unsuitable and inadequate concept of science because it has more often derived its categories and norms from its position within the *universitas litterarum* than from its functional relation to the life of the Church?

Is not theology as true science (and not pseudo science) possible only as a function of the Church? And is not the authentic living connection of theology with the Church precisely its material connection with the New Testament, so that the relations of theology to the Church and to science are not antithetical as they threaten to become again today, but rather condition one another? True science involves an orientation to a particular sphere for the purpose of grasping and defining its subject with adequate categories. These arise from a living existential connection, a "symbiosis," with the subject. Hence at the very outset, true science involves a living connection between subject and object as well as between the categories of thought and the object.

Thus, a scientific, that is, an appropriate treatment of the Bible must proceed with the recognition that the Bible is the Church's Book and only exists as such. The reality of the Church with its needs is the "life situation" of the Bible. It came into existence only from within the Church and only for the sake of the Church. Therefore, one should not a priori have a suspicious and negative attitude toward genuine tradition as the sum of the Church's existential experiences relating to Holy Scripture. Rather, one must first be willing to listen to this tradition and to allow it to guide him. And since continuity with the substance of the New Testament is given and realized in the Church and only in the Church, one must be willing to express the content of the New Testament primarily from the standpoint of the Church's genuine experiences and needs.[5]

Only in the framework of this basic orientation—but not a priori and absolutely—are the historical-critical norms and methods properly to be applied, rather than the reverse, as is the case with the theology of demythologizing, in which alien norms and categories predetermine the general limits. As a result the genuinely theological motifs must see what room remains to them within these limits.

What we have characterized in abbreviated form as the "genuine experiences and needs of the Church" with respect to the New Testament ought not act as a law for biblical hermeneutics which would totally and one-sidedly dominate the entire procedure. This is impossible because the genuine experiences and needs of the Church are not

---

[5] At this point we cannot elaborate further to what degree the scriptural word gives rise to an eminently critical moment for the Church. In any case this critical moment of the scriptural word properly exists only within that living connection in the Church, because otherwise it is applied from some arbitrary external standpoint that evolves out of secular roots—thus handing the Church over to foreign control. Therefore, establishing the critical moment cannot be the primary thing here if heterogeneous standards are not to creep in. "Crisis" and "insecurity" as such are not theological criteria, as so often appears today. It is more appropriate to the youth movement than to theology if one wishes to make "insecurity" as such a virtue and a norm of legitimacy.

fixed in respect to the Bible, for what is "genuine" in the Church must be demonstrated again and again from the perspective of the Bible. There exists then a reciprocal relation in which the experiences and needs of the Church must be methodologically primary and in which the content of Scripture thus developed must be referred to as materially decisive. It is therefore true that the experiences and needs of the Church must be regarded as the heuristic principles to which we give a primary methodological status for viewing the true substance of the New Testament. The historical-critical norms and methods should then be applied within such a framework and relationship. If we wish, however, to avoid taking the wrong course they cannot be the primary heuristic principles, and above all, they cannot be applied in an absolute way; for if they are applied without presuppositions, so to speak, or as an unconditional law, then they are no longer neutral and "objective," but they are filled with the substance of a particular world view. Within this primary orientation of the experiences and needs of the Church the historical and literary critical principles should and must be applied honestly and vigorously, for the pneumatic reality has entered into earthly history and human language.

Guided by this primary orientation of the experiences and needs of the Church as a general inner relation to and as a living connection with the actual content of the Holy Scriptures, the historical and literary-critical norms and methods may and should contribute by helping us to delineate this substance more precisely and by placing it more sharply in our field of vision. Directed to the substance of the New Testament they are preserved from becoming exponents of a world view alien to the substance and are freed for an honest and neutral objectivity. It is necessary to distinguish between philosophy of history and unbiased historical research, between historicism or existentialism as a world view and a relevant application of historical methods or a faithful existential interpretation, just as it is also necessary to distinguish between a late idealistic epistemology as a universally humanistic philosophy and an inherently factual interpretation of literary documents.

The fact that we regard the Bible primarily as a Book of the Church and allow this to provide the primary heuristic principles for understanding the biblical content implies that we also respect the canon as an a priori for our interpretation. Without doubt this respect for the canon is in some way a necessary hermeneutical preliminary decision, and it is clear that we respect the canon primarily on account of the Church. By the canon we mean to indicate primarily the sphere and boundary of the authentic, original witness to the reality produced by the reality itself. There are unquestionably guiding principles with special content for exegesis which arise from the recognition of this sphere and boundary. The boundary of the canon is a decision of faith which the Church has made, or it is the Church's act of confession which comes from an inner connection with the content of Scripture. From this the Church ventured to make a confession which answered to the reality which established her, a confession which confirmed her and placed her existence in union with that reality. This confession points to the sphere and boundary of the authentic, normative, and original witness to the reality. The boundary of the canon is the first confession of the Christian Church respecting the reality which supports and challenges her, and from out of this confession all later confessions concerning this reality have grown. Already implied in the boundary of the canon there is an indication of the actual reality the Church has in mind. If we do not wish to proceed from an arbitrary or alien position, we will respect a heuristic principle for viewing the reality already implied in the fact that we seek that reality here and above all here and not elsewhere.[6]

By regarding the Bible primarily as a Book of the Church and accordingly by respecting the canon, we accept criteria which explain the existence, validity, and meaning of this Book. Now our theological task, part of which is historical and literary-critical study, is that of attempting to confront this claim of the Church respecting the Bible with the claim of the Bible itself. In any case, when we do this we must proceed from the claim of the Church. We cannot approach the Bible without presuppositions, nor seek in any kind of immediacy to understand its claim in a way which might oppose the Church's claim. If we do not approach the Bible from the standpoint of the Church,

[6] This implies that we are also of the conviction that the statements of the New Testament are essentially and basically not rightly understood and interpreted when they are not understood from the perspective of the Old Testament. The theology of demythologizing, however, just as the historical-critical school, by and large ignores this point of view. But it must be stated that when the New Testament is not understood from the "propaedeutics" of the Old Testament, the New Testament is necessarily understood from the "propaedeutics" of some kind of philosophy.

66

we do so from the standpoint of some world view. There is no third possibility such as a neutrality without presuppositions. By proceeding from the previous legitimate experiences and needs of the Church respecting Holy Scripture—but by no means concluding there—we enter into the Scriptures in order that our theology may now "promote the discussion between Scripture and confession" (Schlink) in a living reciprocal relation between Scripture and the life of the Church. Further we must measure, confirm, limit, correct, improve, and increase the claim of the Church by the content of the Scriptures. This means that the concept of the canon is in a certain respect a presupposition, but in another respect the very goal of exegesis, for sound exegesis must always contain both movements—from the outside to the inside and from the inside to the outside.

c) When the historical-critical school and the theology of demythologizing completely ignore this respect for the canon in their study and treatment of the New Testament, or rather deprecate it, then—negatively—this not only involves an inappropriate abstraction and reduction in the viewing of the biblical substance, but also—positively—it results in the adoption of some other course and in the exchanging of the Church's perspective of understanding for some other in arranging the biblical materials. To the degree that we do not receive our main heuristic principles, or "system of co-ordinates," so to speak, from the phenomenon of the Church, we will have to take them from a world view based on a feeling for life and on the natural man's criteria of reality—for we simply must have some kind of heuristic principles. Then the criteria and methods of an allegedly universal *Wissenschaftlichkeit* take the place of the main heuristic principles originating in the reality of the Church. They are given a priori and absolute validity, but in reality they derive from some philosophy. If "biased" witnesses are rejected, then preference must be given to the "unbiased" person and to the postulates and criteria of the person who is not inwardly a participant. Preference is given to the categories and norms of the natural man who is not inwardly grasped by the substance of the Bible over those of the "biased," participating, and believing man.

The real question is whether this is real objectivity and neutrality over against the unique substance of the Bible, for the "unbiased" witness is not at all neutral over against this substance. He makes a definite decision regarding the Bible, however, a decision providing him with his formal and neutral criteria and norms which he postulates as a priori and absolute. A definite feeling for life and a definite world view have already been implicitly accepted along with the a priori and absolute validity of such so-called scientific categories of understanding and interpretation. If they are divorced from their connection with one reality they exist in connection with another. When historical and literary methods are posited as primary and absolute norms they are no longer merely methods; they have become "isms," and they possess the content of a definite philosophy, though such be unintentional. When the living connection and the genuine experiences and needs of the Church are rejected as the primary heuristic principles for grasping and defining the content of the New Testament and are opposed by a certain *Wissenschaftlichkeit,* then they have been exchanged for the axioms of a particular concept of science, which are rooted in a definite feeling for life and picture of the world. These axioms are accepted as normative premises and as unconditionally valid dogmas. The result is subjection to the tyranny of a world picture and of a world view which dictates what is and what is not valid as "reality," and what may still possess validity or "existential significance." Thus the perspective of the world picture—arising from the standpoint of a natural feeling for life—dictates what may be retained and what must be reinterpreted. Does this not mean that ultimately the "world" and the "natural man" are appealed to as the judge and witness of what pertains to the Church, of the sense in which this or that is a concern of the Church, of whether the Church properly describes the concern of the Bible as its own concern, and so forth? With the definite rejection of the reality of the Church as somehow being a determinative factor, the historical-critical method with its own world view—and this entails the categories of the natural man—actually acquires the rank of a dogma. Such "dogmas" are as a rule much more tyrannical in experience than those which stem from the Church's existential experience in relation to Scripture.

While above we asked whether this procedure is really objectively neutral, we must now ask whether it is at all appropriate to the subject matter, whether it is adequate and congenial in relation to the uniqueness of this subject matter. Which heuristic method is more appropriate to the subject matter of the Bible: The "Churchly experience"—to use an expression of Vilmar—which has been gained from, by, and with the Bible, or the categories and standards which have been gained from the feeling for life and from the world picture of the natural man? Can the unbelieving man, can the so-called "modern man," can the "modern world picture" really give us better principles for grasping and defining *this* subject matter? We cannot get anywhere without making some "prior decision" on this question. The question is only what by nature is better suited to give the correct "bearings" on the real content of the Bible and the proper perspective for understanding it.

As we have already said, the universally human and the secular norms should and may not be excluded. For the sake of the incarnation also they must be applied. It is a question of the relative rank of the norms, namely, of those which come out of involvement in the life of the Church and thereby out of a living connection with the substance of the New Testament, and of those which come out of a general empiricism and rationality. Which norms are primary and which are secondary here, whether declared openly or not? Which shall move within the limits of the other? Which shall provide the fundamental concept of science and reality, and which shall stand within the sphere and limits of the other? That is the question. It appears to be a vital question for Protestant theology. We see this relation of rank—in particular because of the *anhypostasis*—in reverse order to the way in which the historical-critical school and its successor, the theology of demythologizing, see it.

III

AN OBSERVATION FROM SYSTEMATIC THEOLOGY

The theology of demythologizing reduces faith to its mere existential significance and abstracts from faith its essence as the assurance of a new, transsubjective reality, a reality from which even the existential significance of faith as such lives and thrives.

a) While with the second observation we had principally in mind that which the theology of demythologizing basically shares with the historical-critical school—and we regard it as revealing that that be seen first—now we will see what is distinctive about it. The common presupposition is that the saving facts attested in the New Testament are essentially "myths" when they cannot be fitted into our "modern picture of the world" as facts. These myths are attempts to express something inherently existential through supernatural facts. D. F. Strauss also held this same presupposition—but it can have different results. On the basis of this presupposition D. F. Strauss rejects practically the whole of the New Testament. The historical-critical school intended to remove and eliminate the "myths" from the New Testament and only give theological consideration to and bestow theological significance upon what remained. The theology of demythologizing, however, intends to interpret the myths existentially, that is, to retranslate them into the understanding of existence underlying them and from which they arose. This retranslation is done in the language and categories of the so-called modern man's understanding of existence. In this way the myths are to be made theologically relevant and homiletically fruitful.

The presupposition is that the nonhistoricity of the saving events in the New Testament has been established. Yet this is interpreted in such a way that it does not stifle theological interest. Even when they are proved to be nonhistorical they possess great theological significance, precisely because of their kerygmatic character. More important than the facts themselves is the fact that they were preached. They are also theologically significant because of the understanding of existence implicit in them and expressed by them—although awkwardly in terms of the framework and by means of the categories of the primitive picture of the world. By means of preaching this understanding of existence is supposed to be continually communicated to others. Thus, the theological task is to decipher the ciphered kerygma, so to speak, to communicate the understanding of existence implicit in and expressed by it, in order to translate the kerygma into the language of the modern picture of the world. (This raises the question whether it is actually possible to make the required separation between "the understanding of existence" and "the picture of the world"; whether one does not rather accept along with the modern picture of the world the feeling for life of the modern man, the former perhaps being the exponent of the latter; or is not the reverse true, namely, that the New Testament's understanding of existence has its only basis in certain facts which burst asunder the so-called modern picture of the world, without being able to be systematized into any definite New Testament picture of the world!)

Even though the saving facts have been demonstrated to be nonhistorical, the attempt is made to preserve what is specifically Christian,[7] rather than allowing it to be dissolved into a generally humanistic religiosity, as was the case with the historical-critical school. Indeed, the theology of demythologizing not only intends to rescue what is specifically Christian, but also to give it more cogent validity by freeing theology from the shackles of historical science and metaphysics, from the "world"—thus enabling it to concentrate entirely upon what is kerygmatic and existential. By such "demythologizing," or positively expressed, by such a kerygmatic and existentialist interpretation, theology will do justice in a quite different way to the specifically Pauline message as the word of the cross, of sin, and of pardon, as well as to the actual concern of the Reformation with its evangelical emphasis on justification. As long as value is placed upon the objective factuality of the saving events, such as the real preexistence of Christ, the virgin birth, the miracles of Jesus, the bodily resurrection, the ascension, and the future eschatological drama, the New Testament message is encumbered and shackled.

Thus the central Christian content is theologically affirmed, but only in a form which is valid and significant for the kerygma and an interpretation of existence, that is, only ontologically, but not ontically —not as real objective facts which have actually happened transsubjectively.[8] There is no place for them within the framework of our modern picture of the world. Therefore, all the central Christian truths are divested of their factual character, are reduced to the mathematical point of mere kerygmatic and existential validity, and have their *raison d'être* only in the shrunken "unidimensional" form of pure significance. The establishment of the kerygmatic relevance and the existentialist interpretation is carried on at the expense of the objective reality of the events. But this is too high a price!

Nevertheless, a theological virtue is made out of a necessity— i.e.,

---

[7] The old understanding of existence in the sense of having my ego enslaved in world-care–sin; the new understanding of existence in the sense of a trusting surrender freed for obedience-justification; the figure of Christ and the event of his cross as an indispensable factor in the transition from the old to the new understanding of existence by placing man radically and finally before decision; the confession that in Christ one stands before God himself, et cetera.

[8] We are reminded of Albrecht Ritschl's statement that religious-theological judgments are not judgments of being but are judgments of value (significance). The *proton pseudos* of this whole matter exists in the "but."

71

the nonhistoricity of the events—by stripping away from faith all false historical and metaphysical "assurances." Thereby faith becomes altogether a plunge into the totally uncertain darkness. The continual attack against everything which could possibly provide any assurance for faith—with the result that everything "uncertain" is *eo ipso* theologically superior—was a fashionable pathos of yesterday's theology, and now recurs as a dominant pathos in the theology of demythologizing. But is this really a theological pathos? Is it not rather one that belongs to the youth movement and the philosophy of existence? Does this introduce any actually serious theological criteria?

It is surely correct that the objective facticity of the saving events as such cannot be the basis of faith. Does this then involve the fundamental rejection of any objective facticity? There appears to be a fatal error of judgment here, no doubt the aftereffect of the antimetaphysical bias of the Ritschlian ethicism and of Wilhelm Herrmann's idea of the relation between the basis and the content of faith. Also certain influences of the "dialectical theology" can be traced here, in particular its concept of transcendence, also its concept of the incarnation, but above all its dialectical method, which wants to make what is theologically significant basically independent of historicity. The theology of demythologizing accentuates the assertion about the irrelevance of the historical into an assertion of nonhistoricity in order to make a theological virtue of this necessity in a dialectical way. But who can actually affirm and decide that something is not "historical";[9] what court and by what criteria? Is this assertion of nonhistoricity really the result of objective historical research (but how can that be historically demonstrated objectively with respect to *these* events?) ; is it a postulate of a dialectical theology of crisis, or is it a prejudice of a world view, the dictatorship of a world picture? We cannot help having the impression that much which is presented as strictly historical is in reality not historically based, but is systematically postulated, or is a philosophical *petitio principii*. In our debate with the theology of demythologizing, it does not seem to be basically a question of a hermeneutical problem, as it is alleged, but a matter of world view.

b) The theology of demythologizing reduces faith together with its object to mere existential significances, but it fails to recognize that

---

[9] See below concerning the ambiguity of this word. Here it is meant primarily in the simple sense of an objective factual event.

faith as faith exists, lives, and thrives on transsubjective realities. Faith (*Glaube* comes from *geleben,* meaning to live on something) points beyond itself to a transsubjective reality by which it has been brought forth and by virtue of which alone it exists. To be sure, the only principle of assurance in faith is the element of *fiducia,* but faith contains more than mere *fiducia.* Within it there is also *assensus, notitia,* and *fides historica.* The Lutheran confessional writings—especially Apology IV—passionately assert that faith is not merely nor primarily *assensus, notitia, and fides historica,* but rather *fiducia.* They still clearly say, however, that faith also contains those elements. In any case they do not recommend a complete reduction of faith to the merely fiducial element. Supported by the fiducial element, genuine faith contains the assurance of new "supernatural" factual realities which are disclosed to it by virtue of the fiducial assurance and without which faith would not exist at all.

The theology of demythologizing is certainly right in stating that here we are dealing with such realities and occurrences which cannot be established by historical means, but which in preaching are disclosed to the heart and conscience in fiducial faith, realities to which there is no other access except in word and faith. But its error lies in concluding that simply because they have no natural reality, they therefore have no objective reality. Here we see the semantic ambiguity in the use of the concept "historical." Does the term "nonhistorical" mean incapable of being established by historical means, or does it mean not having happened at all? Unnoticed, this term oscillates between the first and the second meaning in almost continual confusion, although Kähler had already called attention to the difference between them. The theology of demythologizing is undoubtedly right in regard to the first meaning where we are dealing with realities that cannot be discovered as realities by historical means. Then follows the error in this reasoning which makes this important truth into a disastrous half-truth, namely, that these realities do not exist at all as objective occurrences, but only as kerygmatic power and existential significance. Here it is evident how we stand under the dictatorship of the modern picture of the world, since ultimately we allow this to decide what can be objectively real and what not.

Here we must also refer to the misleading way in which the word *geschichtlich* is repeatedly used. It has been rightly emphasized that in

73

the strict sense *Geschichte* and *geschichtlich* are not concerned with a mere occurrence per se. They refer to something which places me before a decision concerning my existence in the here and now. But now this latter element is taken all by itself, isolated from the objectively real occurrence, and in this sense the word *geschichtlich* is repeatedly used with emphasis. Is this not—at least linguistically—the same as forgery?

It is necessary to point to the objectively real character of the objects of faith, to the biblical and Lutheran *est* in contrast to the mere *significat* to which it has been watered down by the theology of demythologizing, since the *significat* itself only lives from the *est*. Only this must be done in the right evangelical way. It will not do simply to place in unrelated contrast to it a positivistic, historical, or metaphysical concept of reality. It is a matter of showing how a *sui generis* "supernatural" reality discloses itself in faith, how together with faith a consciousness of reality, a *sui generis* sense and criterion of reality are given—that is, how a genuine reality independent of faith has created faith, which faith alone can see and recognize in its objective factuality, from which faith as such lives and thrives, but which just for this reason is objective reality. Along this line Günther Bornkamm has given important viewpoints for overcoming the theology of demythologizing in his essay, "Myth and Gospel." [10] By beginning strictly with justifying faith, he shows how faith in that from which it lives and in that upon which it is suspended points beyond itself to a real, transsubjective reality outside itself. Thus he tries to develop a genuine theological concept of reality.

If in our second observation we called attention to the reality of the Church as an heuristic principle for the correct grasp of the true content of the New Testament, we now draw attention to the reality of faith which itself contains the criteria for this content and whose objects cannot be placed in the Procrustean bed of some alien criteria of reality. Faith should be fundamentally free from the regimentation of the historical both in regard to value and being. Of course, it has no need of fearing a posteriori any historical judgment and of trying to avoid it. The primary positive criteria of reality lie within faith itself, however, and as such it must also have confidence and courage

[10] Cf. pp. 172 ff. in this volume.

to affirm the objects in which it believes and on the basis of which it believes. In order to be really faith it must believe in something with certainty. It should not reduce itself to a mere existential "as if" and thus finally capitulate to a concept of reality essentially alien to it.

Faith knows that as faith it is created, supported, and fulfilled by facts. It is not possible to do as the theology of demythologizing intends, namely, to separate the factual from the actual, the fact from the act, to play them off alternately against each other, and to wish to have the act without the fact. This separation and opposition of act and fact is a false alternative. It results in a whole series of erroneous oppositions—for example, when one says, "not historical fact, but eschatological event of salvation." Just as practically the whole of modern Protestant theology—and Church politics—the theology of demythologizing is shot through with false alternatives in which the modern man expresses his "short-windedness." He falsely radicalizes the one idea he is able to think, and he lacks the mental "long wind" to think several thoughts at the same time as is necessary to do with respect to the truths of Christian faith.

When faith is reduced to its mere existential significance by cancelling out the facticity of its objects, then one advances the exclusive validity of a positivistic concept of reality, in which some criteria of reality outside faith are made to act as norms to determine whether the objects of faith have actually happened and objectively exist or not. Thus in general a rationalistic concept of science long since overcome and the world picture of the old classical physics clearly provide the theology of demythologizing with its negative orientation. Thus, when measured by universally rational and empirical criteria of reality, a myth is something that cannot be real; yet it deserves to be given a religious or some other kind of consideration or validity. "Myth" is essentially, therefore, only a negative concept, a limiting concept from the perspective of the natural concept of reality. Only beyond this limit does what is real emerge.

Only when theology with confidence and firmness actually takes seriously the unique "supernatural" reality which discloses itself in faith will it become free from the "Babylonian captivity" of an alien concept of science, for it is true that every concept of science originates from a corresponding concept of reality. Science is concerned with truth, and truth is correspondence with reality. Hypnotized by the absolute claim of a concept of science derived from a corresponding concept of reality which roots in the natural man's feeling for life, theology, from feelings of uncertainty and inferiority, does not properly rely upon its own concern as it would do if in trust it allowed an actual *sui generis* reality to disclose itself and from that perspective carried on its thinking. Instead, theology, tryannized by a natural concept of reality with its absolute claim, attempts merely to think towards its subject, so far as that is still possible under these presuppositions. But theology can and may not wish to demonstrate its scientific character by submitting to the claim of unconditional validity which the natural man raises for his criteria of reality, permitting these to prescribe the laws of its own activity and to assign it the place for its own object. Rather, theology must have the confidence and courage to acknowledge as fully real a special kind of reality which includes its own objectivity, to carry on its thinking from this perspective, and eventually to receive therefrom its own special thought forms and criteria.

Even if these "supernatural" realities are revealed only to faith, they are nonetheless objectively real and have truly happened. Why this *horror concreti* which continues to afflict modern Protestantism? If we commit the error of a *fideism* which, under the tyranny of positivistic criteria of reality, takes refuge in the shadowy existence of a mere existential "as if," then we deny the reality of the incarnation. ὁ λόγος σάρξ ἐγένετο: It really became flesh, and did not remain mere *logos!* God's Word has really entered the sphere of immanence as a real event and does not have merely so-called "eschatological" meaning at the periphery. God's Word has really entered into our creatureliness and history, and not only into our understanding of existence. Thus the "stories which happened there" [11] make a *sui generis* claim to reality. This claim is not to be piously respected only in relation to these stories, but now all reality is somehow to be approached from such a standpoint, and its claim to absoluteness shattered. What has happened here will not only be an additional reality, but will be the reality of all reality! Now this will confront all natural reality. In such a confrontation, resulting from taking the incarnation seriously,

[11] Why should we not refer to them as *Heilsgeschichte*, an expression which is taboo for the theology of demythologizing? But the expression does not matter, which to be sure is equivocal and therefore subject to misunderstanding.

the "saving historical" realities need not shun dialectically the historical judgment but must endure it in some way. On no account, however, can the Word of God and history be so divorced, as is the case with the theology of demythologizing, that in reality they run side by side unrelatedly, so that history is abandoned to meaninglessness and radical pessimism and the Word of God leads the shadowy existence of a mere hypothetically valid "as if" at the periphery of history.

c) If we affirmed in our second observation that we cannot ignore the reality of the Church in grasping and defining the content of the New Testament, we now affirm that we cannot disregard that which faith claims to be real. This orientation to the Church and this attachment to faith with its assurance of reality are not at all unscientific, but are really scientific because they are true to the facts. There is no legitimate and suitable access to the human word and to what is earthly and historical in the Bible apart from an inner connection with its real supernatural content. Our exegesis of the Bible can and may not expect to stumble suddenly and directly upon a given meaning from mere words. That would be an arbitrary reduction inappropriate to the facts. Rather we can proceed from the word to its existential meaning only by way of an acknowledgment of the objective event attested by the word. That means that we cannot appropriately interpret the human word of the Bible when we ignore that it is at the same time the Word of God, which effects real history. Just as it is not possible to grasp and portray [12] the figure and the earthly life of Jesus with natural psychological and biographical categories, although he was true man; and just as we cannot explain the "saving historical" facts which the Bible recounts only in terms of natural scientific and historical norms, although they have really happened in our world— both are based on the mystery of the *anhypostasis*—so also we cannot explain the New Testament testimonies themselves purely by means of literary principles of interpretation, although they are surely real human words. (In analogy to the mystery of the *anhypostasis* of the human nature by the divine Logos into a *unio personalis,* we could call this mystery the *unio instrumentalis* of the divine and the human word in the Bible, which the Bible characterizes as *theopneustos.*)

---

[12] All the "Life of Jesus" attempts have run aground on the reality of the *anhypostasis.*

Just as we are dealing here with a *sui generis* history, so also in dealing with the biblical testimonies inspired by this history we are dealing with *sui generis* words which simply elude the grasp of purely general literary categories. This is because they proceed from and point to something which likewise eludes the grasp of general historical categories.

Thus it is not possible to apply extra-biblical categories of interpretation as unconditional rules for the understanding of the biblical texts—that is, for grasping their meaning. For the sake of the unique content which has been specifically created by the Word and Spirit of God unique methods and categories are required for grasping the meaning of the original witnesses. But these methods and categories, which quite generally and briefly have been summarized by the slogan "pneumatic exegesis"—which in itself does not say anything definite, but intends something true and important—must not be exempted from the general literary-critical analyses. It is only that these cannot be primary and exclusive. Because of the real character of the Incarnation, neither the historical-critical method with respect to the facts nor the literary-critical with respect to the witnesses can by any means be avoided. Because of the reality of the *anhypostasis,* however, neither one can be the primary and unconditional norm. Thus the historical and literary-critical exegesis can only be "bound" within the "pneumatic" exegesis. Proceeding from the Bible as the Church's Book, led by its genuine experiences and needs in relation to Holy Scripture, in order thereby to be advised of its authentic content, and in faithful personal grasp of its content and in devoted attachment to it, every honest historical and literary-critical treatment of the New Testament can serve to illuminate and sketch the profile of this content more accurately or to further its discussion. Thus in every genuine biblical exegesis there will always occur this double movement from the human word to the divine content and from the divine content again to the human word. While in the first movement the pneumatic reality of the Church provides the heuristic approach to the content, and while the historical and literary-critical methods follow with their contribution, so now in the second movement faith in those supernatural realities through which the divine mind has been existentially disclosed provides the initiative, and also the historical and literary-critical approaches work toward this end with their criteria and methods. Thus the historical and literary-critical methods are embraced here, on the one hand in the movement from word to content, and on the other hand in the movement from content to word. In that way they are "neutralized," or rather freed from the content and tendency of some particular world view for a genuine methodology.

IV

AN OBSERVATION FROM HOMILETICS

The existentialist interpretation of the New Testament message is a task which theology must always undertake afresh. It is only relevant and promising, however, when it is done on the basis of the realities attested in the New Testament, confessed by the Church, and grasped in faith, and not at their expense.

a) We do not intend to depreciate the important concern of the theology of demythologizing; namely, the existentialist interpretation of the great truths of the Christian message and their translation into a form which searches out—or troubles—modern man in his situation, encounters him in heart and conscience, and calls him to decision. Rather, we on our part must take it very seriously. We also try in all our preaching, teaching, and counseling not merely to represent the supernatural facts and events as such, but also the will and action of God revealed in them, to address men existentially and to put to their heart and conscience *tua res hic agitur!* Such a "translation process"— which is part of the condescension and visitation of God both in judgment and grace—always is set as a fresh task before us preachers, teachers, and counselors. It is not to be fulfilled by the system of some fashionable philosophy, for modern man is not a uniform, abstract literary figure. Rather he is a living person who appears in very different forms and in numerous situations which require our continual adjustment and accommodation.

The theology of demythologizing pays too high a price in accomplishing this important and necessary concern of interpreting the Christian message existentially. The existential significance of the great Christian truths is elaborated and proclaimed at the expense of the transsubjective and authoritative realities which stand behind them, so that these truths are reduced to their kerygmatic impact and existential significance. In this way its important concern becomes a half-truth resulting in this disastrous and false alternative: Not ob-

79

jectively factual, but kerygmatically potent and existentially significant; not the fact, but the act; not ontical, but ontological, et cetera. This "but" is false and disastrous.

In addition to this, that kerygmatic impact and existential significance to which the content of the objective facts of salvation is reduced are forced and diverted into only one specific direction, because here the definition of the point of the kerygma and its existentialist interpretation are undertaken in terms of a rather fixed schema; namely, in terms of Heidegger's philosophy of existence, the main elements of which are allegedly to be rediscovered in an exaggerated Paulinism. This is so because this philosophy itself is to be understood only as a kind of secularized Christianity, as a remnant of the original Christian substance. This does not at all result in making the kerygma effective and in disclosing a living existentialist interpretation. It merely works in the service and favor of a specific literary feeling for life of the present day. This means an enormous impoverishment and curtailment of its own—and, as we have said, important—concern, threatening it with intellectual sterility.

The theology of demythologizing is actually oriented more towards the *quo,* the whither of the Christian message, than towards the *unde,* the whence. It receives its categories, norms, and criteria not so much from the reality from whence the message comes, but more from the man and his situation to which the message comes—and, as we have said, only from a definite man in a definite situation. Indeed, in the final analysis the norms and perspectives derived from the life feeling and world picture of a specific man who is addressed so modify the Christian message that the objective reality falls into the background for the sake of a specific interpretation which is now supposed to exhaust the entire fullness of the message. Basically then, the norms for preaching come from the hearer, but this means that ultimately he is left all alone in his picture of the world and in his existential feeling, all alone in a meaningless and merciless environment at the horizon of which there appear only some significant ideas encountering him as a "mathematical point."

To be sure, preaching should be actual, but it must first be substantial. The more genuinely and obediently it is really substantial, the more genuine, living, relevant, manifold, and redemptive will that preaching be in its actuality. There is no competition between a genuine substantiality and actuality. Both of them condition each other, because the motive which prompted God to cause the great facts of salvation to happen was already an expression of his divine will *pro nobis*. Therefore it is not necessary to force the application by any artistic modifications. The Holy Scriptures are by nature the divinely given bridge and rendezvous of fact and act, of substantiality and actuality, so that we derive the norms of genuine actuality best from the Scriptures themselves. The Scriptures know our existence, our flesh, our situation, and our world better than we do ourselves. Genuine conformity to Scripture includes in itself the highest degree of modernity and actuality. Our preaching should not take its categories and norms from the hearer. It must derive them from the substance and the original proclamation authorized by God. Preaching should present this substance to the hearer in its own power and in accordance with the canon ordained by God. It should address him personally so that he is led beyond himself and in judgment and grace is freed for an authentic life. Only the "wholly other" can make man a true "self," because he was originally created in the image of God.

b) The theology of demythologizing does not only bypass the Church's interpretation of the New Testament—our second observation—it not only does not take seriously the uniqueness of faith in its relation to the New Testament—our third observation—it does not even take the self-understanding and self-assertions of the New Testament itself seriously. Instead it chooses and rejects from the Bible according to its own norms. The following three positions are connected: (a) First, one is directed to the content of the New Testament by the scriptural experience of the Church in which the New Testament content continues to live; (b) then, one is inwardly united with this content through a personal faith in salvation which includes its assurance of reality; (c) and finally, one attempts to take seriously the self-assertions of the New Testament. To bring these three things together is an important part of our theological task, and the historical and literary-critical methods and the kerygmatic and existentialist interpretation will also play their respectively important roles—but always within this perspective! This is quite a different perspective than when the historical and literary-critical viewpoints provide the primary postulates, or when the kerygmatic evaluation and existentialist interpretation proceed at the expense of the other. It is the first perspective, however, which renders these things more suitable and scientific, since the latter, with its structures and norms derived not from this unique and specific substance itself, but rather from the standpoint and situation of an outsider, is forced upon the New Testament and necessarily does violence to it.

We must try to realize what strange and artificial figures the New Testament witnesses become for the sake of the theories of the demythologizing theology. What oddly tortuous digressions these somewhat educated men made in order to express things which they really could have said more simply! To support one's own hypotheses one cannot blame everything on their "picture of the world," for if it were true that their picture of the world by its very nature suggested to them such mythological things, then this "new understanding of existence" would necessarily have suppressed rather than kindled them. Not only in respect to their thought forms do the New Testament witnesses appear more than strange according to the myth theory, but even in an ethical respect they appear very much open to criticism and anything but trustworthy, for they affirm quite simply that certain facts have really happened, and they appeal unqualifiedly to the fact that they have seen, heard, and experienced them. Could one bring himself to accept this new understanding of existence—a life and death question —through the mediation of men with such "twisted brains" and with such a twisted sense of truth? If this simple question may be allowed!

On the other hand, how painfully many of the simple, unvarnished, and "massive" self-assertions of the New Testament—for example concerning the resurrection in Paul—disturb the hypotheses of the theology of demythologizing. What complicated and subtle interpretations they force the New Testament to make! And, *cui bono?* Does this not clearly have its origin in a *petitio principii* when, for example, the whole eschatological expectation of the future in the New Testament has to be transformed into an "axiological eschatology" here and now? (In view of the "dismantling"—this expression cannot be avoided here—of the whole eschatological expectation of the future in the New Testament and its reduction to a "mathematical point" of a present existential feeling, it is astonishing that the word "eschatological" has become such an important word, indeed, nothing less than a vogue word of the demythologizing theology which encounters us everywhere. It is given an entirely different meaning, however. But we ask in all seriousness whether we should not cease abusing the word "eschatological" in the sense of a somehow final, or in any case, of an exclusively axiological eschatology and restore this word to its original meaning of *res novissimae* in the sense of a teleological eschatology.)

Should we not simply believe in a purely historical way what the New Testament witnesses say, instead of being a priori suspicious of them—as well as of Church tradition—in respect to certain things that are dictated by the so-called modern picture of the world? Should we not put our trust in them even in regard to earthly and historical things, at least until we are very soundly convinced of the contrary? But the contrary has not yet been soundly proved historically; it is only asserted in line with a world view, and no one can require us to take seriously refutations that are simply determined by some world view. On the contrary, faith is here the first and not the last thing which remains when all the other criteria have uttered their judgment, and surely any theological concept of faith is not true if it does not in some way also include trust in the biblical witnesses. Should we not, or rather, must we not first of all trust what they have to say also about "earthly things" when they have such important "heavenly things" (John 3:12) to tell us which are divine and ultimately decisive for our existence? Now when we proceed from this standpoint —instead of a priori putting everything in question by heterogeneous criteria—and carry our reflections further on this basis, everything else begins to look quite different. The question is always who and what "throws the switch" here: The life of the Church, a personal saving faith with its reality consciousness, and the self-assertions of the New Testament—all three interconnectedly, or the one who is addressed? The first way seems to us to be the truly scientific one because it is more faithful to the facts.

c) In conclusion we will repeat what was expressed in the fourth thesis by the term "promising." It is simply not true that kerygmatic power and existential significance would really be creatively released, reinforced, and increased with the removal of objective factuality. On the contrary, however, when the objective factuality is denied, ultimately the kerygmatic power and existential significance no longer exist. When the fact is eliminated the act is also eliminated, for the act finally lives from the fact alone, and the kerygmatic validity and

83

existential significance ultimately live from the factual occurrence.

If we wish to have the existentialist interpretation at the expense of the objective reality—and the *significat* without, or even against the *est*—then we finally saw off the limb on which we are sitting. Now the existential significance is simply not to be had "nakedly," but only with and on the basis of the factual occurrence. This whole reduction to mere existential validity and significance undertaken here is itself only possible because these facts to be "demythologized" once happened, because they are there, and because until now people believed in them and experienced from their reality a creative abundance of existential meanings. The theology of demythologizing is to be understood basically as the end of a process. It is possible to exclude the facts by an existentialist interpretation only because our "forefathers" believed in the facts. It is very much of a reduction when one no longer believes in the facts but would still like to retain their content, at least in the form of a condensed, reduced, and merely existential significance. One still lives on the capital of the "forefathers," but only the least possible minimal reduction of it remains. Therefore, this kind of theology is no longer capable of reproducing itself. It can no longer carry on its work constructively. It can only produce intellectual subtleties or further be dissolved. How could this kind of theology provide a really creative impulse to the preaching of the future, gather and edify the Church, and evoke in its hearers the existential echo of confession and prayer? It stands at the end of a process. Its spiritual "descendant" will say that he can acquire the same thing more simply, without taking the complicated detour of mythologies and demythologizing, of ciphering and deciphering.

Theology and preaching will be able to be promising, procreative, and constructive with respect to kerygmatic power and existential effect only when they devoutly let the supernatural facts of saving history stand in their transsubjective actuality. Just as faith, preaching lives from something other than itself. It will not do to lay the entire fullness of revelation exclusively within the event of preaching and of one's encounter with it, but preaching and its effect always proceed from the revelation presupposed by it. Although this revelation should continuously become an event in preaching and faith, it should never as such be absorbed in it. Thus we recognize the translation process of existentialist interpretation as a continuously fresh task that is set before theology, but always on the condition that the objective factuality is retained. Otherwise, it is exhausted in only one particular existentialist interpretation—for the sake of which everything would be undertaken—and then peters out. When we retain it, however, it is an inexhaustible reservoir of actual creative existential preaching, for these facts possess this "in themselves."

Further, who or what requires that these facts should not be retained if not the basic standpoint of the world view and norm of the natural man which makes itself the decisive factor? It is just this, however, which we cannot and should not allow, and precisely for his sake. Therefore, we orientate ourselves not to the *quo* but continuously afresh to the *unde* of the message, so that in preaching, so far as the norms are concerned, one relies upon the fact that this is true, and not first of all that it becomes true through preaching. Then also in the event of preaching it becomes true, but preaching as such is not the cause of its truth. We must orientate ourselves to the subject matter and not to the hearer. We do this finally for the sake of the hearer, for his own blessing, that he might be redeemed from himself, from his existential feeling and his picture of the world, and might be led beyond himself, instead of being abandoned in a merciless world.

FOUR

WALTER KÜNNETH

Bultmann's Philosophy and the Reality of Salvation

What occasions our reflection on the problems raised by Bultmann's "demythologizing" in the present situation of the Church and theology? There seem to be two reasons which require us to take up a position.

The need for reflection arises first from the quality and the extent of influence of Rudolf Bultmann's theological theses. An amazing characteristic of our situation is the fact that although Bultmann's decisive publication appeared a decade ago, it has not diminished in significance. Rather, it has enjoyed an increasingly greater scope of action and a still greater depth of influence. Meanwhile something like a Bultmann "school" has arisen. Of course the disciples of the Bultmannian theology interpret and understand their master in different ways and lay stress upon different things.

It is all the more important for us to take up a position because the questions which Bultmann has raised are not peripheral viewpoints; they put in question the very center of the preaching and doctrine of the Church. Thus a *status confessionis* has arisen which goes beyond the framework of a special theological science, and it must be granted that Helmut Thielicke is right in saying that Bultmann's theology affects the "very foundations of the Church," [1] and that it is an "ecclesiastical" event.

If, however, Bultmann's theology involves a new understanding of the substance of Church doctrine and of the New Testament message, then the Church also is affected by these discussions—particularly since

[1] *Theologie der Anfechtung* (Tübingen: J. C. B. Mohr, 1949), pp. 135 ff.

Bultmann's ideas indirectly influence the pulpit and other preaching situations. Therefore we cannot blame Bishop D. Haug for speaking at the "Landeskirchentag" in Stuttgart (1951) of "negative consequences of a theological stream that has been in motion a long time." In his opinion we are faced with a "perilous attack upon the content of our faith." The consequence of this will be a new "distrust of theological work in general and of the trustworthiness of our office."

The second reason which makes it our duty to engage in this discussion must be viewed in terms of the background of this problem in the history of theology and in the history of ideas.

Questions which are essentially bound up in the Christian message, such as faith and history, revelation, myth, and their relations to each other, have been persistently abandoned in serious reflection. These vital problems are brought to expression again in Bultmann's theology. Thus Bultmann becomes a mouthpiece or a representative of a highly significant question in the history of ideas.

In the encounter with the question which Bultmann has posed no doubt a serious gap in the work of modern theology has become evident and its disclosure has become perhaps very painful. Since the triumph of "dialectical theology" about thirty years ago the problems and questions of "liberal theology" with respect to the relations between the history of religion, myth, revelation, and faith—particularly with respect to the problem of historical-critical research—have been left unsolved. The questions were suppressed but not answered. All too readily dialectics elevated itself above the battlefield of historical-critical research with these famous theses of Karl Barth about "supra-history," "primal history," and "transcendence of history." The struggle which was then merely discontinued must be renewed in this arena of historical research and fought through to the end. It is to Bultmann's credit that he has placed this problem again in the center of theological discussion. Therefore, if I may say so, his concern is to heal in his own way the "theological-historical neurosis" which was created by suppressing the problem.

Accordingly, all the disciplines of theology are again summoned to this battle front. It is in fact a question which "will likely preoccupy a whole theological generation and in general remain an abiding question." [2]

[2] *Ibid.*, p. 138.

Our obligation to take up a theological position results from these preliminary reflections. Yet it cannot be clearly enough emphasized that it is by no means a polemic against the person of Bultmann. His personal faith is not part of the discussion—something which Bultmann himself has recently stressed quite rightly and explicitly. Nor is his significance as a venerable teacher to be questioned, a fact which places him perhaps on the level with Adolf Harnack. Rather it is a question of a serious and strictly theological matter of concern. The task consists mainly in arriving at an understanding of what Bultmann's theology means and intends. It would be erroneous to advance cheap and hasty judgments on Bultmann's theses without a basic consideration of the subject. At the same time it gives us the opportunity to offer real help in reflecting theologically on the basis of the New Testament message in the midst of this crisis of faith and in view of the disquiet of the churches. Of course it is impossible in this context even to touch on all the detailed questions which Bultmann's teaching raises. Bultmann's theses actually affect all disciplines. We therefore intend to draw out some essential principles from the standpoint of systematic theology and to offer a small contribution to the decisive question of basic principles.

I

The Meaning of the Programmatic Slogan: "DEMYTHOLOGIZING THE NEW TESTAMENT"

A. THE CONCERN OF RUDOLF BULTMANN

Our question is: What are the intentions which have caused Bultmann to propose this basically new theological view? We think there is a threefold basis to his endeavor.

In the first place, Bultmann's undertaking becomes understandable only if we acknowledge quite frankly his honest concern for the truth. Bultmann suffers from the anxiety of the research historian. He sees contradictions between the statements and results of the New Testament "sources" and the preaching of the Church and tension between scientific exegesis and the message of the Church. Faithful to the Reformation heritage, he raises the question whether in view of this intellectual difficulty the evangelical truth must be abandoned. "The theologian and preacher owe to the Church absolute clarity and ruthless honesty." [3] Accordingly, it is an urgent question for Bultmann

[3] Bultmann, "New Testament and Mythology," p. 9. (Editors' translation.)

88

as to where the authentic proclamation should be found within the framework of an "obsolete picture of the world." Is a theologically valid presentation of Christian truth conceivable apart from the primitive picture of the world? Bultmann is imbued with the scientific ethos of the researcher: "The preacher should make it quite clear what his hearers are expected to accept and what they are not." [4] We will have to agree with Thielicke when he points out that Bultmann's radical interest in the truth "is the most drastic appeal to the conscience of theology which has been issued for a long time." [5]

In the second place, Bultmann's theological aim is nothing less than the rescuing of the kerygma from the consequences of historical criticism. He is therefore concerned about an act of liberation. This is only possible for Bultmann by means of his distinction in principle between the mythological dress, the language, the world picture of the New Testament, and the abiding truth of the proclamation of Christ. For him this is concentrated upon the *justificatio impii*. Bultmann sees the theological task specifically in freeing the "authentic" message of the New Testament from the language veiled in mythology by means of a new appropriate interpretation. In this method Bultmann recognizes the need for guarding against the threat of the "history of religions" approach. It is a question of "establishing the abiding content independent of the mythological form." Bultmann's deepest concern is concentrated in the statement that the task is "to proclaim the decisive action of God in Christ as the event of salvation, although this is presented mythologically; to disclose the truth of the kerygma as kerygma for the man who does not think mythologically." [6]

In the third place, we want to conceive of Bultmann's concern in such a way that we do not lose sight of the pastoral motive underlying his thought. Bultmann takes seriously the modern man. In Bultmann's opinion it is impossible for the nonmythological thought of modern man to understand the New Testament. Its statements move in categories of thought taken from an entirely different picture of the world. Therefore it is inevitable that the modern man will take offence at the primitive picture of the world—including the myth of the New Testament. A repristination of the mythological pictures of the New

---

[4] *Ibid.* (Editors' translation.)
[5] Thielicke, *op. cit.*, p. 137.
[6] Bultmann, "New Testament and Mythology," p. 15. (Editors' translation.)

Testament seems intolerable for the modern man; it is "not thinkable" for him. Also for pastoral reasons a *sacrificium intellectus* must be avoided.

It is, therefore, urgently necessary to provide the modern man with some help so that despite these rational difficulties he may attain to faith. So Bultmann strives in a pastoral way to make faith a possibility for the thinking man of today. "So far as the New Testament speaks mythologically, it is incredible to modern man." [7] The demand that a mythological picture of the world be accepted along with faith is according to Bultmann "senseless and impossible." [8] Conversation with the modern man is so important for Bultmann that he concludes: "The Church can re-establish communication with modern man and speak with an authentic voice only after she has resolutely abandoned mythology," [9] for "by mythology the real points at issue are side-tracked and obscured." [10] It is therefore the duty of theology to prepare the way for a genuine decision of faith.

Bultmann's concern seems to be justified in principle. The duty of theology, according to Bultmann, to carry on an appropriate work of translation is always the basic task confronting every theologian and preacher. But the actual problems which this raises are the following: Is the method of demythologizing really appropriate to the subject matter with which we have to deal here, and is not the content of the kerygma itself changed by this approach? The question thus has to do with the essence or the substance of the theology and the kerygma which Bultmann has demythologized in this way.

B. THE MAIN OUTLINE OF BULTMANN'S THEOLOGICAL CONCEPTION

1. *The influence of the Historical-Critical Principle on Bultmann's Theology*

This thesis should be substantiated by two statements. It seems to Bultmann that the immanent historical leveling of the biblical reports is an established and irrevocable fact. The key to the understanding of the New Testament is exclusively the historical-critical

---

[7] *Ibid.*, p. 3. (Editors' translation.)
[8] *Ibid.*
[9] Bultmann, "A Reply to the Theses of J. Schniewind," p. 123.
[10] *Ibid.* (editors' translation).

method of research. The point of departure for Bultmann's thought is essentially a rational principle—that is, the application of the criteria of the historically given, demonstrable, and discoverable; of the contingent, relative, and correlative. As a result we find in Bultmann a strictly consistent and radical use of text criticism, of the form-critical method and source analysis, as well as the acceptance of the basic principles of the general and comparative study of the history of religions.

The tendency which came out of the "history of religions" type of research consists for Bultmann in attaining an understanding of primitive Christianity, an explanation of the New Testament tradition from out of its contemporary religious environment. Bultmann sees two series of motifs. "The origin of the various themes can be easily traced in the contemporary mythology of Jewish Apocalyptic and in the redemption myths of Gnosticism." [11] The New Testament tradition is inserted into this "framework." Out of such an environment a great number of New Testament ideas and elements can be explained —for example, the beliefs in angels and demons, the eschatology and the idea of world judgment which arise out of late Jewish apocalyptic, but they do not possess any originality. These foreign ideas are then elaborated further by Paul in terms of the Gnostic-Mandaean myths of redemption. The conceptual language of Paul is decidedly Hellenistic, Bultmann observes, following Reitzenstein. Paul takes over ideas and concepts from the "mystery religions and from an oriental belief in redemption." Gnostic influence finds its expression "in the myth of the heavenly man" which allegedly evolved from Iranian origin into various forms of Gnosticism. "The heavenly man, a divine figure, leaves his heavenly home, clothes himself in human dress, in order that, unrecognized by the demons, he might bring salvation through his teaching and devotion to human souls which have been imprisoned in earthly bodies. It seems inevitable that Paul's Christology presupposes this myth (I Cor. 2:6-9; Phil. 2:6-11) ." Like Ernst Lohmeyer, Bultmann is convinced of this transference of the ancient belief in the heavenly man to Jesus Christ.[12]

According to Bultmann the historical-critical result is completely

---

[11] Bultmann, "New Testament and Mythology," p. 3.
[12] Bultmann, "Zur Geschichte des Paulusforschung," *Theologische Rundschau*, I (1929) , 45.

unambiguous. We are faced with a mythological overgrowth in the New Testament, which must lead us theologically to a critical destruction and raise doubt concerning the historical trustworthiness of the biblical tradition.

Now for the second statement: On the basis of these reflections it is significant to ask—what is the "theological locus" of Bultmann's conception? A double statement must be made here.

On the one hand it cannot be contested that in Bultmann's theology we have to do with a fruit and a new blossoming of the "old liberalism." This statement—overlooked and even passionately denied by many today—can be substantiated by the following observations.

We find in Bultmann just as in liberalism the anthropocentric approach resulting in a superficial view of historical occurrences. Reason becomes the absolute norm. Man stands as a neutral critical observer over against the biblical sources. He examines them by the intellectual norms of historical research.

Besides that, methodical doubt is the decisive instrument of legitimate research for Bultmann as for liberalism. This doubt is brought to bear on every report which goes beyond the framework of the historically relative and which affirms the suprahistorical, the inexplicable, and the transcendent. Therefore the critical process of elimination, applied against all texts which contain something unusual or irrational, plays such an eminent role in Bultmann. Thus, for example, all the miracle stories, the "Son of Man" and "I am" passages, and Jesus' statements about his majesty in the Gospel of John succumb to this method. Therefore the assertion so many are fond of making, that unlike liberalism Bultmann refrains from the method of "selection" and "subtraction," must be rejected as erroneous. On the contrary! Bultmann develops further the old liberal approach and exercises the method of elimination in an even more radical way.

This statement is confirmed thirdly by the way in which Bultmann acknowledges the negative results of the history of the Life-of-Jesus research. Even today we should not overlook Bultmann's very decisive judgments in his book on Jesus. His actual conception is understandable only against this background. Bultmann says:

> I do indeed think that we can now know almost nothing concerning the life and personality of Jesus, since the early Christian sources show no interest in either, are moreover fragmentary and often legendary; and other

sources about Jesus do not exist. . . . Whether Jesus believed Himself to be the Messiah or not is a point that remains in obscurity. . . . Thus strictly speaking, this means that we can know virtually nothing of the personality of Jesus. I am personally of the opinion that Jesus did not believe himself to be the Messiah. . . . The sources offer the preaching of the Church. Historical research shows that the whole tradition about Jesus is composed of a series of layers. . . . The Gospel of John cannot be taken into account at all as a source. . . .Within this material many things must be rejected as secondary. . . . By means of this critical analysis an oldest layer is determined, though it can be marked off with only relative exactness. Naturally we have no assurance that the exact words of this oldest layer were really spoken by Jesus. Also this oldest layer is a result of a complicated historical process. . . . Of course the doubt as to whether Jesus really existed is unfounded and not worth refutation. . . . Whoever prefers to put the name of "Jesus" always in quotation marks and let it stand as an abbreviation for the historical phenomenon with which we are concerned, is free to do so.[13]

Further on Bultmann explains: "Jesus did not speak of his death and resurrection. . . . Some sayings of such a character are indeed attributed to him, but they originated in the faith of the church . . . and in Hellenistic Christianity." [14]

Yet, we have not adequately and suitably described the "theological locus" of Bultmann's conception by simply indicating the inseparable connection of his theology with the old liberalism. To supplement the first statement we must add a second thesis of a strongly paradoxical nature, for on the other side of Bultmann we have to do with an attempt to overcome the old liberalism, with a kind of "dialectical dissolution" of historicism. We shall make three observations.

Bultmann renounces the critical method of subtraction which would reduce the whole New Testament to some valid residuum by means of selection and subtraction, since he is not interested in the reconstruction of a "historical Jesus" as the old liberalism. Although Bultmann skillfully uses the well-known critical method of liberalism, he does not see any solution in it; he is not satisfied with a historically questionable residuum, in spite of all, but he wants to maintain the whole fullness of the kerygma.

Then he also breaks with the individualistic mystical concept of re-

---

[13] *Jesus and the Word*, trs. Louise Pettibone Smith and Erminie Huntress (New York: Charles Scribner's Sons, 1934) pp. 8-15. Cf. also Bultmann, *Die Geschichte der synoptischen Tradition* (4th ed.; Göttingen: Vandenhoeck and Ruprecht, 1958) .
[14] *Ibid.*, p. 213.

ligion in liberalism. Schniewind in his discussion has pointed out that Bultmann does not speak as Adolf Harnack of "God and the soul," or propose as Ernst Troeltsch a "mystical religiosity" and a flight into a timeless symbolism or a general self-unfolding of religious ideas in the fullness of their appearances.

Bultmann's intention is further manifest in opposition to liberalism by his proposal of viewing history not with the impartial neutrality and objective attitude of an outsider, but of really "understanding" it from within. According to Bultmann man is "himself a part of history," personally bound up with it. "Hence there cannot be impersonal observation of history in the same sense that there can be impersonal observation of nature." [15] This presentation "must be in the nature of a continuous *dialogue with history*." [16] "Only when we are ready to listen to the *demand* which history makes on us do we understand at all what history is about." [17] Therefore Bultmann does not advocate the method of a neutral investigation of history which ends in relativism, nor the method of psychological explanation, nor the "chronological fixing of what happened" and of actual "biographical details." Rather he affirms the character of history as event which happened once and for all. The actual revelation is important for him. At this point his greatest distance from liberalism is disclosed. Thus Bultmann's thought revolves around the demand that there would have to be a highly "personal encounter with history." It would be a question of "finding a position within history." Therefore Bultmann's object of interest is not "the historical Jesus," not "that which happened," but his attention is directed solely to "what he *purposed,* and hence to what in his purpose as a part of history makes a present demand on us." [18]

2. *Bultmann's Attack on the Mythology of the New Testament*

The main idea in Bultmann's theology is expressed in the question: In what way is the actual validity of the New Testament kerygma to be achieved? The answer does not come by inquiring into the historical "reliability of the tradition," for history reveals only the

[15] *Ibid.,* p. 3.
[16] *Ibid.,* p. 4.
[17] *Ibid.*
[18] *Ibid.,* p. 8.

relativity of the kerygma.[19] Nor does it come by separating the husk from the kernel, so that the kerygma is reduced to the kernel—that is, to timeless truths, to certain basic moral and religious ideas, as Harnack thought. The answer comes rather by way of "demythologizing"—that is, by a systematic attempt to make the New Testament actually understandable. Bultmann points out that this method has been tried long ago, but he thinks that it implies a *testimonium paupertatis,* that it must be said again today.

In this way Bultmann poses the task of ridding the New Testament of its mythological speculation and of discovering its mythological elements.

This attempt of Bultmann brings into evidence six especially pregnant points.

First, Bultmann thinks that the New Testament is essentially determined by a mythical picture of the world, namely, by the idea of a three-storied world, as it were, earth, heaven, and hell. The basic structure of the salvation occurrence is mythical. Within these three stories a mythological drama of salvation and redemption is enacted, with supernatural powers playing their part. Thus it must be that in accordance with the nature of mythology the events characteristic of this picture of the world are presented in mythological language.[20]

Second, "miracles" must consequently be interpreted as the invasion of mythological ideas. "Miracle" is a designation of the divine becoming visible in history, and therefore is a typical expression of the mythical picture of the world. For modern thought the "miracles of the New Testament as miracles" are dismissed.

Third, the "belief in angels" and the "idea of demons" in the New Testament are given no place within the framework of Bultmann's conception. "They are sheer 'superstition.'" "The Church should do all in her power to root it out, for it can only stultify her proclamation. The Blumhardt legends are to my mind preposterous." [21]

Fourth, in line with this the orthodox Christology of the Church can only be regarded as mythology. The doctrine of Christ as a pre-existent divine being or as the "divine Son of Man" rests upon mythological speculation. "The doctrine of the substitutionary satisfaction by the

[19] Bultmann, "A Reply to the Theses of J. Schniewind," p. 116.
[20] Bultmann, "New Testament and Mythology," pp. 1 ff.
[21] Bultmann, "A Reply to the Theses of J. Schniewind," p. 120.

death of Christ cannot be understood." [22] Therefore also the resurrection of Jesus is only a myth, to be repudiated in the sense of a "miraculous event of nature whereby a dead man is brought to life." [23] "Death would not mean a great deal to anyone who knows that he will rise again in three days." [24] "We can no longer accept the story of Christ's descent into hell or his ascension into heaven as literally true." [25] Also Christ's enthronement and heavenly intercession in the New Testament as well as the Church's praying to him, which presupposes a real and personal relation of man to Christ, are to be judged mythological.[26] There is no high priestly office of the risen Christ, for "the prayer relation to the exalted Christ is from the very beginning a misunderstanding." [27]

Fifth, there is no wonder then that the biblical and ecclesiastical doctrine of sin and death are consigned to the mythical. Bultmann says, "Death is not to be understood as the punishment for sin," [28] for guilt is always a responsible deed, as Pelagianism taught. The idea of original sin as an inherited infection is "sub-ethical, irrational, and absurd," [29] and presupposes a primitive understanding of God.

Sixth, to be strictly consistent eschatology must also be interpreted as mythology. "We can no longer look for the return of the Son of Man on the clouds of heaven." [30] The reason for this according to Bultmann is the fact that since Jesus' time world history continued to run its course and the Parousia of Christ has not even yet taken place. Also the Christian hope of "his own translation into a celestial realm of light" is for Bultmann not only "irrational" but "utterly meaningless." [31] Also the idea of the "last day" as a world catastrophe is nothing else than mythological language.[32]

In view of this total attack, this complete calling into question

[22] Bultmann, "New Testament and Mythology," p. 7 (editors' translation).
[23] *Ibid.,* p. 8 (editors' translation).
[24] *Ibid.* (editors' translation).
[25] *Ibid., p.* 4.
[26] Bultmann, "A Reply to the Theses of J. Schniewind," p. 109.
[27] Bultmann, *Glauben und Verstehen,* I (2nd ed.; Tübingen: J. C. B. Mohr, 1954), 249-50.
[28] Bultmann, "New Testament and Mythology," p. 7 (editors' translation).
[29] *Ibid.,* p. 7.
[30] *Ibid.,* p. 4.
[31] *Ibid.,* p. 8.
[32] *Ibid.,* p. 5.

of the entire Christian message, in what sense can we still speak of the validity of the New Testament? That is an urgent question. What constitutes the actual kerygma which for Bultmann is supposed to set forth the substance and content of preaching and faith?

3. The Existentialist Interpretation of Revelation

Bultmann adopts a new course in establishing the binding character of the New Testament kerygma. He selects for his starting point the philosophy of existence.

The premises of Bultmann's thought are the basic ideas of the existentialist philosophy of Heidegger and Jaspers. They are concerned about the "being" and the "self-understanding" of modern man. The being of man is radically fallen to care, to anxiety, and to an encounter with death. The general theme of Bultmann's existentialist philosophy deals with how man attains "true self-understanding" and "authentic existence." In principle Bultmann agrees with their philosophical presuppositions. In his discussion with Schniewind Bultmann attempts to make this philosophical starting point clear. "I *am* trying to substitute anthropology for theology, that is, genuine theological statements are always at the same time statements about eixstence." [33]

Against the charge that it is dangerous to introduce philosophical points of view into theology, Bultmann argues that "the philosophers are saying the same thing as the New Testament and saying it quite independently." [34] "The New Testament confirms the assertion of philosophy that faith and love are the 'natural' or rather the authentic attitudes that man should have." [35]

The method of existentialist interpretation follows from this insight. It is concerned with understanding the existential character of the message of revelation, with grasping the "real intention" of the New Testament regardless of the historical fact that it uses mythological language. As every myth the New Testament myth evokes the question of the way in which man understands himself in his world. Bultmann thinks that he can give the answer by means of the "existentialist interpretation of man." [36] But how does Bultmann define the self-understanding of the New Testament myth?

[33] Bultmann, "A Reply to the Theses of J. Schniewind," p. 107. (Editors' translation.)

[34] Bultmann, "New Testament and Mythology," p. 25.

[35] *Ibid.*, p. 26 (editors' translation).

[36] *Ibid.*, p. 11.

There are three important ideas in connection with the existential understanding of the New Testament revelation.

First, the distinction between "historical fact" and "encounter in history" is essential for Bultmann—that is, between "Jesus of Nazareth" who once lived between the years 1 and A.D. 30 and the "Christ of the kerygma." Bultmann states: "The Jesus of history is not kerygma, anymore than my book was. For in the kerygma Jesus encounters us as the Christ, that is, as the eschatological phenomenon *par excellence*." [37] Therefore Bultmann finds it necessary to abandon all historical data and to direct himself to the unique encounter with the Christ who is preached in the kerygma. "We can see meaning in them only when we ask what God is trying to say to each one of us through them." [38] The teaching and thought of Jesus "are understood in the light of the concrete situation of a man living in time; as his interpretation of his own existence in the midst of change, uncertainty, decision." [39] The words of Jesus "meet *us* with the question of how we are to interpret our own existence." [40]

Second, what is Bultmann's concept of revelation? Bultmann has made a special effort to understand what revelation means. From this study Bultmann has found the following characteristics essential to an understanding of revelation:

"Revelation is an occurrence that places me in a new situation as a self," so that man attains salvation and his authentic self, which he cannot attain by himself.[41] Revelation "cannot be understood as a simple communication, but only as a *personal* address." [42] "In revelation man sees his own limitation," that is, "he is limited by death." "But revelation gives life." Therefore revelation is "not an occurrence within human life, but rather one that breaks in upon it from outside." [43] Revelation can occur "only on the presupposition of faith

[37] Bultmann, "A Reply to the Theses of J. Schniewind," p. 117.

[38] Bultmann, "New Testament and Mythology," p. 35.

[39] Bultmann, *Jesus and the Word*, p. 11.

[40] *Ibid.*

[41] Bultmann, *Existence and Faith*, sel., tr. and introduced by Schubert M. Ogden (New York: Meridian Books, 1960) , p. 59.

[42] *Ibid.*, p. 64.

[43] *Ibid.*, p. 72.

98

... faith *in* an occurrence *in* Jesus Christ, who died and was raised for us." Revelation "consists in nothing other than the fact of Jesus Christ." [44]

But the salvation occurrence is "revealed as *proclamation,* in the word." [45] "Thus revelation must be an occurrence that directly concerns *us,* that takes place in us ourselves; and the word, the fact of its being proclaimed must itself belong to the occurrence." [46] Hence revelation never simply presents an event in the past, but always only in the "present, in my particular present." [47] The fact of revelation has not occurred "in a certain place and at a certain time," [48] but the only question with meaning is how to interpret the occurrence for myself.

What, then, has been revealed? Nothing at all, so far as the question concerning revelation asks for doctrines—doctrines, say, that no man could have discovered for himself—or for mysteries that become known once and for all as soon as they are communicated. On the other hand, however, everything has been revealed, insofar as man's eyes are opened concerning his own existence and he is once again able to understand himself.[49]

From this deduction Bultmann concludes that

the question concerning the "absoluteness" of the Christian revelation can no longer arise. The attempt to rank the various religions—including the Christian one—as phenomena within the world has become meaningless; for all that falls within the range of such a question is relative, not absolute. The question can be raised meaningfully only from the standpoint of faith.[50]

Third, what about the existentialist interpretation of the Christ event? To judge in general, the meaning of the Christ event consists in the fact that "at the very point where man can do nothing, God steps in and acts—indeed he has acted already—on man's behalf." [51] This does not in any way imply that the meaning is contained in the

---

[44] *Ibid.,* pp. 74, 75.
[45] *Ibid.,* p. 76.
[46] *Ibid.,* p. 78.
[47] *Ibid.,* p. 79.
[48] *Ibid.*
[49] *Ibid.,* p. 85.
[50] *Ibid.,* p. 89 (editors' translation).
[51] Bultmann, "New Testament and Mythology," p. 31.

fact of Christ as an event which happened in the past, but the word of Christ becomes the event of salvation only in terms of his existential import.

Specifically this means that "the cross and resurrection of Jesus" are not at all to be believed as facts of salvation which happened in the past, but they become present phenomena, the content of my "self-understanding," to which I stand in a relation of "contemporaneity." [52] It is very interesting how Bultmann answers the question: "How do we come to believe in the saving efficacy of the cross?" Bultmann knows only one answer: "This is the way in which the cross is proclaimed." [53] The crucified and risen Christ encounters us in the word of preaching, and no place else. Easter faith is defined as faith in this word. The word of preaching is the word of God which asks us whether we will believe it or not. This opens up the possibility of understanding ourselves.[54]

Bultmann wants to make it quite clear that "in its redemptive aspect the cross of Christ is no mere mythical event, but a permanent historical fact originating in the past historical event which is the crucifixion of Jesus. . . . As far as the first preachers of the gospel are concerned . . . It presented them with a question and it disclosed to them its meaning." [55]

Bultmann is very insistent that the death and resurrection of Jesus are not to be understood merely "as given facts of history which may be determined and established by evidence." [56] To believe in the cross of Christ means "to make the cross of Christ our own, to undergo crucifixion with him." [57] To believe in the crucified Christ is the same as voluntarily accepting his suffering as a present event for us. Accordingly the "resurrection of Christ" is only an expression of "the meaning of the cross." [58] Whoever looks to the resurrection of Jesus as a fact in the past simply does not understand the actual meaning of the resurrection message. According to Bultmann the resurrection is "not

[52] Cf. H. Thielicke, *Theologie der Anfechtung*, p. 151.
[53] Bultmann, "New Testament and Mythology," p. 41.
[54] *Ibid.*
[55] *Ibid.*, pp. 37-38.
[56] Bultmann, *Jesus and the Word*, p. 213.
[57] Bultmann, "New Testament and Mythology," p. 36.
[58] *Ibid.*, p. 38.

a miraculous proof by which the skeptic might be compelled to believe in Christ," for the resuscitation of a corpse back to life in this world is "incredible." [59] The resurrection of Jesus is "an eschatological event," that is, it is another way of speaking of "rising again with Christ in the present tense." "In everyday life the Christians participate . . . in his resurrection." [60]

The consequences are very significant which Bultmann derives from his existentialist interpretation of the resurrection of Jesus. Bultmann states that "the historical problem is scarcely relevant to Christian belief in the resurrection. . . . We cannot buttress our own faith in the resurrection by that of the first disciples." [61] This accounts for Bultmann's basic indifference to the resurrection narratives of the New Testament. The tradition of the empty tomb is dismissed as legend and the resurrection appearances are reduced to visionary experiences of the disciples. In direct opposition to Paul, Bultmann does not regard these as essential to the resurrection message. They are merely a painful concession to the "weakness of the disciples," for their faith should not have depended upon "seeing." Hence the appearances of the risen Christ art unessential and dispensable. Only the word should have the power to convince. The Easter tradition of the Church presupposes a "false interpretation of reality by the disciples" so that they attached themselves to signs instead of believing apart from visible evidence.[62]

What then in summary is the result of the existentialist interpretation of revelation? It is defined as the attainment of a "Christian self-understanding" based on an encounter with the kerygma. According to Bultmann the process of transforming the self-understanding of man occurs in the following way. First, there is the fact that the New Testament tradition exists in its totality. The preaching of this kerygma becomes a present historical event for me. In our encounter with the "word, our consciousness becomes affected" and because the kerygma

---

[59] *Ibid.*, p. 39.

[60] *Ibid.*, p. 40.

[61] *Ibid.*, p. 42.

[62] Bultmann, *Das Evangelium des Johannes*, p. 539. Cf. also W. Künneth, *Theologie der Auferstehung* (München: Claudius Verlag, 1951), in which an extended discussion with Bultmann's theses is carried on.

strikes us as an event we are enabled to attain a new Christian self-understanding.[63]

The following assertions are presented to us as the content of this new Christian self-understanding, the "authenticity" of man.

The revelatory event is the "act of God through which man becomes capable of self-commitment, capable of faith and love, of his authentic life." [64] Christian self-understanding is nothing else than "faith that the unseen, intangible reality actually confronts us as love, opening up our future and signifying not death but life." [65] All the cardinal Christian concepts are given their legitimate interpretation in this new self-understanding. Thus grace as the forgiveness of sins in the sense of *imputatio* of the *justitia aliena* is the freeing of man from his past.[66] "Accordingly faith means to keep oneself open to the future, to exist without anxiety and care." "Faith in the sense of obedient self-commitment to God and as inward detachment from the world is only possible when it is faith in Jesus Christ" [67]—but of course only in the sense of a kerygmatic event. Bultmann says that his concept differs from the philosophical understanding of existence because he makes the origin of the new self-knowledge dependent upon the kerygma, whereas the existentialist philosophers believe that they can dispense with this maieutic help. Bultmann can also call the new being of man an "eschatological existence." The meaning of this, however, is not anything future or the expectation of coming events, but merely the already actual presence of the time of salvation which meets the believer here and now in the kerygma.

Bultmann's theological conception ends in an anthropology qualified by biblical and Christian ideas. It is already clear then that the demythologizing of the New Testament surrenders the central doctrines of the Christian Church, particularly Christology, hence also any specifically Christian theology, in order to gain a philosophical anthropology that appears to be Christian.

[63] H. Thielicke, *Theologie der Anfechtung*, pp. 142 ff.

[64] Bultmann, "New Testament and Mythology," p. 33.

[65] *Ibid.*, p. 19.

[66] Bultmann, *Existence and Faith*, p. 88.

[67] Bultmann, "New Testament and Mythology," pp. 19, 22, Cf. Bultmann, *Glauben und Verstehen*, I, 263. Plus the sentences in quotation. After quotes (editors' translation).

II

A THEOLOGICAL CRITICISM OF BULTMANN'S POSITION

A. THE MAIN POINTS IN THE DISCUSSION

We will lay emphasis upon the following five problematic areas in which the actual discussion with the philosophy of demythologizing is concentrated.

1. *The Problem of the Modern Man*

In clear distinction from Bultmann's conception it must first be affirmed that faith is independent of any specific picture of the structure of the world. If the biblical picture of the world is mythological in form, to speak with Bultmann, that still does not mean that the content of biblical faith would have to be mythologically determined and hence require demythologizing. A basic error in Bultmann's thesis is the confusion of a world picture (*Weltbild*) and a world view (*Weltanschauung*). A world picture arises out of a wealth of experiences and information about a specific situation, and this picture undergoes change with the progressive increase in the knowledge of facts. On the other hand, a world view has to do with the interpretation or the specific understanding of the world picture. Thus the primitive geocentric world picture as well as the Copernican, or even that of modern atomic physics, can alike be interpreted in terms of a world view. The interpretation of atheistic materialism or of heathen religious mythology are both conceivable, but the same objective material can be interpreted in the sense of the biblical faith in creation. Faith or the interpretation of the events of nature is therefore in principle independent of the nature and structure of the world picture. The Bible itself gives evidence of this; moreover the faith of the biblical man is in no way aware of any dependence upon the knowledge of that time concerning the structure of the world. Schniewind has already rightly shown that the theory of a three-storied picture of the world with its localization of God in heaven was broken through countless times in the Old Testament, to say nothing of the New Testament.[68] There is no normative space-time schema for biblical faith. Knowledge of the omnipotence, omnipresence, and eternity of God fundamentally disrupts the bounds and limits of a naïve view of the world picture.

[68] Ps. 139; I Kings 8:27; Jer. 23:24; Acts 27:28; Heb. 4:14; Heb. 7:26.

This means that Bultmann is fighting against a front that does not even exist. Since Christian faith is not by nature bound to a definite world picture, it also is not in the least interested in defending the primitive world picture. Hence the need to demythologize in Bultmann's sense is pointless.

It is moreover not unimportant to mention in this connection the most recent change in the world picture of classical nineteenth-century natural science due to the results of the study of energy and atomic research. Contrary to Bultmann's opinion this new situation in the natural sciences opens up unexpected possibilities of confronting the modern man with the knowledge of New Testament faith. Bultmann still believes that he has to play the role of an exponent of the already obsolete world picture of the mechanistic and materialistic natural sciences and of the world view built upon it. Surprisingly enough, Bultmann always appeals to a concept of a calculable causal nexus and determinism which makes it appear that every extraordinary event and every miracle is a violation of natural law. We know that the modern world picture of today has brought about a dissolution of this deterministic view. Science has gained a basic insight into the "freedom" of natural phenomena, of the indeterminacy of ultimate constellations. Every serious scientist will take into account the intervention of new energies at any time into the world and therefore allow for the possibility that our previous experiences and our limited knowledge of nature might change. Of course, such a statement does not imply that the new world picture could deliver a proof concerning the truth of biblical faith, nor even any dependence of faith on the results of modern research. It does, however, imply very definitely the recognition of the possibility in principle of miraculous occurrences. The former view of many natural scientists that the biblical miracle stories are "impossible" seems to be no longer tenable today and serious science no longer holds it, but we stress that this admission by natural science of the possibility of extraordinary and unusual occurrences does not in any way whatsoever signify the beginning of faith. It only clears the way for the possibility of statements of faith which can no longer be dismissed with the all-too-cheap gesture that they are legendary embellishments. In any case it is evident from this reflection that Bultmann's thesis is hopelessly obsolete, for natural science offers no argument today against the belief in miracles of the biblical witness.

Bultmann is concerned to do justice to the modern man, but he has overlooked the reverse tendency of the modern man to direct his attention to mythical powers despite the modern world picture. The modern man has obviously run aground on intellectualism. Therefore we find as very characteristic for the understanding of the man of today a recrudescence of an intense longing for the irrational and the transcendent. It is just these irrational phenomena which play a surprisingly great role in the life of the modern man. There is for example the significance of the so-called "archetypes," which in the judgment of psychoanalytic research greatly determine as superindividual powers the subconsciousness of man. There is the flood of superstition, the world of ideas of the grotesque mythological view of the sects, the attraction of spiritism, of "Christian Science"; there are the occult phenomena whose origins in part have still not been thoroughly explored, as well as the passion for magic of the man of today. One could almost speak even of a myth of technology and atomic energy, in reference to that irrational knowledge which couples with certain aspects of contemporary life a religiosity which far transcends the visible and the demonstrable.

Bultmann's conception misses the problem of the modern man in his true situation and actual difficulty. The question which agitates the man of today is quite a different one. He does not by any means deny the fact of unexplainable processes, but in parallel with the primitive Christian situation he poses the question as to what power causes them. Is it a cosmic energy within the world or a demonic influence or an intervention of God? In view of this aspect of modern times Bultmann's solution is antiquated, and as such is not able to provide any real help.

2. The Problem of History and Revelation

There is no doubt that Bultmann's concept of revelation contains two elements of truth which cannot be overlooked. Quite rightly Bultmann stresses the present actuality of the revelatory event and emphasizes as well the connection of the believer's destiny with the Christ event. Yet, Bultmann's concept of revelation is not satisfactory because of its complete one-sidedness. What Bultmann construes as revelation has in any case very little to do with the biblical understanding of revelation. Revelation is not merely "address" *in actu*, but also

105

communication of a *factum,* the message of a completed event of salvation, in the past. Three critical arguments must be established over against Bultmann's position.

First, Bultmann's theory threatens the once-for-allness, the uniqueness, and the singularity of the Christ revelation, which occurred and still takes place independent of our consciousness. Bultmann is not secure from slipping into the famous universal "truths of reason" (Lessing) which possess validity apart from historical facts. Bultmann's dissolution of the category of the "historical past, of the once-for-all, and the perfected" in favor of that which is "presently actual and which calls to decision" leads to the mystical concept of religion.

Second, Bultmann's manner of expression is so intolerably ambiguous that the events of revelation and history are thrown into a befogging twilight and their contours disappear. We must ask with all urgency whether Bultmann's concept of faith is necessarily bound to a quite definite fact of revelation in history as the decisive foundation of faith and the indispensable content of faith. Up to now Bultmann's answer to this question has been only evasive and indecisive. We ask: Could not the Christian self-understanding be evoked by some entirely different "stimulus"? Why does the movement toward the rise of the new self-understanding originate from a point completely embedded in historical darkness, a point which bears the name Jesus of Nazareth, though some other name could serve as well according to Bultmann? With Bultmann the saving fact of the Christ revelation dwindles to a merely imaginary point, an X, concerning which no details can be given. The tiny stone which set loose the avalanche is for Bultmann completely unessential. What counts is only the impression which this avalanche of the kerygma evokes in the actual encounter with it.

Therefore we must emphatically ask whether Bultmann intends to affirm the Christ event as a reality appearing once-for-all in the historical Jesus of Nazareth, who was crucified on Golgotha and arose on the third day. It must be clear, however, that this reality also possesses validity independent of the immanent content of human consciousness. In Bultmann's conception, however, there seems to be no doubt that not the *est* but only the *significat* possesses meaning, that merely the subjective validity and interpretation take the place of the actual reality. Bultmann's position appears to be impossible as soon as the connection of revelation with history is taken seriously, for in accordance with his understanding every event of revelation which really happened in the past would have to be interpreted as myth.

Bultmann's "theology" actually dissolves the historicity of the saving event and thereby loses the ground of history from under its feet. While Bultmann places the situation of the moment into the bright light of day, the saving reality bound to history is lost for Bultmann in the dark clouds of night.

Third, with this interpretation of revelation Bultmann falls into an irreconcilable opposition to the message and the faith of the evangelists and apostles, indeed, into a contradiction with the total witness of the New Testament. In direct reversal of the Bultmannian ideology, the stress here is on the eyewitness, which founds the apostolate. The primitive Christian witness reads: We have seen the Lord who is risen; we saw his glory! "That . . . which we have seen with our eyes, which we have looked upon and touched with our hands . . . that . . . we proclaim . . . to you" (I John 1:1, 3). This indicates that uniquely qualified events are always the cause of faith. The fact of saving revelation is here the primary presupposition, and faith is secondary, but with Bultmann conscious experience is the primary cause of faith. Only from this point can one possibly infer a historical datum which stands unknown and unclearly behind the kerygma. It is entirely typical when Bultmann calls the eyewitness accounts of Paul and his argument in I Cor. 15:3 ff. "fatal." In this way he perverts the primitive Christian message. Bultmann's volatilizing of the historical fact is a blatant antithesis to the basic meaning of the *logos sarx egeneto* (John 1:14). Here all the stress is upon the entrance of God's revelation into history, into the time-space schema, into the language structure of the world. The more revelation is divorced from history, however, the more a new Gnosis remote from history becomes victorious. Bultmann's "theology" bears the stamp therefore of a new "Gnostic myth."

In opposition to Bultmann's concept of revelation, we must rather speak positively of the historical potency of the biblical revelation, especially of the Christ revelation. Revelation is therefore always more than history, not only history, but not without history. Revelation structures history as "signs" and draws them into the saving event. Therefore the Christ revelation in its activity both transcends history and is immanent in history.

From this it follows that we have also to do with historical knowledge of the historical deposits of revelation. This *notitia* is also accessible to unbelief, just as even the enemies of Jesus did not deny the actuality of his miracles and the Pharisees also witnessed what happened on Gologtha as a historical fact (John 11:47), but the authentic knowledge of such events as God's revelation is only accessible to faith. Here only *assensus* and *fiducia* are valid. This knowledge of faith is not a human possibility, but the work of the *Spiritus Sanctus*, and thus of divine revelation itself.

Historical research can thus neither prove nor contest the reality of saving revelation. The truth and validity of faith's statements concerning revelation cannot at all be answered by historical research. As Leopold von Ranke claimed, it can only ask what has been delivered, what has been asserted, what has been believed. At this point the inquiries of Ethelbert Stauffer are justified. To be sure, revelation is not historically demonstrated by his inquiries, but its truth is secondarily confirmed.[69]

With respect to this problem also the result is evident that Bultmann misses altogether the essence and uniqueness of biblical Christian faith by his relativizing of history. He is not able to recognize the foundation of faith; namely, the revelation which is bound to history. As a consequence of this dissolution process all his partially justified theological statements hang in the air and thus lose their validity.

3. The Problem of Myth and Revelation

The concept of "myth" is the basic concept with which Bultmann attempts to understand the phenomenon of religion, including the world of the Bible and Christianity. The decisive question is whether myth is at all identical with revelation. How is the biblical revelation differentiated from the mythical? These fundamental questions are not answered by Bultmann!

According to Johann Jakob Bachofen the rise of the mythical is characterized by three factors. First, myth is the product of the creatively active subconscious, an inheritance of prehistorical recollections. The explanation of legends, sagas, and myths is best understood from

---

[69] Cf. Stauffer, "Entmythologisierung oder Realtheologie," *Kerygma und Mythos*, II, 9, 16 ff., 19, 21 ff.

this perspective. Secondly, myth is the result of the experience of numinous impressions due to strong impulses of certain appearances of nature and of historical life. This gives rise to the stories of gods, theophanies, and myths of divine redemption. Finally, myth can also be the result of the creative power of the human spirit, therefore, so to speak, the objectification of an emotion.

The nature of the mythical is not characterized by the word phantasy, for the mythical also contains a reality, a "nucleus of event." It remains, however, characteristic that a myth presents always the product of an anthropocentric interpretation of the world. Myth expresses the effort of man to get control of the world and to interpret its appearances spiritually. Myth is therefore what man knows of his own, what he can know, and over which he has control.

In sharp contrast to the mythical world of ideas, the witness of biblical revelation speaks of an antimythical reality. We will develop this proposition in three directions.

First, the revelation of God in the biblical sense is that which "no eye has seen, nor ear heard, nor the heart of man conceived" (I Cor. 2:9), and therefore the absolutely "totally other," the Transcendent, the mystery of the *oikonomia,* of God's plan for the world in Jesus Christ. Revelation is *apocalypsis,* that is, the unveiling of the hidden, unknown, silent God, who now through revelation becomes *Deus revelatus.* Revelation means *Deus dixit* or *Verbum Dei* and signifies the exclusive action of God. It is not a possibility of the human spirit.

Second, since revelation always has the reality of God in view and does not mean an idea or an interpretation of man, the expressions "myth" or "legend" are essentially inadequate for the revelation of God. For this reason also the biblical "stories of the creation and the fall," while indeed not historical reports, are witnesses of revelation to a reality, which man cannot at all grasp on his own, that is, mythologically. Thus, for example, the statement "God, the Almighty Creator of heaven and earth" is not an historical statement, but it is definite knowledge of revelation. The form of this message of revelation, however, is a pictorial presentation (Gen. 1-2), the only human possibility of expressing in earthly terms the unutterable and the inconceivable. This necessary and appropriate pictorial form should not, however, be confused with myth or legend. Here then the task is not that of demythologizing, but of translating.

109

Third, biblical revelation is to be understood as the answer to all mythology and thus as its crisis and its fulfillment. In relation to the late Jewish apocalypticism with its quest for the future world, the answer of biblical revelation is that with the resurrection of Jesus a new world has dawned and with it the promise of eschatological fulfillment is given. In relation to the Gnostic myth with its intense longing for light and life and its preparing the way to heaven, the witness of revelation answers that Christ is the way, the truth, the light, and the life absolutely. Myth and the Christ revelation stand therefore in the relation of question and answer, of promise and fulfillment. They are not identical, but stand over against one another in strict diastasis.

In view of the overemphasis on parallels in the history of religions, the limits of analogical relationships in the history of religions should not be overlooked. An apparent similarity of form is not to be equated with identity of content.[70]

Bultmann succumbs to a twofold error in his capitulation to the idea of myth. First, the explanation that myths in the history of religions have exerted an influence of content upon the apostolic message is arbitrary and bears the stamp of scientifically unfounded phantasy. Second, the diametrical difference in content between the a-historical myths and the gospel of Jesus Christ as the unrepeatable event in history has been overlooked by Bultmann.

4. The Problem of a Legitimate Theology

The thrust of Bultmann's thought is not essentially determined by theology but rather by philosophy. The premises of existentialist philosophy provide the direction for his theological conception. Thus it necessarily happens that theological statements are perverted in the sphere of philosophical thought. Four points will make this situation clear.

First, we confront in Bultmann's ideology a repetition in principle of the process which already occurred in classical idealism. Just as in Hegel, Fichte, and Kant we meet in Bultmann statements that sound Christian, whereas in reality the concepts mean something

---

[70] For more detailed statements about the difference between faith in Christ and the mythical ideas in the history of religion, cf. Walther Künneth, *Theologie der Auferstehung.*

entirely different from what they say and present some other content. Therefore we are dealing with a specially dangerous concealment of the change in Christian substance under the guise of preserving the Christian forms. Bultmann's preaching bears the external stamp of a legitimate Christian theology of the Church, but it actually denies the content of the biblical theology of the Reformation. Philosophical opinions are substituted for it, resulting in a metamorphosis of the theological content. According to Bultmann, Christology is nothing else "than the explication of faith's understanding of the new being." [71] When Bultmann says kerygma, for example, he does not mean the gospel of the evangelists and apostles, and when he says Christ, the word is only an ideogram. It does not mean Jesus Christ as the four Gospels and the apostolic preaching bear witness to him. When Bultmann speaks of the cross and resurrection, these are not saving facts which happened in history, but they are constructions which interpret processes occurring in human consciousness.

Hence with Bultmann demythologizing means abstraction, that is, the detachment of Christian statements not only from their original imagery, but also from their historical ground which alone renders them possible and meaningful. For example, what does sin mean for Bultmann? It is philosophical knowledge concerning the lostness, the fall from authenticity, from the authentic being of man. But the biblical notion of sin is to be conceived only in terms of a relationship to the living God, to the Creator and Lord, to whom man is responsible and in relation to whom he stands in guilty rebellion. Bultmann defines the forgiveness of sins as freedom from the curse and indictment. This explanation—in itself right—is only legitimately founded in biblical terms upon the atoning sacrificial death of Jesus on the cross, a statement, however, which is repeatedly denied by Bultmann. The same goes for the statement concerning the love of God, which according to the New Testament witness is meaningfully and clearly manifest only in and through Jesus Christ.

Further, in line with his rationalistic starting point, Bultmann's theology is not secure against a philosophical "metaphysics of timelessness." The Christian words and concepts such as "Christ," "love," "faith," "forgiveness," "eschatology," et cetera, become timeless sym-

---

[71] Bultmann, "Die Christologie des Neuen Testaments," *Glauben und Verstehen,* I, 267.

bols of a universal truth. The denial of attachment to history leads to a philosophically abstract spiritualization. Because of this tendency towards abstraction, these concepts attain the arbitrariness of a new philosophical mythology, which exists divorced from its original historical ground. Thus these philosophical ideas become stimuli or motors of a transformation of consciousness, the content of which possesses no meaning *extra hominem*.

Finally, this philosophical dilution of Christian truth bears in itself the consequences of a self-dissolution of theology into an atheistic philosophy, a course which has been pursued by Kamlah, a student of Bultmann. Bultmann separates the Christ-kerygma from historical facticity, while Kamlah goes even further to separate self-understanding from the Christ-kerygma, just as is the case with Heidegger and Jaspers. Hence, the ultimate consequence of Bultmann's perspective is that Christ has become unnecessary for anthropology, and the way has been prepared for a modern anthropology with no dependence upon Christianity.[72]

In opposition to Bultmann a legitimate theology must be characterized as a thought movement of faith. Its point of departure is the revelatory fact given from beyond the immanent possibility of human thought. As over against Bultmann's anthroponomous method of proceeding, the essential thing here is the theocentric-theonomous starting point.

Consequently the norm of truth and validity does not reside in man himself, but is situated outside man. The principle is characterized in terms not of anthropological ontology, but of christological theology. It is a question here of turning 180 degrees away from philosophical thought. The knowledge acquired by modern theology —above all since Karl Barth and Karl Heim—that theology is not a section of the history and philosophy of religion, but presents a unique content of its own, should not be lost once again.

The knowledge of faith in the form of theological statements does not need the support and confirmation of philosophical insights and arguments. Christ is "foolishness" for the wisdom of the world, but the wisdom of Christ—herein Bultmann is right—should prove its worth in the new understanding of man and the world. Theology is

---

[72] Wilhelm Kamlah, *Christentum und Selbstbehauptung* (Frankfurt: V. Klostermann, 1940).

not anthropology, but it provides the basis for a genuine anthropological and cosmological knowledge.

The theology outlined by Bultmann does not offer a legitimate knowledge of revelation and faith, rather philosophical wisdom in Christian dress. Thus, despite all the Christian terminology, the real Christian substance is attenuated and dissolved.

5. The Problem of Forming Theological Concepts

Bultmann is hardly to be praised for rendering a special service when he indicates the need for translating the Christian message, for this translation has been a self-evident missionary task of preaching from Pentecost till now and to the end of time.

The reason a translation is needed is due to the transcendence or the otherness of the divine revelatory event. It completely bursts the framework of our earthly thought and imagination. "The revelation of God has become flesh" and enters into human language, and this earthly form of the human word comprises the "Word of God." Thus the preacher has the obligation to make clear to his hearers the "authentic" meaning of these earthly words, pictures, parables, and concepts and the real significance of the "substance" of revelation in the earthen vessel. Therefore we cannot avoid the question of what in the preaching has a divine claim and what is only human speech; what in a certain picture is eternal, divine, and true and what is only an outdated idea; what is the "substance" and what is only a peripheral remark.

The posing of this question conditions the task of every single preacher, namely, to undertake the translation and clarification of the biblical message in our mode of thought and our faculty of imagination. So, for example, the plastic eschatological images of the Apocalypse of John—the City of Jerusalem, pearls, trumpets, et cetera—are not the expressions of religious phantasy, but the materially necessary references to the coming of a real new world—including corporeality —which is distinguished by glory and beauty, by a new language and a new community.

This unavoidable work of translation does not, however, involve us in a special kind of demythologizing in Bultmann's sense, for the objective content which finds expression in this language of picture and parable is preserved and disclosed in its actual meaning. It is merely an admission of the basic fact that the revelation of God as something invisible, suprahistorical, and indemonstrable is necessarily accessible for human thought only in pictorial language. Without the pictorial language and conceptual matter which must be derived from the sphere of experience in our earthly world in order to become understandable, there would be no message at all, no genuine kerygma, but only a mystical silence, only a nothingness, only a rejection of every form of expression altogether.

The decisive question can be posed only in this way: Which pictures, which concepts, are adequate to the revelation of God? In a real sense a total adequacy in this eon is not to be had. According to I Cor. 13 we all see through a "mirror dimly." Only the eschatological fulfillment shall bring the total knowledge from "face to face." But the essential decision concerning the selection of the appropriate concepts and modes of expression has already been made by the apostles and evangelists. Their selection qualifies certain words and concepts as archetypal, which are not exchangeable or replaceable. When the New Testament borrowed terms and partly also concepts which had been used mythologically from its environment—we have in mind mainly the Logos speculations and the Kyrios concept— a specific process of recasting and transvaluation of meaning began in regard to these concepts. Those concepts are not simply husks which are filled with a new content. Instead they become changed and recoined through the new usage itself. It is therefore basically incorrect to speak of a new revelatory content in mythological form, for the pictures borrowed by the New Testament and the contemporary forms and concepts lose their mythological quality as soon as they have reference to revelation and are molded by it. Hence the New Testament itself has already carried out whatever demythologizing is necessary and relevant to the matter. Indeed the biblical message must at first appear to be mythology to the extra-Christian world of religion, because unbelief of itself is not able to recognize and understand the revelation of God. Therefore it necessarily confuses religion and revelation, religion and the gospel, myth and revelation. In view of this it is an indispensable task of theology to distinguish these concepts and ideas very clearly and to exercise the greatest caution in the selection of concepts and pictures.

In this connection there is still an epistemological question. Is there any possibility at all of dispensing with pictorial language? Even Bultmann is not in the position to do this. He also speaks of "God," of the "act of God," of "Christ," of "grace," "sin," and "love." Either these expressions are empty concepts, mere ideas and products of consciousness, behind which there stands no reality whatsoever—then theology has arrived at the point of self-dissolution—or Bultmann is also required to acknowledge a "residuum" which can no longer be demythologized and which is accorded basic and decisive significance. To complete a demythologizing of our thought is therefore denied in principle. Even the modern man is required in practice to think in the form of the primitive mythical picture of the world. He speaks naïvely of "below," "above," of the "rising and setting of the sun," of "movement and rest," although these judgments are all only relative and scientifically incorrect—yet indispensable and vital for making ourselves understood. The pictorial outlook is the form of our thought without which a suprahuman reality cannot be described.

In view of this problem Bultmann's concern is an impossible attempt to eliminate the materials of pictures and images which are inseparably bound up with human existence. Demythologizing is also epistemologically doomed to failure. The knowledge of the world becomes intellectualistically narrowed and abbreviated, but fails to grasp the totality of the world in its depths and foundation. By using the standard of demythologizing the distance from actual reality increases. No one can breathe or live any longer in the rarefied atmosphere attained in that way. The concepts and pictorial ideas of the New Testament are indissociably connected with what they express. They do not need demythologizing, but only translation into the language and conceptual world of any given time in accordance with the method which Paul already used of becoming a Jew to the Jews and a Greek to the Greeks.

B. THE TRIUMPH OVER BULTMANN'S PSEUDO-THEOLOGY

1. The Question Concerning Decision

The basic question upon which everything depends and which stands "before" and "above" all theology and philosophy is to be posed in the following way:

Is there an actual revelation of God in this world, a real invasion of God in history; has God in a unique sense acted and spoken—not only symbolically or ideally but really—in Jesus Christ or has nothing new happened in reality; does the New Testament tradition present only a subjective belief and piety of the Church, which I today must first interpret anew if it is to be valid for my present situation?

Either the latter is true—then there are only religions and myths in the world; then everything is relatively without validity; then also the biblical reports contain in principle nothing new and once-for-all; then the result is a general leveling of everything into the history of religions (but practically this means that there is no deliverance, no salvation); then everything is somehow illusion, a "pious fraud"; then we are the "most wretched among men." Or, the former is true —then there has actually happened a breaking-in of a transcendent revelation of God culminating in Jesus of Nazareth, in his cross and in his resurrection; then this fact is an objective event of a unique kind, a completed salvation *extra nos,* an *actio Dei* in Christ; then Jesus Christ is *pro nobis;* then God's grace and love have been unveiled for all the world *propter Christum.*

This either/or requires a decision. It is not made on the level of scientific research and its results, for this decision precedes every scientific work. It is only a question of a decision of world view, of faith. Bultmann is right. Revelation is always a demand which calls me to decision now and today. It is always an event *pro me.* In opposition to Bultmann, however, this decision is only a real one when I decide "for something" which "God has done outside of me," when I decide for the real Christ. With Bultmann the kerygma has no objective foundation and is therefore deprived of its power and ultimately of its very meaning. Therefore the decision in Bultmann comes dangerously close to autosuggestion, to self-deception, to illusion.

It should also not be forgotten that the true decision is not primarily concerned with the self-understanding of man, but with the deliverance of man, with the *justificatio impiorum.* This does not set forth a process of consciousness but rests upon an objective judgment of God which the plain language of the Church expresses in the sentence: "Jesus, Thy blood and righteousness, My beauty are, my glorious dress."

Bultmann's "decision" is thus not a genuine one, for the keynote of his theology is not faith but *ratio*—that is, unbelief based on reason to which the real revelation appears "untrustworthy" and therefore "mythical." Here the theological flank has been falsely exposed to all research and therefore all further constructions necessarily end in error.

The genuine decision of faith for the revelation of God in Christ was basically and initially made by the eye- and earwitnesses, by the apostles, by the primitive Church. Their faith was no self-created product of their soul and consciousness. It was an answer, an echo to the claim, to the reality of Christ which was occurring independent of themselves. Here Bultmann confuses cause and effect. Accordingly we do not find in Bultmann's theology either genuine revelation, genuine decision, or genuine faith.

2. *The Decision of Faith as the Basis of Theological Research*

Historical inquiry as well as the whole of theological knowledge are never presuppositionless. One precondition is the fact of the resurrection of the crucified Christ, the "theology of resurrection." Only this key and cardinal point makes possible a proper and meaningful hermeneutics of the New Testament. Thus it becomes self-evident that the saving events in the sense of "facts" in a history of salvation possess fundamental importance not only for the Synoptics, but in the same manner also for Paul and John. The Church arises from "hearing" the "mighty works of God" (Acts 2:11). It further becomes self-evident that the cross without the resurrection of Jesus remains an enigma and a disturbance for the disciples. The resurrection is not an expression for a subsequent interpretation of faith, not a ceremonious kind of thing upon which the intended significance of the cross is to stand. It is a hidden turning point of the world, a break-through of a second creation and the beginning of a genuine and real eschatology. From this perspective it also becomes self-evident that miracles, angels, and demons are not fanciful mythological notions, but rather new illuminating realities in which the true being of the cosmos and of man is unveiled in its "authenticity."

The decision for the saving reality of the Christ revelation signifies indeed an encounter with the scandal. Bultmann thinks that he can also sequester this concept for his theology. But for Bultmann the scandal implies the "non-demonstrability of the kerygma, man's not being open for the cross of Jesus." Here also a totally different meaning

117

is given the word "scandal" than is set forth in the New Testament. According to Bultmann man experiences the offence merely in the sense of the claim which extricates him from his fallenness to the world and requires a transformation of his self-understanding.

According to the New Testament, however, the authentic scandal is the paradoxical event of revelation that the crucified man Jesus of Nazareth is the Redeemer and Ruler of the world. Therefore we are under the impression that in Bultmann's theses the primitive Christian situation is repeated in regard to the revelation of Christ, the irrational paradox of which is felt as a scandal. Is it too much to say that Bultmann utters a "no" in the name of philosophical reason to the real Christ of the New Testament? The result of his demythologizing is summarized in the following judgment: "There cannot have been such a revelation of God as the primitive Church handed down to us, judged by the standard of reason of the modern man. The belief that the crucified historical Jesus is at the same time world-transcending Lord cannot be demanded of our thought, cannot be the real content of faith." [73] In the face of this result the Pauline judgment is repeated: "Unto the Jews a stumblingblock, and unto the Greeks a foolishness" (I Cor. 1:23 K.J.V.). Bultmann's theology founders on the witness of I Cor. 1:17-23.

We will now summarize the results of our examination.

Rudolf Bultmann's effort confronts us with two positive contributions of knowledge: First, the emphasis on revelation as an event of present concern to men, and next, the obligation of making the biblical truth intelligible and of translating it into a living witness which sets the man of today before decision.

Yet we must critically judge that even from a methodological standpoint it appears especially difficult to carry on a discussion with Rudolf Bultmann. This is true not only because extremely difficult and complex issues are in question, but also because Bultmann with all his erudition is not able to express himself clearly and without equivocation. The complaint whch he always makes against his critics, "I have not been correctly understood," gives us pause. Bultmann seems to feel that he is always misunderstood, but we can hardly say that the

---

[73] The editors have not been able to determine whether this is a direct quote. The author is frequently accustomed to omitting bibliographical references. The quotation does not appear to be unambiguously characteristic of Bultmann.

critics are always responsible for this. When it is a question of life and death, it is an original sin for a theology not to make clear and unmistakable statements.

Our examination has shown that there can be no compromise or peaceful agreement between the truth of the New Testament message of Christ and the "pseudo-kerygma" of Bultmann. It need not be stressed that this judgment refers to the issues involved and is not meant personally. The confusion of minds is a sign of our turbulent time, but in the realm of theology and the Church we should not forget what Paul in Galatians 1:6 recalled to his congregation in a most intolerant way. The decisive question remains: Is not that which Bultmann's theology presents actually a "different gospel"? In any case Bultmann should have offered an unambiguous proof that it is the same gospel and that the error lies with his critics.

There is no doubt that from the standpoint of the Church Bultmann's theology must lead to unwholesome consequences. With this theological knowledge one cannot preach, cannot approach the youth, cannot appear at the bedside and at the grave, cannot conduct missions!

Still we can see that Bultmann's attack can be of service. He proceeds in a "wholesome unrest"; he threatens a false security and offers the occasion for clarifying and deepening one's own theology. His ideas have led to a new *status confessionis*. But the confession can only read: "For no other foundation can anyone lay than that which is laid, which is Jesus Christ" (I Cor. 3:11).

FIVE

REGIN PRENTER

Myth and Gospel

The conflict between the contemporary form of the Christian message and its essence, independent of all historical changes, is not a new problem. Each generation takes part in the solution of this problem in its own way. In order that the gospel might not appear to be an anachronism, it must in a certain sense be adapted to the language and ideas of today. This is the cause of most of the debates in the history of Christian thought. What actually caused the heretics to look for new formulas if not the need to present the message in the language of their time and in conformity with their way of thinking? And what caused the orthodox to react against these new formulations if not the feeling that in trying to make the evangelical doctrine conform to the language and thought of a given time, not only the external appearance of the message, but also its very substance was being changed? They suspected that it was not the language and the thought of the time which became servants of the evangelical message, but on the contrary it was the gospel which was placed in the Procrustean bed of modern thought and language, so that it "obediently" said what thinkers of the period had already said.

If we disregard for the moment the concrete formulations which this problem has assumed in every epoch, we find that the problem always remains the same. How can the following problem be avoided when it seems absolutely unavoidable: Either preach the biblical message according to its original substance—though it be entirely incomprehensible and indifferent to the modern man—or preach it in the language appropriate to the time, so that it answers contemporary problems—with the risk of no longer preaching true Christianity. Most often it has been this alternative which in every period has

120

provoked the separation between liberal and orthodox tendencies in the theological conflicts. It is obviously not easy to find a third point of view beyond this alternative and this line of demarcation which would unite the theological substance with a modern formulation and thus put an end to the sterile opposition between the orthodox and the liberals. Yet this is the task of evangelical theology.

Rudolf Bultmann's theological program, when he proposes to "demythologize" the gospel, can be understood as the quest for a third point of view which would do justice to this double requirement: Conformity to our contemporary way of thinking and yet essential agreement with the kerygma of the New Testament. He has sketched out this program in his earlier writings, but recently he has formulated it in a particularly frank way in his essay "New Testament and Mythology." This essay has aroused comparatively great attention in Germany and Denmark—but apparently less in the other Nordic countries.

Bultmann is trying to find a third point of view beyond orthodoxy and liberalism. In asking us to renounce all antiquated concepts, he is allying himself with liberal theology, but in criticizing liberal theology for eliminating the "mythology" of the New Testament and thereby relinquishing the substance of the gospel itself and in suggesting, rather than elimination, a method of interpretation whereby this same mythology would retain the essentials of the kerygma, Bultmann is actually defending the cause of orthodoxy. To demythologize the gospel means to replace the clothing of mythological images in which the gospel is presented in the New Testament with an existentialist interpretation of the mythology. This program was intended to satisfy the whole present problem, for on the one hand existentialist philosophy is the form of self-understanding peculiar to our time, and on the other hand the true intention of the gospel itself, in Bultmann's opinion, is to give us an understanding of existence and not a mythology.

This program appears extremely seductive, but can it be realized? This all depends on the answer to two very important questions. First, has Bultmann succeeded in carrying out a systematic demythologizing, or does there still remain a residuum of mythology which an existentialist interpretation cannot reduce? And what then is the place of this residuum in the kerygma of the New Testament?

Next, does this existentialist interpretation of the mythology truly reproduce the understanding of God and of man in the New Testament? These are questions which we cannot treat lightly if we wish to judge Bultmann's program of demythologizing.

We will take up these questions one right after the other.

Has Bultmann succeeded in carrying out a methodical demythologizing? He has recognized the problem. He has himself demanded that the demythologizing be done radically without anything remaining. The problem cannot be solved by "selection and subtraction." That would be only a half-way measure. But at the end Bultmann himself sees clearly that there still remains a residuum—the idea of a God who acts. This inconsistency is bound up with the way we define the idea of myth, of mythology, and of demythologizing. Hence we must enlarge upon this awhile. Only when these concepts are clarified can we take a position and see whether in the final analysis a demythologizing is possible, and if so, whether this can contribute to the resolution of the conflict between the demand that preaching conform to every epoch and that it remain faithful to the substance of the gospel.

Bultmann's ideas on New Testament mythology and on demythologizing are very complex, and we can only understand their inconsistencies when we have seen the different components of his thought.

According to Bultmann, the mythology of the New Testament which is to be interpreted has a double origin. On the one side there is the mythical picture of the world—more a formal consideration. On the other there is the concrete interpretation of the redemption in Christ which is inserted into this picture of the world—more a material consideration.

Part of this mythical picture of the world is the idea, for example, of a world divided into three stories—heaven, earth, and hell. The middle one, the earth, has become the battlefield for the powers of the two others, the angels and demons—God and the devil. This battle culminates in a world catastrophe, which puts an end to the eon dominated by the powers of evil and, after the final judgment, will inaugurate a new eon in which God alone will rule. Man finds himself caught in this battle, for the devil as well as God can act upon him by magic and by sacraments.

A mythological conception of salvation is added to this picture of the world. According to the ideas of Jewish apocalypticism and the

122

Gnostic doctrine of redemption, Jesus Christ is actually a pre-existent divine being which has become man in order to pay for the sins of humanity and bring the message of salvation by his death and resurrection. Powers are communicated to believers by the sacraments—baptism and communion—for their new and true life, the life of the Spirit.

To this duality in the mythology of the picture of the world and of religion there also corresponds in Bultmann a double motif in working out this demythologizing. If the mythology contains a particular picture of the world, it is *eo ipso* unacceptable and unbelievable to those who no longer hold to that picture. Now, however, it is a fact that neither a person nor an epoch chooses its own picture of the world. It is a heritage which conscious thought receives from all past centuries. We who live today and whose picture of the world is determined by the natural sciences of the modern age cannot simply accept the mythical picture of the world which belongs to the New Testament without committing a *sacrificium intellectus*—and that would be dishonest. Thus it happens that in proceeding from the picture of the world which is given to us by our historical situation and the natural sciences, a whole series of New Testament images are subjected to criticism. These are simply disposed by the sole fact that they share in an obsolete picture of the world. This is the case, for example, with conceptions such as the ascension of Christ, his descent into hell, the belief in spirits and demons, the miracles, and the eschatological images of the final catastrophe. Modern science has put an end to these pictures which are no longer acceptable. We cannot on the one hand use electric lights and the radio and on the other hand continue to believe in such conceptions.

However, the picture which we construct of the world is not only determined by physical science, but also by psychology. It does not matter whether this psychology is idealistic or naturalistic; it still considers man as an independent personal reality and not as a battlefield for celestial and demonic forces. The "Spirit" and the sacraments of which the mythology speaks are thus incomprehensible, and the same goes for the ideas of a vicarious atonement and a resurrection understood as a liberation from death. Modern psychology understands man either as a product of purely natural forces (naturalism) or as a creature responsible for his own actions (idealism). In both

123

cases the idea of an infused force which can transform man's ethical quality is absurd. The same is true of the idea of a martyr who can suffer death for another. For naturalistic philosophy the resurrection is nonsense, for death is the natural end of life; for philosophy the only possibility of an eternal existence is that which springs out of the depths of one's own nature, and not the physical resurrection of another being.

Thus a good part of the New Testament has to be set aside by the sole fact that our view of the world is entirely different. According to Bultmann, however, that is neither the only nor even the most important reason which necessitates a demythologizing, for the New Testament mythology is not composed only of a picture of the world, but also of a doctrine of a concrete redemption; namely, the Christ event. After all, it is this doctrine which forms the central point of the New Testament mythology. The picture of the world is only a framework. If we interpret the mythology from the standpoint of its center, we see that the purpose of the myth is not to present a picture of the world. To the extent that the myth speaks of a redemption— not only the New Testament speaks of this—its purpose is not cosmological but existential. The concept of salvation is existential, not cosmological, but if salvation is at the center of the myth—as in the most pronounced myths in Christianity; *viz.*, those of apocalyptic and Gnostic origin—then there is already in the myth itself a motif which calls for a demythologizing—that is, a suppression of the cosmological in favor of the possibility of an existentialist interpretation. Moreover, according to Bultmann, this motif is reinforced by the cosmological contradictions which the mythology of the New Testament contains: The death of Christ as a sacrificial victim is opposed to the death of Christ understood as a cosmic event; Christ as the Jewish Messiah is opposed to the Christ as the new Adam; the kenosis of the pre-existent Son of God to the miracles of the Messiah as signs of power; the pre-existence to the miraculous birth, et cetera.

Let us pause for a moment in order to see the exact meaning of the concepts of myth and of demythologizing which we have been using. Let us first observe a peculiar contradiction which is apparently connected with the nature of myth—i.e., it is both cosmological and existential. In the first part of Bultmann's argument the mythical picture of the world is so essential, so indispensable to mythology, that a slight change in this picture makes demythologizing necessary. In opposition to this, however, the second part of his argument seems to make the picture of the world entirely accidental. The true intention of the myth is not cosmological but existential. That is why the myth already contains within itself a motif for demythologizing.

Then, where is the truth? Do the cosmological tendency and the mythical picture of the world constitute such an integral part of the myth that the myth itself must disappear when science destroys its cosmological significance? Is it not rather the case that the under-standing—not cosmological but existential—of the human condition in relation to the good and evil powers (as concrete as one might care to imagine them) is the essential thing, so that the myth, deprived of its cosmological content, might still be interpreted existentially in accordance with its deepest meaning? Bultmann seems to operate with both answers as the occasion presents itself. When he is combatting orthodox theology which opposes all demythologizing the cosmological aspect becomes such a decisive part of all mythology that it would be simply dishonest for a modern man to retain the slightest part of it. It is all or nothing; neither "selection" nor "subtraction." The myth-ology as such disappears with the cosmological aspect. In contrast to this, the bell has a different sound when Bultmann is discussing the existentialist interpretation of mythology. If he wants to undertake a true interpretation and not an elimination of mythology, as Bult-man himself criticizes the liberal theologians for having done when they attempted to demythologize, he is naturally obliged to maintain that the myth in its essence is based upon an existentialist interpreta-tion. If it is not in the nature of myth to provide the meaning of existence instead of a cosmology, if consequently mythology is not in its essence cosmological but existential—this in direct opposition to what was previously defined as essential to the myth—then Bultmann's interpretation is not really an interpretation but an elimination.

Thus the third point of view which Bultmann opposes to both orthodoxy and liberalism ends in an obscure and wavering definition of mythology and demythologizing. When he is attacking orthodoxy, the essential thing in mythology becomes in his view its cosmology and its picture of the world, so that merely the existence of the modern picture of the world makes it impossible to grant the New Testament conceptions their original value. Hence, "demythologizing"! Away

125

with all mythology! The position taken by Bultmann is typically liberal: Science is employed as an argument in theological questions! In contrast to this, when he is attacking liberal theology, mythology becomes suddenly existential and not cosmological, since the nature of myth is to define man in relation to good and evil powers. This makes possible an existentialist interpretation, which is not arbitrarily chosen as one among others, but really grasps the deepest intention of myth. This is obviously an orthodox attitude; for what else does orthodoxy propose if not an interpretation of the essence of the soteriological myth over against all the liberal digressions into metaphysics and cosmology? Thus if Bultmann were logically consistent, he would not in fact speak in this way of demythologizing. The central content of myth is in effect retained in an existentialist interpretation; a rather important residuum of mythology still remains—the idea of a God who acts. This does not mean of course that mythology in the old sense—i.e., mythological cosmology—is justified. The concept of demythologizing simply does not fit this kind of interpretation. In reality it is not a question of demythologizing but of what one might call "decosmologizing"—that is, a suppression of a mythical metaphysics in favor of an existentialist (soteriological) interpretation of the myth.

Hence, the position adopted by Bultmann is not a third beyond orthodoxy and liberalism, but only a position which alternates between the two, playing off liberalism against orthodoxy and orthodoxy against liberalism. This accounts for its many inconsistencies. This also accounts for the fact that the very idea of demythologizing does not accord with the solution of the problem which Bultmann suggests; namely, the distinction between what is bound to the time and the very essence of the gospel message. If the idea of demythologizing were to be applicable here it would have to be defined in such a way as to make it systematically applicable. The terms "demythologizing" and "mythology" should be so clear that no misunderstanding will arise concerning the essence of the kerygma and the nature of myth. Otherwise there is a contradiction in speaking of demythologizing.

Now, that is what has happened in Bultmann. The two terms "demythologizing" and "interpretation of myth"—as opposed to elimination—are also incompatible. Either we dispose of the myth and do not interpret it, or we interpret the myth and do not call it demythologizing. The aim of every interpretation is to shed light upon the essential value of its object. In order to be systematic a real demythologizing must always eliminate all of the mythology as liberal theology did. But would not Bultmann's interpretation result precisely in an elimination? Is not his point of view, despite everything, that of the liberals, so that he ultimately undertakes a demythologizing of the gospel? We will see whether this is true when we try to answer the second question.

Does Bultmann's existentialist interpretation of New Testament mythology with the aid of the philosophical categories of existentialism really correspond to the understanding of the situation of God and man given in the kerygma of the New Testament, or does it not rather result in an elimination of the essence of the kerygma? This is the decisive question for us if we wish to judge Bultmann's whole program and his whole theology.

In accordance with Bultmann's idea of the nature of New Testament mythology, including both cosmology (the mythical picture of the world) and soteriology (the doctrine of salvation), he also develops his existentialist interpretation in two steps. In regard to the mythical cosmology, the Christian conception of existence is like an existentialist interpretation of cosmology. In regard to the mythico-eschatological doctrine of salvation, it is an existentialist interpretation of the death and resurrection of Jesus in terms of their historical significance (*geschichtliche Bedeutsamkeit*).

Does it really correspond to the New Testament message when the Christian conception of existence is connected with the idea that Jesus' death and resurrection—however these might be understood—form the historical basis and even the condition of this conception of existence? Bultmann thinks "yes," but this assumption is hazardous.

In the Christian conception of existence man is bound to the world of death and instability—but not understood as subjection to matter, and therefore in opposition to spiritualistic Gnosticism. If man is "flesh," this does not mean that he is a slave of his sensual nature, but that he wishes to govern his own existence by tangible means. Man does not wish to abandon himself totally in faith to the future which comes from outside. He wishes to make himself master of his own future by employing the possibilities of his own life and by dominating the concrete world at his disposal. Therefore man without faith is delivered over to care. It is a life lived in perdition, outside

127

true human existence. Man thus loses the authenticity of his own existence when he becomes attached to the concrete world and thinks he can secure his own future, for the true existence of man consists of faith, of surrender to the real future, to the invisible, to the intangible. Authentic existence involves "desecularization" (*Entweltlichung*) and liberation from everything that is visible and tangible in the world. It is an unconditional surrender to God who gives man his future at every moment. It is this existence in faith which, according to Bultmann, the New Testament eschatology describes by the two "eons." Faith is the coming of the new "eon." The Spirit is the new possibility of the life of faith.

How does the transition occur from inauthentic existence in unbelief to authentic existence in faith? The answer would not seem to be difficult. If faith is understood as the category of "authentic existence" in terms of existentialist philosophy, then the transition from one kind of existence to the other must also be understood in terms of that philosophy. This amounts to saying that man decides concerning his own existence when he chooses to understand it, not from the standpoint of those means of self-assurance which are found in the concrete world, but when on the way of truth, of the incalculable and intangible future, he chooses to abandon all security and to surrender himself to all the uncertainty and instability of life. The transition from inauthentic to authentic existence is man's decision of faith—his existential decision. Bultmann says this also. "The Spirit does not work like a supernatural force, nor is it the permanent possession of the believer. It is the possibility of a new life, which must be appropriated by a deliberate resolve." [1] Faith is the "natural" attitude of man and not a mysterious supernatural faculty.

This understanding of faith as an existential decision confronts Bultmann with a difficult problem. In the final analysis, is there room in this understanding of faith for the event of salvation, for the Christ event? When faith is understood as man's authentic existence, does this not make faith as such a possible form of existence for man? What happens then to the eschatological event of salvation?

In reality Bultmann has not succeeded in resolving this thorny question, and the solution which he offers is not satisfactory. It is self-evident that when one takes an existentialist point of departure, the

---

[1] Bultmann, "New Testament and Mythology," p. 22.

result will be existentialist in kind. If New Testament mythology is to be interpreted in an existentialist way it must be done radically, and things are such that the concept of redemption is completely foreign to the viewpoint of the existentialists. It is unacceptable to them. This is why, despite his efforts, Bultmann does not succeed in finding room for the event of salvation in his existentialist interpretation. The salvation of which he speaks is not a true salvation; it is simply an element in the existential decision of man.

In his effort Bultmann starts from the following position: It might seem possible to secularize the Christian conception of existence— that is, to divorce it from the Christ event. The existentialist philosophies of Jaspers, Heidegger, and Kamlah are in fact such secularizations. The decisive point, however, is not that man's authentic existence can be recognized apart from the Christ event. The decisive point, rather, is knowing whether man can of himself achieve authentic existence or whether his fall into inauthenticity is so complete that he is unable, merely by a knowledge of his true existence, to rescue himself from his lost condition and to live an authentic life. Whereas philosophy judges this to be possible, the New Testament believes it to be impossible. The New Testament regards man's perdition or "sin" as being so absolute that man cannot of himself create his own true existence. Sin is bound to the man who attempts to secure his own existence instead of being willing to abandon himself to the uncertainty of the future. This also applies to Heidegger's "resolve" and Kamlah's "abandon." If a man is a conscious sinner in the sense of the New Testament he can receive his authentic existence only as a gift. It is precisely by salvation in Christ that God offers man his authentic existence. It is only by receiving his authentic existence through the forgiveness of sins that man can be delivered from himself, from his inauthentic existence. Man cannot obtain the forgiveness of sins by some kind of resolve, however. Forgiveness is an act of divine love in man's favor. "The event of Jesus Christ is therefore the revelation of the love of God. It makes a man free from himself and free to be himself, free to live a life of self-commitment in faith and love." [2]

It seems that Bultmann finds room here both for the existentialist interpretation of faith and for the necessity of salvation. But it only appears that way. A logical examination reveals that his proposed

[2] *Ibid.*, p. 32.

solution contains an inner contradiction. Either the forgiveness of sins must be conceived as a real event, in which case the existentialist approach to the problem is overturned; or the existentialist approach to the problem is still determinative, in which case the words "redemption" and "Christ event" are used in an improper sense as only elements of an existential decision. There is no third possibility.

If it is only by an act of divine love—a real event—that man can attain his true existence, then the terms "authentic" and "inauthentic" no longer correspond to the possibilities of our existence, and the basis of existentialist philosophy is abandoned. Existence is defined as the possibility of life which man himself creates by his own decision. To say that man cannot create his authentic existence because he is unable to deliver himself from his fall into inauthenticity is not a way of speaking existentially, but mythologically. The concept of sin as a judgment from which the guilty man cannot deliver himself by a mere transition into authentic existence as well as the concept of grace as a divine act in a real sense are ideas which come from mythological philosophy and not from existentialism. If the inauthentic is understood as a possibility of existence, it lies in the nature of the guilty man to be able to accept it and out of it to actualize an authentic existence for himself. Judged by the standards of existentialist philosophy the idea that man can receive his true existence only as a gift is just as mythological as the idea of the inbreathing of the *pneuma* into the depths of the soul.

Hence, if it is seriously a question of salvation and the gift of eternal life, the existentialist point of departure must in principle be abandoned in favor of a return to a mythological point of view. Bultmann has not done that. Upon closer inspection we can observe that what Bultmann says about salvation and about Christ are only metaphorical expressions for the existential "decision." This is evident by the way in which he speaks of the cross and the resurrection as events of salvation.

The New Testament regards the crucifixion of Christ as an eschatological event which signifies the change of "eons"; it is an event actualized by baptism and communion. This is why Bultmann thinks this event should be understood historically and not mythologically. This eschatological doctrine expresses the historical significance (*geschichtliche Bedeutsamkeit*) which belongs to the cross as a historical (*historisch*) event. We will have to distinguish between the words "*historisch*" and "*geschichtlich*." The first presents the crucifixion as an event of the past; the second underlies its importance for my present existence in terms of its historicity (*Geschichtlichkeit*).

In the last resort mythological language is only a medium for conveying the meaning of the past event. The real meaning of the cross has created a new and permanent situation in history. The preaching of the cross as the event of redemption challenges all who hear it to appropriate this significance for themselves, to be willing to be crucified with Christ.[3]

This passage is extremely important, for it shows what Bultmann really means by redemption.

According to Bultmann the fact that the crucifixion is the history of salvation means that it contains a historical significance which goes beyond the isolated event of the past. But how does this significance enter into my existence? It asks me whether I will appropriate it for myself, whether I will let myself be crucified with Christ. This means that the crucifixion as a historical event is only important as an example. (Bultmann rejects every idea of satisfaction or sacrifice as mythological!). The crucifixion represents the true existence of man, and it asks me whether I will accept that kind of existence. Belief in the Crucified is thus understood—to use the medieval term—as an *imitatio Christi*. The cross of Christ, it is said, is a historical (*geschichtlich*) happening (*Geschehen*) which has its origin (*Ursprung*) in the historical (*historisch*) event (*Ereignis*) which constitutes the crucifixion of Jesus.

This interpretation of the cross of Christ as the history of salvation is entirely accommodated to the categories of existentialist philosophy. This crucifixion in the past is only an illustration of the decision in my own existence, an illustration which acts as a concrete inspiration —an indispensable inspiration just as Schleiermacher's Christ-prototype was also indispensable for the triumph of the God-consciousness over the sense-consciousness—upon my present existential decision in terms of the existence of faith. Is faith also understood as an existential decision inspired by the historical example of the crucifixion of Christ? But then what remains of the forgiveness of sins as a gift unto existence? Nothing! That God offers sinners forgiveness by the crucifixion of Christ only indicates that the impulse of the existential

[3] *Ibid.*, p. 37.

decision does not come from man himself, but it comes to him from the outside by a historical example. In this conception liberation from the past means both the forgiveness of sins and grace. Man does not deliver himself from perdition by his own resources, but he receives an impulse for it from the significance (*Bedeutsamkeit*) of the historical example of Christ. (We see how close this idea is to Schleiermacher's Christ-prototype.) Nevertheless, faith is still an existential decision; the existence offered is still understood as a possibility of existence. This is why Bultmann underlines so strongly that redemption should not be understood mythologically, but only historically (*geschichtlich*).

But is this the way that the New Testament kerygma understands the death of Christ as the history of salvation?

Similarly, the resurrection is understood existentially. According to Bultmann the resurrection is not a verifiable miracle (*ein beglaubigendes Mirakel*) which could be acknowledged as a historical fact, but it is an eschatological fact accessible only to faith. But what does that mean? It must be understood existentially. This eschatological fact signifies our redemption by Christ, symbolized in baptism and expressed in our life (again we see here the *imitatio* motif) as "a struggle for freedom from sin and casting off the works of darkness." [4] The resurrection as an existential reality is only faith in the redemption of the cross which gives birth to our Christian doctrine. Easter is only a picture of the resurrection of faith—the form of a man's existence born out of the encounter with Christian doctrine. This concept of the resurrection remains entirely within the framework of existentialist philosophy. The resurrection is spiritualized here to the point of becoming the genesis of the existential decision in the encounter with Christian doctrine. It is self-evident that we need such an intermediary between a historical episode as the crucifixion and its present significance for existential decision. If an event of the past is going to have real historical significance in my existence it has to be announced. But was this really the intention of the New Testament kerygma when it proclaimed that Jesus rose from the dead on the third day according to the Scriptures? Is this really an interpretation of the kerygma? Is it not rather a total elimination of its whole substance?

[4] *Ibid.*, p. 40. (Editors' translation.)

We have seen that neither of the two decisive conditions for carrying out the program of demythologizing has been fulfilled. Demythologizing cannot be carried out systematically without eliminating all the mythology, and as a result, all the Christian kerygma. The concepts of "demythologizing" and "existentialist interpretation of mythology" are mutually exclusive, and the alleged existentialist interpretation of the Christian mythology does not conform to the kerygma of the New Testament. The salvation occurrence is not understood as a real event, but it is spiritualized to the point of being only a metaphorical expression for what is peculiar in the Christian understanding of existence. It indicates that the existential decision is motivated not merely from within, but by the crucifixion of Jesus as an indispensable historical example. The doctrine of the kerygma of the forgiveness of sins, which the early Church understood as a paradoxical event, is here reduced to an existentialist ethic of "imitation." Perhaps Bultmann would not approve of this interpretation. This would prove that Bultmann does not draw out the implications of what he says, for when we go to the bottom of his thought, this is what he is saying and nothing else.

We can therefore say that Bultmann's program of demythologizing is disposed of (*erledigt*). Yet the problem still exists: The tension between what is conditioned by the time and the unalterable essence of the kerygma, between the liberal and the orthodox points of view. In reality we have not advanced a bit and the rest is peripheral, for it is better not to try to solve a problem than to let oneself be deceived by a fallacious solution. Nor is there any doubt that we shall not now achieve that magnificent third point of view where orthodoxy and liberalism are joined in a higher unity. No doubt our generation will not manage to transcend the dialogue between liberal and orthodox theology. On the other hand, if such a dialogue had really taken place we would have already come a good part of the way, whereas up to now we have only had a pseudo-dialogue, proceeding from Bultmann's liberal point of view.

Yet the dialogue will not stop here, for some of the questions which were raised along the way should once again be more carefully examined. For example, there is the question of the relation between mythology, cosmology, and soteriology, or between mythology, philosophy, and theology.

We have seen that Bultmann has used an ambiguous concept of mythology in order to justify the need for demythologizing. On the one hand, the picture of the world, the cosmological side, is said to be something essential for the myth; on the other hand, the picture of the world is said to be so secondary that the myth not only permits an existentialist (soteriological) interpretation, but even aims at it.

What then are the respective relations of these magnitudes—the picture of the world, mythology, and soteriology? Is it entirely certain from the outset that every kind of mythological expression contains a fatal implication of a definite picture of the world? That there are cosmological myths is a fact. It is also most clearly evident that a number of mythologies have a cosmological character; for example, the Gnostic myths of ransom, of redemption, which Bultmann traces back so close to the origin of Christianity.

Nevertheless, Bultmann has made several correct observations when he asserts that myth has the tendency to suppress the cosmological in favor of the soteriological. This applies particularly to those mythologies which interest us in relation to Christianity and its environment. The cosmology contained in myth, however, is not independent. Its principal function is not to explain the composition or the origin of the world—that is a task of philosophy. As soon as the cosmological interest prevails, we are dealing with philosophy and not mythology. Of course, we cannot see any clear line of demarcation in the transition from mythology to philosophy. Philosophy—we know this from Plato—often used myth in constructing its cosmology. Still, however, when the cosmological interest dominates, it is no longer a question of true mythology, but of philosophy in mythological form. The true intention of myth is not to give an explanation of the world, but to bring redemption. From its very origin myth is connected with the cultus, and its cosmological elements do not serve to explain the enigmas of the world, but to procure divine power indispensable to man. We could also express it this way: Myth does not necessarily contain a definite picture of the world, even though it may contain cosmological elements. On the contrary, it contains a definite picture of God, and in that light, it also contains a definite concept of man. In any case, what is decisive in myth is not its picture of the world, but its picture of God. This is particularly true of Christian mythology which gives a certain picture of God.

134

Hence, Christian mythology is not bound to any certain picture of the world. It is highly significant that in comparison with the other Gnostic myths the cosmological side in Christian mythology—i.e., the explanation of the world by metaphysics—has been almost entirely eliminated, whereas the Gnostic systems are full of cosmological speculations about the "eons." Thanks to its very marked reserve in the area of cosmology, Christian mythology does not collapse because of the transformations which science has imported into the notions of the make-up and history of the world. Copernicus did not compel the Christian Church to dismiss the day of ascension.

On the other hand, it is of decisive importance to Christian mythology that it present the Christian view of God. It is this which makes it impossible to demythologize the gospel. The progress of science can indeed change what Swedish theology has called "the clothing of the idea" (as opposed to the "motif of the idea"), but nothing is changed in the fact that God—when it is the God of whom the gospel speaks—can only be proclaimed mythologically. The "clothing" of the idea can change as far as the cosmological accessories of mythology are concerned. In any case, the New Testament does not hide the fact that the clothing of the idea cannot fully express by itself the mythical reality. God dwells in an "unapproachable light" (I Tim. 6:16); here below we can see things only partially as in a mirror (I Cor. 13:12); and when God is described, we are not left in doubt that it is only in terms of coarse pictures (Rev. 4:3-11). All in all, Bultmann has undertaken quite a trivial task when he thinks he has to inform us that modern science has rendered unacceptable such concepts as the ascension, the descent into hell, Spirit, sacraments, ransom, et cetera. First of all, myth does not pretend to give a cosmology to be taken literally; next, it is important to know that it is not only mythology which must have recourse to a language of symbols. This is also the case with the existentialist philosophy admired so much by Bultmann. Its symbolic language which is often so difficult to understand —we are thinking of Heidegger—frequently points to phenomena which do not conform to the picture of the world presented by modern science. Just to mention one of several examples—the concept of "historical existence." From the scientific viewpoint, is not this concept just as mythological as the ascension of Christ?

And does not modern science proceed in the same way? When

science returns to its ultimate principles, the concept of phenomena which it fashions for itself, as far as I can understand, is no longer mechanistic, but rather, we could say, mythological.

The symbolical language of mythology is not therefore sufficient to disqualify it, since the sphere of its reality cannot be conceived in any way other than mythologically, and according to the spirit of the Christian gospel God can only reveal himself in a mythological way. A demythologizing of the gospel would consequently falsify its picture of God.

In summary, what is the result of demythologizing? Simply this, that the picture of God is replaced by a concept or a feeling of God. In this sense demythologizing is not at all a new idea. The history of Christian thought records two very important tendencies which have had far-reaching consequences. The one is metaphysical, the other psychological.

When mythology disappears metaphysics takes its place. The metaphysical tendency of scholastic theology, with all its consequences, is an example of demythologizing. In contrast to this, Luther's theology is a tremendous "remythologizing." This is the way to understand his preference for the coarse images of the early Church and his contempt for all the artifices of metaphysics. Mythology preserves in effect a picture of God as a living and acting being, which is the true picture of the God of the Bible and of the gospel who manifests himself in the incarnation of Jesus Christ. The true relation between mythology and history, or this dependence which constitutes the enigma in the sacred history of the New Testament, adheres to the picture of God who is an integral part of the gospel. The gospel does not proclaim Jesus as a teacher or example. It proclaims him as a real act of *agape* which God offers to me. Through him God deals with us. But this can only be said when myth and history are joined together: The Word became flesh and dwelt among us. In the moment that we suppress the myth, Christ is transformed into a teacher or an example, and the picture of God becomes a different one, that of a distant God, inactive and majestic, and not the God who becomes history.

In post-Reformation theology we have a different example of demythologizing which has had incalculable consequences. When mythology disappears, feeling takes its place. In an excellent study appearing in *For Kirke og Kultur,* 1936, by Einar Molland and Alex L.

Johnson, entitled "Kristen Mythologi?" a study which in its brevity teaches us more than Bultmann on the problems of myth and mythology, it is shown how the hymns after the Reformation betray a persistent tendency to suppress mythology in favor of psychology. The ascension and the resurrection become, for example, events which take place in the soul. In a certain sense, the pietistic tendency as a whole shows such a tendency towards demythologizing. Moreover, it is evident that when demythologizing does not end in metaphysics, it leads necessarily to psychology. In reality, Bultmann's demythologizing contains some psychology, only disguised in existentialist terminology. For him, as for Emanuel Hirsch, the crucifixion and the resurrection —under the title of eschatological events—become facts in the "soul" or in "existence." This psychologizing results in another kind of deformation of the picture of God. God is no longer the living God, active, sovereign, and compassionate, but the object of religious feeling or the inspiration of existential decision.

Mythology, philosophy, and theology are thus to be seen in terms of this reciprocal situation, in which theology at the start differentiates itself by means of mythology from all the philosophical and metaphysical problems. The world and its explanation are abandoned to philosophy. By the same token, however, mythology also bars philosophy and metaphysics from having access to theology. Mythology keeps watch over the Christian picture of God.

Today mythology must be reinforced so that the substance of the gospel will not be volatilized into metaphysics or psychology. That this "remythologizing" will contain new problems is quite another matter. But an honest, sincere, atheistic existentialist philosophy and an orthodox Christianity equally honest and sincere are—despite all the problems posed by their disagreement and incompatibility— far more desirable than a kind of compromise which is neither real Christianity nor genuine existentialist philosophy.

SIX

Nils Alstrup Dahl

The Problem of the
Historical Jesus

The historical Jesus has become a problem for us. That does not mean that Jesus generally or primarily is a problem. Whatever the problem, we have a direct impression of Jesus as his figure encounters us in the Gospels. This is enough for the simple, believing Christian; in life and death he may set his hope on Jesus as he learns to know him through the Holy Scriptures. The *problem* of the historical Jesus first arises in connection with critical reflection which raises the question as to what can be ascertained about Jesus in purely historico-scientific fashion. The concept of the "historical Jesus," as I use it here, designates Jesus as the object of methodical, critical, historical research, and the picture of him which can be drawn by such research. It is this historical Jesus which has become a problem for us.

In the form in which it is posed today, this problem is of relatively recent date. The older Catholic and Confessional Christianity was certain that the Gospels as canonical Holy Scriptures give information about Jesus which is absolutely reliable historically. The question was merely how the individual Scriptures could be brought into complete harmony with each other. For the rationalistic and liberal theology the relation between the historical Jesus and the Christ of Church dogma became a problem, but for it the doctrine of the Church was problematic and not the historical Jesus. Rather, it was assumed that the real picture of Jesus could be reproduced by critical historical research, and that this picture could serve as the basis for a purification and renewal of Christianity.

For present-day theology, however, it is precisely the historical

Jesus which has become a problem. A symptom of this is that our time abounds with Jesus novels, descriptions of Jesus' life which raise more scientific claims but which are written almost exclusively by outsiders and dilettantes. New Testament scholars know only too well how difficult the task is and how uncertain the attempts at solution are. The leading spirits among them content themselves with writing terse and sketchy descriptions, in which, on the basis of their detailed research, they emphasize the elements which they regard as essential. It is peculiar, moreover, that the popularity of literature on the life of Jesus appears to be on the increase in the Catholic sector, while at the same time it has become altogether suspect for German Protestantism, the classic sphere of research on the life of Jesus.

The problem concerns not only the question whether it is at all possible to give a scientifically founded and tenable description of the life of Jesus; it also involves the question concerning the relevance of such a description for theology and the Church. It is of the nature of the case that such can only be attained by means of the usual historico-scientific method, "the profane scientific" method, as it is sometimes put in theological circles. Already, however, the methods employed prevent the recognition of what is essential for faith; namely, that Jesus Christ is the Son of God and the living Lord. It is understandable that the question is raised whether or not faith, the Church and theology must keep to that which is written in the New Testament, without troubling with the alleged historical Jesus of critical science.

Today the uncertainty in face of such questions appears to be very great. The following essay represents an attempt to contribute to the clarification of the historico-scientific and theological problem.[1] First of all, the present state of the problem and its presuppositions in the history of research must be viewed somewhat more precisely.

I

THE HISTORY OF THE PROBLEM

The concept "the historical Jesus" as well as the scientific research

---

[1] This essay originally appeared in a collection of lectures entitled *Rett lære og kjetterske meninger* (Oslo, 1953). The revised German draft still gives evidence of the fact that the author has attempted to write in an intelligible way also for non-theologians, which accounts for a certain breadth and scope in presentation.

on the life of Jesus came into being in the period of the Enlightenment. Their presupposition was the appearance of a historical source-
criticism and the application of its methods to the Gospels, first of all
in a quite naïve, rationalistic manner, then later in a more methodical
fashion. Albert Schweitzer in his *Quest of the Historical Jesus,* written
with ingenious one-sidedness, has correctly pointed to a second presupposition: "This dogma had first to be shattered before men could
once more go out in quest of the historical Jesus, before they could
grasp the thought of His existence." [2]

Liberation from dogma could now assume various forms. A few
scholars went to work in a radical way and utilized the "historical"
description of Jesus as a means of getting free from Christianity as
such. That holds true for the pioneer of the German Life-of-Jesus research, Hermann Samuel Reimarus. Strongly influenced by English
deists (a fact which Schweitzer conceals!), he portrays Jesus as a political messianic pretender and his disciples as frauds. For such radicalism, however, he found relatively few disciples in the following
century. The Life-of-Jesus research, in its classic period of the nineteenth century, was in the main a gigantic attempt to get free from the
christological dogma of the Church, but at the same time to maintain
the uniquely religious significance of Jesus. In carrying this through
there were many possible variations on the sliding scale between
strictly conservative and quite radical views. Differences could occur
in the way in which they maintained the unique position of Jesus.
Rationalism emphasized especially the teaching of Jesus and his moral
example. Later, Jesus' portrait and his God-consciousness assumed the
center of the stage. For Ferdinand Christian Baur's research, carried
on under the influence of Hegel, the decisive thing was that in Jesus
the consciousness of the unity of God and man had first broken
through. On the basis of this presupposition, the historical Jesus could
now indeed become a problem; Baur himself saw in the speculative
theology of German idealism a Gnosticism of a higher order. The
problem was actualized by David Friedrich Strauss and his radical
scepticism over against the historicity of the Gospel tradition. Indeed,
the solution of the problem for Strauss was given in advance by the
Hegelian philosophy: The essential thing is the Christ idea, the idea

[2] W. Montgomery tr.), (New York: The Macmillan Company, 1948), p. 3. Used
by permission of The Macmillan Company and A. & C. Black, Ltd.

140

of God-manhood, realized in the total history of the human race. What Jesus as a historical person was or was not was therefore irrelevant.

The speculative theology rapidly drew to a close. The crisis called forth by Strauss led to an even more intensive preoccupation with the historical Jesus. Thereafter the Life-of-Jesus research not only stood under the aegis of the struggle for freedom from dogma, but also under that of the apologetic defense against Strauss. In the period of empiricism there was also the desire to erect a secure historical basis for Christian faith. It was assumed that the necessary basis in the sources had been found by means of the Marcan hypothesis and the Two Source Theory.

In contrast to rationalism and speculative theology, the later liberal theology was more anti-metaphysical and anti-intellectualistic. To be sure, Jesus' proclamation—e.g., of the Father love of God and the infinite worth of the individual human soul—could be strongly emphasized, but that which was really decisive and unique was found in Jesus' personality, his religion or his "inner life." Jesus lived in a unique relationship of sonship to God and thus made it possible for us as well to live in divine sonship of faith. Following upon such an evaluation of the person of Jesus it was possible for a "liberal-positive" mediating theology to preserve or gain a positive relation to the apostolic proclamation of Jesus as Savior and Lord. Liberal theology has been of influence within the Scandinavian churches chiefly in this mediating form.

In its more radical form, interest in the historical Jesus not only led to liberation from dogma, but also to a break with the apostolic proclamation of the Christ underlying that dogma. That came sharply to light in the debate concerning Jesus and Paul, so intensively carried on at the turn of the century. Paul was represented as a second founder of Christianity, who replaced the simple teaching of Jesus with his complicated doctrine of redemption. Of course, this debate in its extreme was quite senseless, as leading liberal theologians soon recognized; for the main features of the Pauline preaching of Christ already existed in the Church before Paul. The real problem is not "Jesus and Paul," but rather, "Who was Jesus and what has the Church made of him?"

We would misinterpret this whole stream of research if we were to overlook the fact that a real piety was joined to this interest in the historical Jesus, his life, and his portrait. But we will have to agree with Albert Schweitzer's evaluation of the Jesus-research of the nineteenth century that each epoch in theology rediscovered its own ideas in Jesus, "otherwise it could not endow Him with life." "But it was not only each epoch that found its reflection in Jesus; each individual created Him in accordance with his own character." [3] Modern religiosity not only gave rise to the quest of the historical Jesus behind and beyond the New Testament, but also to the method by which it was done. This was candidly expressed by the otherwise so critical and level-headed Adolf Jülicher in the masterpiece of his youth: "I could not understand the Lord, and thus could not love him, if a Galilean spring, sunny days with an inspired view of high mountains, had not preceded His Easter-death in Jerusalem." [4] This contrast between the bright spring in Galilee and the dark days in Jerusalem was common to all presentations in the life of Jesus.

All the liberal biographies of Jesus shared the conviction of having in the historical Jesus an ally in their efforts toward a modern theology and a broad-minded Christianity. Accordingly, the historical Jesus was modernized. This liberal Jesus-religion which wished to build on a historical Jesus freed from churchly dogma and isolated from the apostolic preaching has become an impossibility for us today. That same critical-historical research on the Bible which grew in connection with the liberal theology is responsible for it. It is to the unfading glory of this latter movement that it had the courage and the truthfulness to carry on a historical research which undermined its own dogmatic views.

The decisive blows against the liberal interpretation of the historical Jesus were already dealt at the turn of the century, though their effect only became gradually clear. The blows came from various sides. One of them struck at the sources for a presentation of the life of Jesus. In the Gospel of Mark some deletions had been made and were attributed to the theology of the Church; otherwise it was thought to be a historically reliable source of the life of Jesus. However, Wilhelm Wrede in his *Das Messiasgeheimnis in den Evangelien* showed that this approach was fundamentally uncritical and unhis-

---

[3] *Ibid.*, p. 4.

[4] *Die Gleichnisreden Jesu*, I (Tübingen: J. C. B. Mohr, 1910), 144.

142

torical. The oldest Gospel, according to its basic structure, was already dogmatic, dominated by the faith in Jesus' messianic secret. The significant thing about Wrede's book was above all its new orientation in method. He put his finger on the sore spot: "Scientific research on the life of Jesus suffers from psychological conjecture." [5] A genuinely critical and historical treatment must abandon psychological hypotheses in order in all candor to study the extant sources, and, first of all, of course, as witnesses to the faith and theology of the evangelists and the communities in which they lived. From this standpoint there was no longer any principal difference between Mark and John, and in respect to the gulf which had developed between Jesus and Paul, the Gospels now were to a certain extent removed from the historical Jesus and ranged on the side of Paul.

Julius Wellhausen's contributions to Gospel research moved in the same direction. As a direct result of the radicalizing of criticism he came to the conclusion in his *Einleitung in die drei ersten Evangelien* that "without his later influence in the community we can visualize nothing of the religious personality of Jesus. It always appears only in a reflection, broken by the medium of the Christian faith." [6] In our century the form-critical school has attached itself to Wrede and Wellhausen—although the form-critical method in itself does not need to be bound to this specific tradition of research, as some have incorrectly supposed. It has become a main concern of Gospel research to understand the evangelical tradition in connection with its life situation in the Church. This function of the tradition and the interest of faith connected with it has determined the selection, formation, collection, and writing down of the recollected words of Jesus and episodes from his life. The theology of the Church, therefore, is not only a disturbing element which appeared subsequently and falsified the genuine picture of Jesus; rather, it was there from the very beginning and explains why any recollections about Jesus were retained in the tradition.

Another blow against the leading liberal theology came from the school of the history of religions. In this school there was opposition first of all to the modernizing of primitive Christianity which is

[5] *Das Messiasgeheimnis in den Evangelien* (Göttingen: Vandenhoeck und Ruprecht, 1901), p. 3.
[6] Berlin: Georg Reimer, 1905, p. 114.

rather to be placed within the framework of Hellenistic syncretism. Significant for our problem was the fact that whereas the earlier liberal theology laid the chief emphasis on the ethical sphere, now the specifically religious was more clearly featured; for primitive Christianity the uniqueness of Jesus lay not in his religious-ethical personality, but rather in the fact that he was the Redeemer and Lord of the community, the "cult hero," as it was put. It was thereby made clear that for primitive Christianity the significance of Jesus was totally different than the evaluation placed upon him by modern Christianity.

When the need arose, radical Gospel criticism and the "religio-historical" view of primitive Christianity could still be joined to a typically liberal picture of the historical Jesus, although in that case the historical connection between Jesus and primitive Christianity threatened to break completely. The attacks were also directed against the liberal picture of Jesus itself. Within liberalism Johannes Weiss gave the storm signal. In his *Predigt Jesu vom Reiche Gottes* he demonstrated that "the idea of the Kingdom of God in Ritschl's theology and in the preaching of Jesus are two very different things." [7] The message of Jesus was eschatological. Albert Schweitzer proceeded further on this course. For him not only the kingdom of God in the preaching of Jesus was to be understood eschatologically, but also "thorough-going eschatology" offered him the key for understanding the whole life of Jesus. The dogmatic conception of his mission was not something added later; Jesus himself understood his life and suffering in the light of an eschatological dogmatic. Of course, less notice was paid Schweitzer's own attempt at solution than his settlement with the history of research "from Reimarus to Wrede." Contrary to the author's intention, the *Quest of the Historical Jesus* introduced a period of scepticism into this research. Schweitzer could maintain that the result of the Life-of-Jesus research was negative:

The Jesus of Nazareth who came forward publicly as the Messiah, who preached the ethic of the Kingdom of God, who founded the Kingdom of Heaven upon earth, and died to give His work its final consecration, never had any existence. He is a figure designed by rationalism, endowed with life by liberalism, and clothed by modern theology in an historical garb. [8]

[7] Göttingen: Vandenhoeck und Ruprecht, 1892, p. v.
[8] Schweitzer, *op. cit.*, p. 396.

144

The study of the Life of Jesus has had a curious history. It set out in quest of the historical Jesus, believing that when it had found Him it could bring Him straight into our time as a Teacher and Savior. It loosed the bands by which He had been riveted for centuries to the stony rocks of ecclesiastical doctrine, and rejoiced to see life and movement coming into the figure once more, and the historical Jesus advancing, as it seemed, to meet it. But He does not stay; He passes by our time and returns to His own.[9]

The eschatological expectation is not the only aspect uniting Jesus with Judaism of the first century, however. That he was part of it has also become clear in many other connections. In this area, of course, scholars of another school have accomplished more than the liberals. The latter had generally presented *Die Predigt Jesu in ihrem Gegensatz zum Judentum* (Bousset, 1892), and had drawn rather a caricature of Pharisaism, a dark background for the portait of Jesus' personality which shone all the brighter. The school of the history of religions was primarily interested in primitive Christianity as a syncretistic religion and emphasized the influence of oriental Hellenism. The conservative theologians showed a preference for the Jewish background in order to find a support for the historical credibility of the Gospel tradition. Of course, it was hardly their intention to bring to light what was strange and ancient in the Judaism of Jesus himself.

Jewish scholars also took pains in a most profitable way to illuminate the Palestinian background of the gospel history. Influenced by Jewish emancipation and religious liberalism, they began research on the historical Jesus. The strange thing now was that liberal Jews could draw an ideal picture of Pharisaism strikingly reminiscent of the liberal picture of Jesus. Even in Judaism could be found faith in God as loving Father, emphasis on the significance of principles in morality and many other things. It is not surprising that they made contact with the research on Jesus done by Christian theologians, in order to utilize it to the advantage of reformed Judaism,[10] for this historical Jesus belonged to Judaism as one of its noblest figures, though a few prejudices and exaggerations on the part of his followers could explain why he became the Founder of a new, non-Jewish religion. It

[9] *Ibid.,* p. 397.

[10] Gösta Lindeskog has written the history of this research in *Die Jesusfrage im neuzeitlichen Judentum* (Uppsala, 1938). Cf. also *Judaica,* VI (1950), 190-229, 241-68.

also became clear to them that it was faith in Jesus as the crucified and risen Son of God which was at the heart of Christianity, and which alone differentiated it from a reformed Judaism. Wellhausen expressed the same insight briefly, tersely and somewhat brutally: "Jesus was no Christian, he was a Jew." [11]

In order to discover the essence of Christianity in the "religion of Jesus," theology, characterized by the slogan "back to the historical Jesus," had lost the historical ground beneath its feet. The lectures which Adolf von Harnack delivered on "What is Christianity?" at the turn of the century were not the program for a new era, but were rather the epilogue to an epoch in the history of theology which was fast coming to a close. The dilemma into which liberal theology had fallen was clearly seen by one such as Wellhausen: "Without the Gospel and without Paul even Judaism would still have to cling to Jesus. . . . We cannot go back to him, even if we wanted to. . . . For if the Gospel were removed, the historical Jesus would be a very dubious and unsatisfactory substitute as a basis for religion." [12] Even Wrede, so it is reported, is supposed to have suffered from the discrepancy between the results of his research and the piety of liberal Christianity. But these men could not indicate a way out of the dilemma.

Albert Schweitzer found his own way. His criticism of the modern liberal picture of Jesus not only originated in scientific research; it was the result of a reaction to his contemporaries who lacked the sense for the "elementary." Philosophically and religiously he found the solution in an ethical voluntaristic mysticism for which Jesus was not the basis of religion, but indeed an enlivening and inspiring factor: "He comes to us as One unknown, without a name, as of old, by the lake-side, He came to those men who knew Him not. He speaks to us the same word: 'Follow thou me!' " [13] Obedience to this word led Schweitzer from scientific theology to the primeval forest of Africa. His lifework attests to the power which can lie in a liberal Christianity, but may also raise the question whether it can exist elsewhere than in the shadows of a churchly Christianity. Schweitzer's intensely personal solution could not guide the further work of theology on the problem of the historical Jesus. Whatever fruitful begin-

[11] Wellhausen, *op. cit.*, p. 113.
[12] *Ibid.*, p. 115.
[13] Schweitzer, *op. cit.*, p. 401.

nings his conception contained were first made clear by the publication of his work *The Mysticism of Paul the Apostle.*

In the main, little note was first taken of the theological crisis which resulted from the work of Wrede and Wellhausen, Weiss and Schweitzer, the school of the history of religions and Jewish research on Jesus. The consequences became clear only gradually, and that is understandable. These scholars and schools of research were in part mutually opposed, and each of them could properly be criticized for its one-sidedness and exaggerations. Liberal theology disintegrated only after the First World War, but more with reference to studies on Paul and the Reformation than to research on Jesus. This theological reversal would not have been possible, however, if New Testament research had not undermined the liberal Jesus-religion a few decades earlier.

Conservative theology had remained somewhat reserved over against the Life-of-Jesus research. Hence, without concerning itself with the crisis in this research, it could continue working in the old way relatively undisturbed—more so in Scandinavian countries than in Germany. To a certain extent, these conservatives took a kind of morbid pleasure in the dissolution of liberal theology. For the most part, however, they were too preoccupied with the apologetics of defending the genuineness of New Testament Scriptures and traditions to have been able to make a decisive contribution to the critical research on the life of Jesus.

There were also theologians of a churchly conservative temper who combined a deep anchoring in biblical Christianity with an openness to the questions with which scholarship had to deal. Even before the problem of the historical Jesus had become critical, and when the Life-of-Jesus research was still in full bloom, Martin Kähler had written his book *Der sogenannte historische Jesus und der geschichtliche, biblische Christus.* In it he pointed out a way which was to be significant for the future. Kähler stated that the foundation of faith cannot be a scientifically reconstructed and therefore necessarily hypothetical historical Jesus, but rather must be a Jesus Christ as proclaimed by the apostles in the preaching which established the Church. The Gospels are not sources for the biography of Jesus, but rather are "sermons on the Messiahship of the Crucified," "passion stories with a rather lengthy introduction."

147

Upon publication Kähler's book aroused lively discussion, but it had no decisive influence at first and could be ignored in Schweitzer's *Quest of the Historical Jesus.* It had its real effect only in our century, following the crisis in the Life-of-Jesus research. After the First World War his ideas were taken up and further elaborated. Once more it has become clear to us that Christian faith relates to the Jesus of Nazareth who is preached in the apostolic proclamation as the crucified and risen Lord. That which gives the various New Testament writings their inner unity is, of course, not a theoretical dogma, nor is it the inspiring impression of the personality of Jesus, but rather the Gospel of the act of God in Jesus Christ, in whom forgiveness of sins, righteousness, and life are given to us. The message of the apostles is the proclamation of a kerygma for which they are commissioned by the appearances of the risen Lord. The resurrection of Jesus stands at the center of the New Testament and cannot be removed from this place without a resultant collapse. The recollections of the historical Jesus were preserved, formed, and interpreted within the framework of the proclamation concerning the risen Lord, and for Christian faith this interpretation is the proper and legitimate one. Only by faith in the apostolic Gospel is it possible to hold fast to the unique religious significance of Jesus. For a purely immanent, historical view he can only be unique in that relative sense in which other great men may be called unique. If the liberal theologians wish to hold fast to the unique significance of the historical Jesus in another and more absolute sense, that is conceivable only as an aftereffect of ecclesiastical, dogmatic Christianity.

Reducing it to a brief formula, one may say that the Life-of-Jesus theology was superseded by a kerygma-theology. To some extent, a historical formulation of the question was now more or less consistently rejected: The extant Gospels are the only things to which we must hold fast. My honored teacher Ragnar Asting said, e.g., that the Gospels are "directed forwards," bearers of a creative proclamation; we should believe them, instead of inquiring into the historical verifiability of what is reported. He was not the only one who tended to regard the attempt to penetrate behind the Gospels to the historical Jesus as a scientifically insoluble and unfruitful task, as well as a theologically illegitimate inquiry. This new kerygmatic-theological orientation does not imply, however, that New Testament scholarship has landed in a neo-orthodoxy free of problems instead of working with serious historical questions. Just as the Life-of-Jesus theology, so also the kerygma-theology appears in an ecclesiastically conservative as well as in a more radical form. The question for debate is not merely to what degree the old dogma of the Church is a legitimate and necessary interpretation of the apostolic kerygma, but also the question, how the kerygma is to be interpreted today—the problem of demythologizing.

In spite of all its dependence on the older critical research, even Bultmann's existential interpretation must be viewed as a variant of the kerygma-theology; it is concerned neither with the Christ idea nor with the personality of Jesus as accessible to historical research, but rather with the Jesus Christ proclaimed in the gospel. The debate on demythologizing, however, has shown that we cannot so quickly dispense with the problem of the historical Jesus. Already a certain re-action to a thoroughgoing kerygmatic theology appears to have set in. As Ernst Käsemann has recently pointed out, an interesting shift in fronts has come about; in reaction to Bultmann's radicalism, an attempt is being made to counteract a separation of kerygma from tradition.[14] In a most spirited manner, Ethelbert Stauffer has begun to advocate a renewal of the Life-of-Jesus research on the basis of an inquiry into the historical period of the New Testament.[15]

It is impossible to return to the precritical evaluation of the Gospels as historical source documents. Of course, archaeological discoveries and more recent researches on some questions have invalidated radical critical hypotheses and strengthened trust in the tradition, but even if this should continue to a much greater extent in the future, we will not be able to avoid the new method of reading the Gospels primarily as witnesses of the primitive Church. It is true, however, that it would be premature to conclude from Kähler's theologically significant and exegetically fruitful ideas that the question concerning the historical Jesus is not to be put at all. To be sure, faith comes from preaching and is not dependent upon the historico-scientific work of New Testament professors. It would be something quite different, however, to deny to scholars their work on historical

[14] Cf. Käsemann, "Das Problem des historischen Jesus," *Zeitschrift für Theologie und Kirche,* LI (1954), 125-53.
[15] Stauffer, "Der Stand der neutestamentlichen Forschung," *Theologie und Liturgie,* ed. L. Henning (1952), pp. 35-105.

questions or to oppose the use of methods which in themselves are completely profane, but which are the only ones at the disposal of the historian. That the essence of Christianity cannot be found by a return to the historical Jesus does not mean that it would be senseless and improper to ask what we already know and are able to know about Jesus in a purely historical way. The fact that the problem is extremely difficult and its solution only approximate does not mean that we may simply abandon it permanently. The curiosity which underlies all science will certainly lead to a continually new treatment of the problem. If we theologians ignore this task, others will undertake it. Even if the question should be theologically irrelevant (more of this later), we cannot call it illegitimate. The scientific ethos requires that we do not avoid it, but rather work at it in all sincerity, for God's law lies behind the scientific ethos. The historico-scientific concern with the problem of the historical Jesus is at least an honorable task which is subject to the distress and promise of every honorable profession, and certainly to the Pauline ὡς μή as well.

II

THE HISTORICO-SCIENTIFIC PROBLEM

The fact that objectively assured results can only be reached in an approximate way does not in itself distinguish Jesus-research from other historical science. The point is rather that the difficulties with which *all* historical science must grapple are especially perceptible in this area. All historical work is influenced by the presuppositions of the historian, and he himself is a child of his own time. That becomes particularly noticeable when Jesus is made the object of historical research, and even the historian obviously cannot deal with Jesus without being involved in a positive or negative way. It is a real question whether personal involvement is not a positive presupposition for a scholar's attaining to any kind of historically fruitful results. To a certain degree, wishful thinking and subjective errors can be eliminated by methodically scientific work, when the will to truth is present. Scholars with different starting points co-operate and are able mutually to correct each other. For that reason also, it is not desirable that non-Christian scholars remain aloof from this work. In certain respects even antipathy can be illuminating; Jewish scholars, e.g., can have a clear eye for what is characteristic of Jesus.

Other difficulties for research on the historical Jesus lie in the *nature of the sources*. We have no documentary reports and no traditions concerning Jesus by his enemies or other contemporaries. Even the oldest extra-Christian references to Jesus appear to rest not on direct recollections, but on encounters with Christians in Palestine or Rome. They may suffice to corroborate the historical existence of Jesus, but nothing more. Only on the basis of the New Testament writings are we able to construct for ourselves a real picture of Jesus. Of these the oldest were written about two decades after his death, and all aim at nourishing faith in him; none of them can be regarded as a neutral historical record. Once we recognize the nature of these sources, we will the more easily be amazed at how much we still know of Jesus historically. A great part of the tradition consists of brief, pregnant expressions and characteristic episodes which are easily committed to memory. Very early, the tradition must have taken on a relatively fixed form and, of course, in a milieu where it was customary to preserve recollections with great faithfulness. The interest of faith in the tradition about Jesus served not only to shape, but also to conserve the tradition; flights of fancy were confined within much narrower limits than is the case, e.g., with the legends of the apostles.

Only by methodically pure and critical work can the received traditions be made useful for a historical description of Jesus, but thereby personal and current views concerning what Jesus may have said or done may not be made a criterion in the evaluation of the material in question. The history of research has taught us what a dangerous source of error this can be. If we want to avoid all subjective arbitrariness historico-critical research on the Gospels becomes an extremely complicated work requiring the highest degree of precision. The extant Gospels are first of all to be studied and interpreted as literary wholes. Their relationship to each other must be accurately examined, but even the relatively certain results of literary criticism have only limited value for the historical question, for we must reckon with the fact that the oral tradition still existed in addition to and following the first written records. The possibility exists throughout that an older variant of the tradition may have been preserved in a secondary literary source.[16]

---

[16] Cf. my essay, "Die Passionsgeschichte bei Matthäus, *New Testament Studies*, I, No. 3 (1955).

In addition to the literary investigation of the Gospels we must consider the traditio-historical study of the small or smallest units of the tradition. In addition to the Gospels, material from later sources —e.g., quotations from the church fathers—textual variants, and fragments of apocryphal gospels has a significance which cannot be ignored. The new material which such sources offer is of course extremely small and of dubious value, but the subsequent history of the Gospel tradition is illuminated, and from it the cautious scholar will be able to draw a few conclusions regarding its earlier history. In further research, critical viewpoints concerning the form, language, and substance are also to be observed. No single road leads to the goal; in spite of the very fruitful beginning of form criticism, the result has been, e.g., that the study of form has not yielded objective criteria for separating older from later traditions to the degree expected. The linguistic criteria, in their turn, lead with great probability to old traditions where the original Semitic tongue shines through but do not allow any positive decision regarding the *ipsissima verba* of Jesus. Preference for one certain method as is shared by the schools should be regarded as a calamity and should, where possible, be replaced by the co-operation of a variety of specialists.

On the basis of numerous individual observations, a more comprehensive picture of the history of the tradition can then be outlined. Certain statistical, not absolute, laws and regularities emerge which leave their imprint on the formation and transformation of the tradition. It is well known that the individual sayings and narratives as such have been relatively faithfully preserved, while the evangelists and the narrators before them were much freer in the collection and arrangement of the material. Within the individual sections of the tradition greater freedom is exercised with respect to rendering introductory and concluding data than with regard to the central point. Among the different variants agreement is greatest in the rendering of the words of Jesus, but the words have not been preserved because of any reverence for the antiquarian, but because they are words of the Lord to his community. Loosed from their original situation, the words have been used and construed in a new way, a factor which has affected not only their arrangement, but also their formation. That can be most easily observed in the case of the parables.[17]

[17] Joachim Jeremias, *The Parables of Jesus*, tr. S. H. Hooke (New York: Charles Scribners Sons, 1955), pp. 20-28.

The goal of critical Gospel research is to make clear the history of the tradition about Jesus within the Church. With some certainty, moreover, distinction can be made between the core of the tradition and its later elaboration. It is much more difficult to find objective criteria which can determine whether the core of a tradition is authentic or secondary. It is theoretically possible that migrant sayings have been transferred to Jesus, that words of Jewish wisdom or utterances of primitive Christian prophets have been put in the mouth of the historical Jesus, et cetera, but only very seldom can positive proof be adduced that such is really the case. Here, generally, the total perspective of the scholar is decisive for an evaluation of the case in point, and not vice versa. That can easily be observed in Bultmann's *Die Geschichte der Synoptischen Tradition,* but also applies to scholars who, like myself, are inclined to believe that on the whole the Church did not produce the traditions about Jesus, but rather reproduced them in a new form.

In no case can any distinct and sharp separation be achieved between genuine words of Jesus and constructions of the community. We do not escape the fact that we know Jesus only as the disciples remembered him. Whoever thinks that the disciples completely misunderstood their Master or even consciously falsified his picture may give his phantasy free reign. From a purely historio-scientific point of view, however, it is more logical to assume that the Master is to be recognized from the circle of his disciples and its historical influence. But then it is also possible to work methodically when an attempt is made to advance from the analysis of the Gospel tradition to the description of the historical Jesus.

Even without a clear differentiation between pure history and the Church's theology the Gospel tradition permits us to draw a very clear picture of what was typical and characteristic of Jesus. Cross sections of the tradition bring to the fore what was characteristic, e.g., of his proclamation of the Kingdom of God, of his position toward the law, or of his attitude toward various groups of men. Words and reports of differing form and genre, transmitted within various layers of the tradition, mutually illumine each other and yield a total picture in which there appears something that is characteristic of Jesus. Whether the historicity of individual words or episodes remains uncertain is consequently of lesser importance. The fact that the word or occurrence found a place within the tradition about Jesus indicates that it agreed with the total picture as it existed within the circle of the disciples.[18]

The cross-section method must be supplemented by drawing longitudinal lines leading from Judaism beyond Jesus to primitive Christianity. While the time when Zarathustra and Moses lived has long been the subject of debate, we know that Jesus was crucified under Pontius Pilate. The fixed starting point of all our knowledge about him is that he is the crucified One whom the community, originating in his band of disciples, believed to be the risen Messiah. We also know that Jesus worked in Israel and that he himself was born and grew up a Jew, was "born of woman, born under the law." The historical Jesus is to be found at the crossroad where Christianity and Judaism begin separating from each other, although it only became gradually clear that the paths parted in such a way that Christianity appeared as a new religion alongside Judaism.

From the oldest Christian sources we must work our way backwards in the direction of Jesus. It is of great advantage that the most important groups of New Testament writings are independent of each other; Paul, the Synoptists, John, the Epistle to the Hebrews, et cetera, cannot be arranged into one straight line of development. Rather, each in its own way reflects the impression made by Jesus and the events connected with his name. Between the historical Jesus and the New Testament writings there are, of course, the Easter occurrences, but that does not alter the fact that the historian who works backwards from the various formulations of primitive Christianity toward the common starting point by this method also approaches the historical Jesus. The investigation of the tradition lying behind the Gospels is, of course, the most important, but not the only part of this work.

On the other hand, we must view Jesus within the context of Palestinian Judaism. Everything which enlarges our knowledge of this environment of Jesus indirectly extends our knowledge of the historical Jesus himself. Since the results in this area are relatively certain, it is a very real question whether or not the insights gained here in

[18] Julius Schniewind's remarks in "Zur Synoptikerexegese," *Theologische Rundschau,* II (1930), 129-89, are still of value, and particularly his discussion of "longitudinal" and "cross-section exegesis." On the questions of method, cf. also C. H. Dodd, *History and the Gospel* (London: James Nisbet & Company, 1938).

the long run involve the greatest enrichment of our historical knowledge about Jesus. Only by saving the honor of the Pharisees, e.g., has the unheard-of radicality of Jesus' words against the Pharisees really come to light. It is still not possible to estimate what the textual findings from the caves may yield; in any case they impel us to resume the quest of the historical Jesus. As never before we have the possibility of tracing the trends and ideas which, both positively and negatively, form the presuppositions for his ministry.

When, on the one hand, the historian works backwards in this way from oldest Christianity to Jesus and, on the other, attempts to clarify the presuppositions of his appearance on the basis of Jewish sources, quite a clear picture can be gained of the setting into which Jesus appeared and of the changes which his ministry effected. By this method it is also possible to insert the transmitted words and episodes into their original historical situation. Thus we can form an idea of what Jesus wanted to say to the Jews of his own time and can attempt to construct a historical picture of him.

The historian's attempt to reconstruct the historical Jesus by the historico-scientific method may be compared with the work of the archaeologist who attempts to restore an old monument of which only the foundation and a few scattered stones remain. He may try to draw sketches on paper in order to show how the structure probably looked. No one will deny him that, and it can be useful and necessary for his work. He misleads his readers, however, when he publishes his sketch without calling attention to the place where exact knowledge leaves off, where he has good grounds for his reconstruction, and where he has further drawn free hand. When he finds the precise spot where one or a few of the scattered stones originally lay, it means more in the long run than such reconstructive attempts. Similarly, it is permissible to write a description of the historical Jesus, but hypotheses may not be advanced as exact scientific results. If there is an ingenious element in the hypotheses, as e.g., in Albert Schweitzer's case, then they may give important impulse to further research. But over an extended period an expansion of our exact knowledge of primitive Christianity and of Judaism in Jesus' time means more for our historical knowledge of Jesus than many books about his life.

Historical science can only approximately achieve exact results. This does not merely apply to the Jesus-research, but such a general truth is most particularly to be observed in the Jesus-research with its involved problematic. Whoever has to fix an uncertain chronological datum, e.g., the year of the origin of a work, is only seldom in the position of finding new arguments which allow him to make a completely accurate decision. He must begin by establishing the *termini a quo* and *ad quem* and, on the basis of these two limits, try to approach the precise point of time. Even the more involved historical problems will, *mutatis mutandis,* have to be dealt with in a similar way. So far as Jesus is concerned, the scholar must search, on the one hand, for what could be established in any event and cannot justifiably be called into question however great the historical scepticism. Radical criticism, even the most radical, has a necessary, historico-scientific function here provided one adheres to the rule that it is not the nongenuineness, but contrariwise the genuineness of the individual piece which is to be demonstrated and that a genuine transmission concerning Jesus is established only when the "tradition, for various reasons, can be neither derived from Judaism nor attributed to primitive Christianity." [19] This radical criticism and its results may not be dogmatized, but must rather be regarded as one necessary heuristic principle among others. Whatever is discovered in this way is only a critically assured *minimum.*

On the other hand, the total tradition concerning Jesus must be taken into consideration. In its totality it is theology of the Church, but at the same time it is also in its totality a reflex of Jesus' activity—a *maximum* which contains everything of importance for our historical knowledge about Jesus. To delineate this maximum more precisely is a problem for the solution of which Stauffer's "iron rule" applies: *In dubiis pro tradito.*[20] The further task consists in harmonizing the maximum of the tradition with the critically assured minimum to the highest degree possible, in order step by step to approach more closely to the historical Jesus. The chief reason why the older Life-of-Jesus research became sterile and scientifically unfruitful might have been that it set too directly and rashly toward its goal. If today

[19] Käsemann, *op. cit.,* p. 144.
[20] Stauffer, *op. cit.,* p. 93.

we face a renewal of interest in Jesus-research, we will have to be on our guard against committing the same error again.

Although we are still far removed from the desired degree of exactitude, we may still construct quite a clear picture of the manner of Jesus' appearance as well as of the content of his proclamation and his teaching, and of the impression which he made on the adherents and opponents among his contemporaries. The sources do not permit us to say much regarding his inner life, since they were not interested in it. The question, however, is whether we may detect only characteristic individual features or whether it is possible to give a scientific description of the life of Jesus founded on objective arguments. That a biography of Jesus cannot be written is a truism today. We cannot even write the history of Jesus' development within the period of his public ministry. The contrast between the Galilean spring and the subsequent period of defection and opposition is not sufficiently attested to in the sources, as Albert Schweitzer correctly emphasized. But Schweitzer's own theory, which did not proceed from the beginning but rather from the climax of Jesus' public life and which found the key for understanding the history of Jesus in the delay of the Parousia at the time the seventy were sent out (Matt. 10:23), rested on an entirely arbitrary combination of the sources.

The difficulty of the task does not mean, however, that it would be senseless to work at it scientifically. There is a point in the life of Jesus which is unconditionally established. That is his death. A historico-scientific description of the life of Jesus would only be possible in the form of a description of his death, its historical presuppositions, and the events preceding and following it. In other areas it has proved a fruitful method to begin with a very definite event in order from out of it to throw light on the preceding and following periods. In our case this could be the only practicable way. Such is due to the nature of the sources. Kähler's statement, "passion stories with a rather lengthy introduction," is important not only for the proper interpretation of the Gospels, but also for their use as historical sources on the life of Jesus. Historical considerations of a more general character point in the same direction. In the historical development which led to the rise of Christianity, the death of Jesus is the axis on which everything turns. "Without his death he would not have become historical at all," said Wellhausen.[21] Historical research must begin with the death of Jesus if it will inquire not only into the preaching but also into the life of Jesus.

Of course, a historical description of the death of Jesus is still a most difficult and complicated task. No doubt the Gospel reports at this point, but only at this point, are somewhat detailed and coherent and up to a certain degree are chronologically arranged. The interest of the evangelists, however, lies in describing Jesus' death as saving event and as the basis of the New Covenant, and not in presenting him as a world historical phenomenon with certain historical causes and effects. Before written Gospels existed, the oldest passion narratives which Christians read were such Old Testament texts as, e.g., Psalm 22, a practice which can often be traced in the Gospel accounts. One must be extremely cautious about employing them in the service of historical reconstruction.

In other respects, also, our historical knowledge is extremely limited. The debate over the Sanhedrin's authority to levy the death sentence, a debate which still has not been finally settled, provides one example. It is further questionable how much of rabbinic penal law can be traced back to the time of Jesus. Even where that is possible, the gain is dubious, for we must reckon altogether with the possibility that the trial of Jesus was conducted according to the rules of presumably Sadduccean legal practice—if, indeed, there was any intention of conducting before the Sanhedrin a trial against Jesus according to regular juridical forms, which is equally uncertain. The motives which induced the Jewish authorities and Pilate to proceed against Jesus are very difficult for us to detect. With all the existing difficulties, however, the attempt would have to be made once or even several times at beginning with the death of Jesus in order, with all the available means of historical science, to clarify the more proximate details, and from that point on, at attacking the remaining problems of Jesus' life. There will always be much that remains doubtful, but we may be confident that research which works energetically in this direction will attain to significantly surer results than the previous Life-of-Jesus literature.

In any case it is clear that what we know quite certainly of the life of Jesus is that it ended on the cross. That must also be kept in mind in the attempt to understand the preaching and teaching of

[21] Wellhausen, *op. cit.*, p. 115.

Jesus. An obvious weakness of many descriptions of Jesus as a very pious and very humane, but somewhat harmless teacher lies in the fact that it is not understood why high priests and Romans had any kind of interest in the execution of this man. The end of Jesus' life helps to sharpen our view of the challenging claim to authority manifest in his appearance and which, e.g., is also evident in the Sermon on the Mount. We must observe the same in the exposition of the parables; in many instances the real meaning becomes clear only when we keep in mind how, in veiled form, they express the decisive meaning which Jesus attributed to his own mission.[22] Accordingly, no one can maintain that historical research has access only to the preaching of Jesus and not to his life. Rather, we must state that an historical understanding of his preaching can be attained only when it is seen in connection with his life, namely with the life which ended on the cross.

III

THE THEOLOGICAL PROBLEM

In spite of all the problems and difficulties, the inquiry into the historical Jesus is a legitimate and a not unfruitful historico-scientific task, but the more difficult task is whether this work is also of significance for faith, for the Church and theology. The problem becomes clear at this point when we presuppose hypothetically that it would be possible to give a scientifically founded description of Jesus' life in the form of a presentation of his death and the events preceding it. It would have to reach such a degree of scientific objectivity that everyone, regardless of his presuppositions of faith, would have to admit that everything happened in just this way and not otherwise. In this way not only the external course of Jesus' life would be illuminated, but also a series of factors influencing it. In addition to other factors, say, of a political and social kind, the nature and content of Jesus' preaching would also come into consideration as important elements which unleashed the opposition and reaction to him. With

---

[22] Here, the starting point of C. F. W. Smith, *The Jesus of the Parables* (Philadelphia: The Westminster Press, 1948) , p. 17, is correct: "Jesus used parables and Jesus was put to death. The two factors are related and it is necessary to understand the connection." On the exposition of the parables cf. also my essay, "The Parables of Growth," *Studia Theologica,* V (1951) , 132-66.

good reason, I would assume, it can be made probable that Jesus not only foresaw his own death, but actually ascribed to it a vicarious significance and saw in it a necessary presupposition for the coming of the kingdom of God and his own enthronement as Son of Man. For the historian, such ideas of Jesus would come into consideration as one factor among others illuminating the course of Jesus' life. Then it would be understandable why Jesus did nothing to avoid the threatening danger, but through his purification of the temple seems to have provoked the intervention of the high priests.

It is obvious that the Christian faith and the Church would have only a very limited interest in such a presentation of what actually occurred, though it could be given with a very high degree of historical probability. What alone is decisive for faith and the Church, namely, that Jesus' death was a dying *for us*, would not at all appear in such a historical description of the causes and effects of his death. The historian *qua* historian can say nothing concerning what really took place in that which occurred here—that God showed his love to us, that while we were still sinners, Christ died for us. The believing community could therefore tranquilly disregard the historical description of Jesus' death and his previous life for the sake of holding to the Gospels and to the rest of the New Testament writings. Once more it would be clear to the Church that only the resurrection of Jesus from the dead and the witness of the Holy Ghost through the apostles disclose the meaning and the significance of Jesus' death and his previous life. It will therefore firmly maintain that in the New Testament and nowhere else is it revealed who Jesus really was—without being required to contest the results of historical science.

Faith is concerned neither with the immanent effects of Jesus' death nor with an evaluation of his personality. Jesus' life and death have their significance in and with the message that God raised him from the dead. But in contrast to the life and death of Jesus his resurrection cannot be made an object of historical research. Only the Easter faith of the disciples is accessible to the historian, the origin of which he can illumine only to a certain degree. Good reasons can be advanced for the fact that the tradition of the empty grave is historical in essence, as von Campenhausen has recently shown.[23]

[23] Hans Freiherr von Campenhausen, *Der Ablauf der Osterereignisse und das leere Grab* (2nd ed.; Heidelberg: Carl Winter Universitätsverlag, 1958).

Even though it were raised beyond every doubt, however, the historian would still find only an empty grave and no risen Savior. The possibility of some kind of a misunderstanding or an inexplicable accident would remain. Similarly, the revelations of the risen Lord to Peter and to the disciples can be explained as visions and hallucinations, and even if it could be proved that no psychological explanation suffices, the possibility of a parapsychological interpretation remains, and we would not be one step nearer the Christian faith, which praises God for the fact that he has begotten us again to a living hope through the resurrection of Jesus Christ from the dead.

Whoever knows what historical research is and what the resurrection of Jesus from the dead means cannot suppose that he is able to prove the resurrection by historical arguments. That Jesus of Nazareth is the Son of God who died for us and rose from the dead is visible only to him who believes in him. Objective, historically scientific arguments do not decide concerning belief and unbelief, but rather only the personal relation to the apostolic message of the crucified and risen One, the Son of God, our Lord. Faith arises from the fact that grace is given us to believe in this gospel. The emphasis of kerygma-theology that faith comes through preaching and that it is relatively uninterested in a historical Jesus-research may not merely be regarded as an escape from an acute crisis in the Life-of-Jesus research, but actually rests upon a proper knowledge of what the Christian faith is.

That faith is *relatively* uninterested in the historical Jesus-research does not mean that it is *absolutely* uninterested in it. To draw this conclusion would be a kerygma-theological Docetism, or even a denial of faith in God as Creator, under whose worldly rule even the historian does his service as a scientist. The fact that Jesus can be made an object of historico-scientific research is given with the incarnation and cannot be denied by faith, if the latter is to remain true to itself.

The Jesus-research, with its more or less debatable results has, at all events, made it clear that Jesus was really a true man with human individuality, belonging to a definite time and a definite milieu. The message of the New Testament that *this* man is the Son of God, the Word become flesh, can neither be proved nor refuted by the Jesus-research. One thing has become clear, however: incarnation signifies not only the assumption of an abstract human nature by the

Godhead, but the Word really become flesh, concrete, human history. By making this clearer, historical research has contributed toward clarifying the offence of the Christian message and the possibility of its scandal. In this way the Jesus-research can occasion offences and inner conflicts from which many difficulties for Christianity have arisen and may still arise. But this has not made it more difficult to have a living faith—at all events not more difficult than in the first period of the Church when there was still an immediate remembrance of Jesus as a man among men and when the foolishness and the offence of the cross were not yet tempered by a traditional symbolism. The possibility of offence was not less for the contemporaries of Jesus than for us who today can make him an object of historical research. By having made this clear, historical research can help us to hear the word of the Master with new joy: "Blessed is he who takes no offence in me." Whoever in anxiety over Christianity wishes to keep critical-historical research away from Jesus should ask himself whether or not he in reality is seeking to avoid the possibility of the offence and the inner conflict in which faith must now live in the world.

In any case, the Life-of-Jesus research has this negative relevance, that it uncovers the possibility of the offence. The question is whether it has or at least can have positive significance. A tendency towards a negative answer can be observed not only in such representatives of kerygma-theology who would hold simply to the canonical Gospels, but also in a radical critic such as Bultmann. In the case of the existentialist interpretation of the New Testament, it is only of consequence that Jesus lived and died on the cross and that this is proclaimed as the saving event to be grasped in the obedience of faith. On the other hand, faith as an existential attitude is not supposed to be interested in the question of the *how* of Jesus' life. The understanding of faith may not be interpreted as an objectifying knowledge, irrespective of whether the things to be regarded as true are dogmatic mythologoumena or are demonstrable historical facts. In this form, therefore, the kerygma-theology does not lead to indifference over against the historico-critical question, but, on the contrary, to the fact that a radical historical criticism is pressed into the service of a definite theological conception. Criticism itself receives a theological function since it serves, e.g., to make clear that faith cannot hold to a historically unequivocal picture of Jesus' personality and that in his character a

162

"messianic consciousness" cannot be demonstrated as an observable phenomenon.[24] Faith has no historical security, but only the assurance given by the word of preaching. The Gospel of John is for Bultmann the chief Gospel, not *although* he regards it as completely unhistorical, but precisely *because* he does so. In it Jesus is described "not as a reliably attested person in the past, but in such a way as he is always present in the word which proclaims him in the power of the Spirit." [25] In such a way the significance of Jesus becomes clear for faith.

It is important to understand that historically mediated knowledge can create no security for faith and that, conversely, much that is unhistorical may be in the Gospels without the need for faith to feel itself seriously endangered. The existentialist interpretation carried out consistently signifies, as I have pointed out elsewhere, not only a demythologizing, but also a dehistoricizing of the New Testament.[26] This dehistoricizing of the New Testament is an ultra-Pauline extreme conditioned by existence philosophy which does not do justice to the Gospels. Though it may be true that the Gospels are proclamation and witness, still it would be completely contrary to the intention of the evangelists to declare as irrelevant the inquiry into the historicity of the narratives. In all philosophical naïvete it may be regarded as natural and normal that even the present-day believer shares the interest of the evangelists in preserving reliable information concerning what the Lord and Savior did at the time of his earthly life and how his life took shape. This interest may lead to error, for example, when the history of Jesus is interpreted by means of improper historical categories or when a false and illusory security is sought. As a warning against this possible error, the Pauline refusal to know Christ after the flesh retains its abiding justification, but the necessity of this critical corrective does not mean that positive interest in the history of Jesus is objectionable *per se*. Even without seeking a false historical security, the Christian may rejoice when historical research not only brings inner conflicts for faith but shows that the historically

[24] Cf. Bultmann, *Glauben und Verstehen,* I (Tübingen: J. C. B. Mohr, 1933), 174.
[25] Bultmann, *Theologie des Neuen Testaments* (Tübingen: J. C. B. Mohr, 1953), p. 172.
[26] On this cf. my discussion of Bultmann's *Theologie des Neuen Testaments* in *Theologische Rundschau,* XXII (1954), 21-49.

demonstrable facts of Jesus' life are not unambiguous proofs, but are indeed visible signs to faith that Jesus was the One as the New Testament proclaims him to be. When the how of the life of Jesus is declared to be theologically irrelevant, the incarnation of the Word threatens to become a paradox devoid of content. We must raise the question whether or not the dehistoricizing existentialist interpretation leads to an avoidance of the possibility of offence and of inner conflict lying in the concrete history of Jesus and thus fails to see his hidden glory.

To require that the Jesus-research should establish the glory of Jesus, conceived this way or that and by means of objective arguments, would be the demand for a sign on the part of an unbelieving generation. On the other hand, we must openly admit that it would be really fatal theologically if the result of this research would be the establishment of an irreconcilable opposition between the historical Jesus and the witness of the New Testament to Christ. Even Bultmann cannot avoid it; theologically he is not so uninterested in the question concerning the historical Jesus as might perhaps appear from some of his statements. That Jesus' preaching must be interpreted as a call to decision and in such a way that his own person as Bearer of the Word signifies the demand for decision[27] is rather a materially necessary presupposition for Bultmann's interpretation of the New Testament. It follows from this that after his death the preaching of Jesus could only be taken up in the form of a message concerning the saving deed of God in Jesus Christ calling to decision, and not in the form of a literal reproduction of his sayings or of a biographical description of his life.[28]

Bultmann calls attention to the fact that the Jesus-research is theologically questionable and dangerous when it results in interpreting the historical Jesus in categories which originate elsewhere and which are not appropriate to him—for example, when he is presented as a teacher of timeless ideas, as a personality or as a charismatic miracle worker or a religious hero. The use of such categories is conditioned by the respective presuppositions of the scholar, however, and is not a necessary result of historical inquiry; its inappropriateness

[27] Bultmann, *Theology of the New Testament*, tr. Kendrick Grobel, I (London: S. C. M. Press, 1952) , 8.
[28] Cf., e.g., Bultmann, *Glauben und Verstehen*, I, 205.

is proved by the continuing research itself. It is pertinent to ask now whether, in view of the historical sources, it is not an impermissible extreme, conditioned by existence philosophy, to describe the historical Jesus merely as the Bearer of the Word which calls for decision. It must be the object of historical research to eliminate, as far as possible, all modern categories in order to ascertain how Jesus was understood by his contemporaries and how he himself wanted to be understood. It will best serve theology and the Church when it limits itself to this task with complete impartiality. (The historian only has access to an interpreted history of Jesus, not to the *nudum factum* of the *Verbum Dei incarnatum,* which Stauffer supposes he is able to illuminate by a research into the historical period of the New Testament.)

Whoever does not share Bultmann's existentialist interpretation will agree with him that the relationship between the historical Jesus and the preaching of his apostles is not a problem which threatens theology to the extent it appeared to do so at the turn of the century. At first, of course, it appeared that the radical Gospel criticism and the history-of-religions school would lead to the assumption of an unbridgeable gulf between Jesus and the Church; in this situation it is quite understandable why outsiders proceeded to deny the historical existence of Jesus. Theologically, the most important result of Albert Schweitzer's grand conception was that it pointed a way out of this dilemma: The eschatological message and the eschatological expectation bind Jesus and primitive Christianity into a unity.[29] Jesus proclaimed the nearness of the kingdom of God; indeed, as we express it today, in our correction of "thoroughgoing eschatology," he preached that in and with his own mission, his word and work, God's kingdom had already broken in. The primitive community and Paul share the same expectation, but their place in the eschatological history of salvation is different. Neither a proof of the difference between Jesus' preaching and the teaching of his apostles from the standpoint of the history of ideas nor a proof of their connection from the standpoint of the history of their development can really lead us anywhere. On

---

[29] Cf. especially Albert Schweitzer, *Mystik des Apostels Paulus* (Tübingen: J. C. B. Mohr, 1930), pp. 114-16, 378-85; in addition, cf. also Rudolf Bultmann, "Jesus and Paul," *Existence and Faith,* tr. Schubert M. Ogden (New York: Meridian Books, 1960), pp. 183-201.

the basis of the presuppositions common to Jesus and the primitive Church, it is impossible that after the death of Jesus the disciples could have preached the message of salvation in the same form in which he himself preached it. Between Jesus and the primitive community there lie his death and resurrection as decisive events: Jesus is appointed to the position of messianic ruler in which he shall some day be revealed; those who call upon his name now already assemble themselves as the *ecclesia* of God in the new time of salvation. Jesus-research thus leads us to this alternative: Either the events of Easter and Pentecost are the preliminary fulfillment of Jesus' eschatological promise, or this promise, at the heart of his message, remained unfulfilled. Then in spite of all the inspiring impressions emanating from him, we would have to classify him among the messianic pretenders of Judaism.

Accordingly, we might say that instead of isolating the historical Jesus from the apostolic gospel and the Church, the critical test of historical research has enabled us to see them in their unity. The question today is whether we may proceed still further and establish a direct connection in the sense that the historical Jesus himself intended the Church. A whole series of investigations has shown what a great role the Church, worship, sacraments, et cetera, have played in primitive Christianity. There has also been the attempt to show that all this must have been rooted in the earthly life of Jesus. In the more recent Swedish theology, but not only there, much was accomplished in this direction in the last decades. Anton Fridrichsen, e.g., has most pointedly remarked: "Everything that Jesus does and says points toward that goal, His *ecclesia*." [30] With such an emphasis, the kerygma-theology takes on the form of a new ecclesiasticism in which the kerygmatic-theological denial of the historical Jesus on the one hand and its positive interest in referring the Church with its Christology and its sacraments back to this historical Jesus on the other seem to contradict each other.

To what degree this view of the Church may correctly appeal to the results of New Testament research is still debatable on many points. The methodological difficulties are very noticeable here. Wherever we

[30] *This is the Church,* ed. Anders Nygren *et al.,* tr. Carl C. Rasmussen (Philadelphia: Muhlenberg Press, 1952) , p. 22.

see in the Gospels a direct agreement with the Christology and the community life of the primitive Church, the critical question arises as to whether or not such ideas were only subsequently dated back into Jesus' earthly life. On the other hand, the christological interpretation of the resurrection appearances and the subsequent formation of the Church can hardly be understood if the words of Jesus had not already paved the way for both the Christology and the Ecclesiology of the primitive Church. Therefore, in such questions it is extremely difficult to attain negatively or positively to any objectively certain results; the classic example of this is the ever-fluctuating debate concerning the word of Jesus to Peter in Matt. 16. In other instances, e.g., in the choosing and sending out of the twelve or in the case of the words of the Lord's Supper, we may assume with a greater degree of certainty that the words concerned refer to Jesus himself. As far as Christology is concerned, not only the post-Easter proclamation of the disciples, but also the fact of Jesus' crucifixion proves how easy it was to assume that he himself intended to be the Messiah even though he did not proclaim himself publicly as such. The consciousness of authority back of his total preaching and his total attitude over against the Jewish authorities and persons points in the same direction. This supports the traditional, directly messianic words of Jesus as the hidden Son of Man about to be enthroned after his death.

It would be unnatural if the Church did not have an interest in what can be rendered probable on this issue, but historical research never proceeds beyond probability. That which is to be unconditionally affirmed is that the certainty of faith rests upon the proclaimed Gospel and not upon what science does or does not have to say concerning Jesus' messianic self-consciousness. Likewise, our certainty of belonging to the Church of God is connected with the fact that by his death Jesus gained a people for God's own possession, and not with the fact that present-day research can advance good arguments for the idea that the ministry of the historical Jesus had the formation of a Church as its goal.

The "new ecclesiasticism" has avoided a danger which threatens other forms of kerygma-theology—namely, the danger of disengaging the gospel from real history, the danger of the kerygmatic-theological Docetism. In place of it another danger threatens. It would not only

167

be historico-scientifically but also theologically suspect if the interest in the historical Jesus should limit itself exclusively or even primarily to rendering it probable that Jesus' own work aimed at his *ecclesia.* It is essentially correct when Fridrichsen asserts that the unity of the New Testament can only be affirmed when Jesus is seen in his unity with the Church and not in categories of personalistic idealism.[31] The danger in such a formulation lies in the fact that this unity between Jesus and the Church can be understood as a kind of identity by which Jesus Christ is dissolved in the Church, in its proclamation and dogma, its cultus and office.

Thus it is also a theological necessity to keep the question concerning the historical Jesus open and living, and, of course, not least for the reason that the independence of Jesus over against the Church must be maintained. Jesus is already in existence before and outside the proclamation and the Church; he may neither be absorbed by the existential here and now of the kerygma nor by the tradition and the Church. This independence of Jesus is not to be understood as an isolation, as was the case with the "back to Jesus" slogan. It does mean, however, that Jesus is present not only in the Church and its proclamation, but also—and that is the first and basic thing—that he stands over against the Church in sovereign freedom. Research on the historical Jesus must continually refer to this independence. It must do so primarily and simply by recalling the basic historical fact that Jesus was a Jew, "sprung from the seed of David according to the flesh." Through Jesus the Church is bound to the Scriptures of the Old Testament and to the sacred history of Israel. That the Church is the legitimate successor of the people of God of the Old Covenant cannot, however, be proved with historical exactitude. The people of Israel continued to exist alongside the Church in midst of many sufferings which were often inflicted upon them by the believers in Christ, but Christ is an Israelite according to the flesh, and research on the historical Jesus makes this explicitly clear to us. For the Church this fact signifies a continual warning against ecclesiastical self-sufficiency and self-confidence. Paul was aware of this (Rom. 11), but the Church after him has only too often forgotten it.

[31] Anton Fridrichsen, *et al., The Root of the Vine* (London: Dacre Press, 1953), p. 60.

Not only the fact that Jesus belonged to Israel but also the nature of his historical influence within Israel constitutes a warning against that form of self-contented ecclesiasticism. The preaching and the appearance of Jesus attest to his deep unity and solidarity with his people, the people of God. In this solidarity, however, he appears as a man whose word and work are a judgment upon all Jewish ecclesiasticism; temple worship, scriptural erudition, pious practice, the basic attitude of those who trust in the privileges of the people of God—nothing of all that is spared. This Jesus who chastens and reprimands the people of God is the Lord of the Church in whom we believe. This is made unmistakably clear by research on the historical Jesus and has certain necessary consequences, namely, that even the Church of the new people of God stands under his judgment and under the reprimand which proceeds from him, the living Lord, who is none other than he who once lived in Israel, the historical Jesus. When the Church is unconcerned about the historical Jesus, this will only too easily lead to its ignoring his warning against all ecclesiastical self-sufficiency. Already in the case of the evangelists, and especially in Matthew, we can observe how Jesus' warning words of judgment to the Jews have received a new addressee and serve as a warning to the members of the new community (cf., e.g., 7:22 f. as over against Luke 13:25 ff.).[32]

To be on principle indifferent to the concrete, earthly history of Jesus might further involve the danger that the kerygma also is not related to the concrete, everyday life of man, but is validated only in the abstraction of an understanding of existence or only within the sacred realm of the Church. The preacher stands basically in the same post-Easter situation as the evangelists and is bound to the interpretation of the history of Jesus by the apostolic proclamation transmitted in the New Testament, but he must be allowed to go back to the alleged original meaning of a word in order, analogous with the procedure of the evangelists, to proclaim it, in view of the post-Easter situation and the change of audience, as a word of the Lord to the community of his time. Because of the special authority already ascribed to the words of the Lord in the New Testament, we cannot regard the question concerning the historical genuineness or non-

[32] Cf. Jeremias, *op. cit.,* pp. 25-28.

169

genuineness of a word as completely irrelevant for theology.[33] Yet, for preaching and dogmatic reflection this question really becomes actual only in the possibly or actually critical cases when there is no real agreement of a word with the central kerygma; then we will more easily be able to disregard the word when objective historical criteria suggest that there is no authentic word of Jesus.

We have not given a dogmatic answer to the question of the theological relevance of Jesus-research but have only stated a few viewpoints and random observations. I think that this must be the case if it is true that scientific research on the historical Jesus can neither be of fundamental significance for faith and the Church nor can it be totally irrelevant. Neither the historico-scientific nor the theological problem of the historical Jesus is to be answered definitively, so that we could ever dispense with it. This problem signifies an element of unrest for the Church, but this unrest is salutary and should remind us of the fact that Jesus is Lord of the Church and that the Church may not make itself lord over Jesus. To the question: Who was Jesus? the Church answers with its praising confession. It will not go astray because of the alleged results of the Life-of-Jesus research. It would not, however, be fidelity to its confession but rather pride if it were to declare itself on principle uninterested in the work of a sober historical research.

For a while it can be of benefit to New Testament research to leave behind the attempts at historical reconstruction in order to work at other tasks, where there are greater possibilities of attaining to fruitful and certain results. But we cannot on principle or for any length of time pass by the problem of the historical Jesus. Even the scholar who stands in the Church and who would serve the Church by his work cannot allow himself to be ordered by ecclesiastical courts regarding the results he must attain. Indeed, the New Testament scholar will be interested in a co-operative effort with his colleagues in systematic theology, because they can make clear to him whether, with the historical methods necessary for his work, he has also appropriated a definite historical and ideological tradition which is not appropriate to the object of his investigations. We should neither expect nor desire

---

[33] On this question cf. W. Michaelis, "Notwendigkeit und Grenze der Erörterung von Echtheitsfragen innerhalb des Neuen Testaments," *Theologische Literatur-Zeitung* (1952), pp. 97-402.

that the Church's preaching and dogmatic reflection be built on the uncertain ground of research on the historical Jesus. On the other hand, we should retain an openness and truthfulness toward this research. We must expect of dogmatic work in Christology that it not avoid the problem of the historical Jesus, but really have a concern for a better solution than the historical Life-of-Jesus theology and the dehistoricizing kerygma-theology.

SEVEN

GÜNTHER BORNKAMM

Myth and Gospel:
A Discussion of the Problem of
Demythologizing the
New Testament Message

Theology too is bound to be wise and to build its house upon a rock. For that reason it cannot for one moment avoid the question concerning its foundations. When this question is put to it afresh, then it must face up to it and must even suffer gratefully the shock and disquiet meted out to it. Any attempts to suppress or dispose of such questions with alarm and undue haste could only be symptomatic of the fact that the foundations of our theology are not in the best repair, indeed, that the concern for a firm foundation is not at all a genuine concern in a theology which behaves so anxiously and waxes so indignant.

Rudolf Bultmann's publication *Offenbarung und Heilsgeschehen,* and in it particularly his essay on the "New Testament and Mythology," has put anew and with most pressing urgency the question concerning the foundations of our theology—that is, concerning the proper appropriation and exposition of the New Testament message. For a long time no theological writing has aroused such a storm and such passionate literary and oral discussion in theology and in the Church—even far beyond their confines. It appears that this storm will agitate us still further and keep us in suspense for some time to come. Moreover, any perceptive person knows that it is not a problem peculiar to the theological disciplines which is involved here, but rather an unsolved question which affects everyone who is thoughtfully concerned about appropriating the Christian message or indeed, about

172

merely taking an honest position over against it. In addition it is a question which concerns primarily the theologian who must present that message.

The question is certainly not new. It is in a certain sense as old as the gospel itself; it is woven into the whole history of the Church and of the Western spirit, however that spirit undertook to accept or reject the Christian message and however it solved or capitulated before the question put to it. We must consider the question in the form put to us, however, and would do well not to begin at an earlier stage of the discussion. Hence, in the following, a survey[1] shall first of all be given of Bultmann's development of the problem and his attempt at solution; then, a critical coming to grips with the discussion thus far; and finally a few theological observations on the problem as newly sketched by Bultmann.

I

BULTMANN'S PROGRAM OF DEMYTHOLOGIZING

Bultmann's train of thought is as follows: He sees that the problem implicit in the question consists in the complete and profound discrepancy between the New Testament world of ideas and modern thought as irrevocably shaped by science. The three-story world pictured in the New Testament (heaven, earth, hell) is mythical; its idea of man whose existence is determined by supra- and sub-worldly powers (God, Satan, angels, demons) is mythical; its idea of history as the arena of these divine and demonic powers, its notion of the two aeons—of the end of the old world period now under the form of antidivine powers and hastening on to its end in the midst of cosmic catastrophes and of the coming of a new time of salvation, a new creation—is mythical. Accordingly, the idea of the saving event set within the framework of this mythical view of the world and of history is also mythical, i.e., the idea of a divine being which descends in human form, performs miracles, conquers demons, vicariously dies an atoning death for men; which arises, ascends to heaven and will soon return upon the clouds of heaven for the resurrection of the dead and for judgment.

[1] The following brief summary of Bultmann's ideas, already considerably condensed, ought merely to serve some as an aid to memory and a guide, and others as a stimulus to read Bultmann himself.

This mythical world of ideas is irrevocably shattered for the modern man. His world no longer has room for mythical figures and occurrences. Hence he can no longer understand the Christian message together with all the ideas which have been added to it, particularly from late Jewish apocalypticism and from Hellenistic Gnosticism. The question, therefore, is whether the New Testament proclamation is essentially bound to these ideational forms. If it is not, then the task of demythologizing the Christian message in a radical and methodical sense is required, and without arbitrariness and sporadic deletions.

According to Bultmann, the necessity of this task is twofold. First of all, it is indicated by the nature of myth itself in so far as it does not intend giving an objective picture of the world as outlined by science, but rather a form of expression in which man, not yet awakened to reason, expresses his own understanding of the world and of himself. Into such an understanding every genuine interpretation of myth must inquire. That interpretation must distinguish between what the myth says and what it intends. The myth, of course, speaks of the figures and the occurrences of a world accessible to the senses, but it has in mind that which transcends the realm of the disposable world, though it conceives the other-worldly in terms of this world and the divine in terms of human life. Therefore the question in light of which the myth will be expounded is: How does man understand himself in it? What idea of human existence is expressed in it? So the question is not: How is the world described in it? An exposition which puts such questions Bultmann terms existential interpretation.[2] The necessity of such an exposition, however, really arises out of the New Testament itself, for we can see from the mainfold fragmentariness, imbalance, and discrepancy of the ideas in the message that what is intended in the gospel is not bound up in those mythical forms of ideas.

Bultmann thus understands the theological task of appropriating

[2] The concepts "existential" and "existentiell," which are continually confused, are to be sharply differentiated. "Existential" interpretation is an exposition which inquires into the understanding of human existence given in a text. The concept originates with Martin Heidegger who distinguishes as existentialia the characteristics of being pertaining to existence (of the human being), from those characteristics pertaining to objectively extant things (categories). Cf. Martin Heidegger, Sein und Zeit (Tübingen: Max Niemeyer, 1927), pp. 44 ff. "Existentiell," on the other hand, is a speaking and listening in terms of one's own concrete concerns. ("You are the man," II Sam. 12:7.)

the primitive Christian message in a way quite different than did the liberal theology of the history-of-religions school (Harnack, Troeltsch). If the latter attempted to peel off the mythical forms of ideas as temporally conditioned husks in order to discover the kernel of a timeless truth or a religious experience, Bultmann sees his task not in the elimination of the myth, but rather in its interpretation, and always in terms of the question: What conception of human existence is expressed in the mythological statements?

Therefore, Bultmann's attempt to carry out his demythologizing according to its basic features is so consistently structured that he does not begin with the Christ event, but inquires first of all into the New Testament understanding of existence. For that reason, in all of his New Testament and theological works[3] Bultmann begins with the description of unredeemed man, of the "fleshly" man (Paul) who has fallen prey to sin, care, self-praise, anxiety, and death; in short, who has fallen prey to the world but who in his lostness still never gets free of God because God's law calls him to his destiny, a destiny which the fleshly man (either as lawless or as zealous for the law) can indeed never realize. It is not accidental that Romans 7 plays such an important role in Bultmann's theological thought and work. In contrast to this unredeemed man the believer is one who abandons all security and in reliance upon God's grace frees himself from whatever is disposable and exists in terms of a critical distance over against the world.[4] Bultmann describes this attitude by the concept "desecularization," a concept not to be misconstrued in terms of mysticism or asceticism. He characterizes faith as eschatological existence, whereby again "eschatological" does not contain ideas of a catastrophic world destruction occurring within time, but rather the end of the world as an event within the attitude of faith itself. For the believer it is true that the world is crucified to him, just as he is crucified to

---

[3] Cf. Bultmann, *Theology of the New Testament*, tr. Kendrick Grobel (London: S. C. M. Press, 1952); *Primitive Christianity*, tr. R. H. Fuller (New York: Meridian Books, 1958), pp. 189 ff.; "Paulus," *Die Religion in Geschichte und Gegenwart*, ed. Hermann Gunkel and Leopold Tscharnack, IV (2nd ed.; Tübingen: J. C. B. Mohr, 1929), 1019 ff. It is not an accidental principle of arrangement, but a very specific and theological intent, a very specific hermeneutical principle which underlies this general sketch of his presentations, which, in that respect, are basically different from e.g., Ethelbert Stauffer's *New Testament Theology*.

[4] For this reason Bultmann so frequently quotes I Cor. 7:29 ff.

the world (Gal. 6:14). This understanding of eschatological existence removes the basis from those worldly ideas of the end which primitive Christianity appropriated from apocalypticism and Gnosticism. Paul, of course, is still bound to them. John is the first to have completed the conquest of a mundane, traditional eschatology in that word which for Bultmann constitutes the decisive witness of eschatological faith: "He who hears my word and believes him who sent me, has eternal life; he does not come into judgment, but has passed from death to life" (John 5:24).

Thus far, Bultmann has unfolded the New Testament understanding of existence (in regard to unredeemed, as well as redeemed, believing man) without any reference to the Christ event. On the basis of his theological and hermeneutical presuppositions, he could not, as should now be clear, first develop a drama of salvation in factual objective fashion, in order to draw from it specific conclusions for man and the world—that is, he could not at the outset place man within the course of a history of salvation capable of being demonstrated or mythologically represented.

Does this mean that Bultmann's theology dispenses with what we call the saving event in Christ? Must not theology admit that this "saving event" is a mythological residue which must be dissolved into statements about man's existence? Bultmann sees this question put most urgently by modern philosophy (Dilthey, Graf York, Heidegger, Jaspers, Kamlah), which has been greatly influenced by Paul and Augustine, Luther and Kierkegaard, and which now, though disregarding a saving event, can also speak of the fallenness of man and of his real destiny. Is it, perhaps, theology's task to liquidate, so to speak, the mythological heritage of the tradition and to surrender what is existentially intended in that tradition to the philosophy of existence? Bultmann views philosophy in an intimate closeness with theology, but he also views its difference from theology at a fundamental point, namely, at the point of deciding how fallen man achieves his authenticity, how the one who is lost becomes redeemed. If philosophy views the realization of man's real destiny as lying within the realm of his own possibilities, theology knows and maintains that just such an assumption is nothing but the *hybris* of despair, for it is God's love alone which frees man, indeed, which has freed him through Jesus Christ. "This is precisely the meaning of that which was wrought

176

in Christ. At the very point where man can do nothing, God steps in and acts—indeed He has acted already—on man's behalf." [5]

Of course, the primitive Christian proclamation speaks of this Christ event in such a way that the mythical and the historical are remarkably interlaced in it: The Son of God coming from heaven is the man Jesus of Nazareth. The cross, interpreted with ideas of the Old Testament concept of sacrifice, is a historical fact. But what does this "interlacing" of the mythical and the historical mean? Bultmann answers that the mythological mode of speaking intends to make visible the significance of the person and history of Jesus Christ, and it is precisely that significance which the interpretation must bring out. Interpretation may not simply content itself with describing the crucifixion in objectifying ideas. It must rather unfold the cross of Jesus as an eschatological event—that is, as an event which has once for all changed my history and with it the history of my world. To believe in the cross of Christ, therefore, means to take up his cross as my own, to let myself be crucified with him. I do not understand the cross when I merely demonstrate it to be a historical event within the relational context of the world, nor do I understand it when I accept the objectifying ideas by which this crucifixion is portrayed. Rather, I understand it in the sense of the primitive Christian message only when I allow my own existence to be determined by this event.

That which is true of the cross of Christ is true also of the resurrection; both belong inseparably together. Indeed, for Bultmann, there is a notable difference. Unlike the cross, Jesus' resurrection is not a "historical" (*historisch*) event; language about the resurrection is rather an expression of the "meaning of the cross." [6] It is not surprising that this formulation has caused offence. (Nor do I regard it as simply misunderstandable, but rather as disastrous.) That which is correct in this very questionable thesis is that historical science which only demonstrates what is objectively present cannot demonstrate the resurrection of Jesus Christ. What it succeeds in demonstrating are, in terms of its own categories, the visionary experiences of the disciples. It is an absurd undertaking as Stauffer recently attempts, to verify historically the message of the resurrection of Christ

---

[5] Bultmann, "New Testament and Mythology," *Kerygma and Myth,* ed. Hans-Werner Bartsch, tr. R. H. Fuller (London: S. P. C. K., 1954), p. 31.

[6] *Ibid.,* p. 38,

by archaeological means—for example, by reference to an inscription found in Nazareth from the time of Tiberius, placing severe penalty upon the robbing of corpses and the desecration of graves.[7] That is impossible. And the interpretation of the resurrection as a miraculous proof certainly does not suit the meaning of the Easter message, although such ideas play a role in the New Testament. In this respect, Bultmann is obviously correct: The resurrection of Jesus Christ is based alone upon the word of proclamation. Indeed, the proclamation itself is part of the Easter event. "In the word of preaching and there alone we meet the risen Lord." [8]

All in all, Bultmann's effort has one aim, as expressed in the conclusion of his essay: To give validity to the paradox of the New Testament proclamation in its genuine form—that is, not to fasten that paradox to the mythological forms of ideas of the New Testament kerygma, but rather to give to it its place where it also puts to man today the question of decision, namely, in the message that God has acted eschatologically upon the world in a man of flesh and blood, Jesus of Nazareth, and in a history which lies open without limitation to historical, sociological, and psychological considerations. Only in this way, as Bultmann says, is the paradox of the presence of the transcendent God in history maintained, a paradox which the prologue of the Gospel of John expresses as "the Word become flesh."

II

THE DISCUSSION OF THE PROBLEM

Bultmann's essay affected some as a liberating word. To others it appeared and still appears as a unique, fearful heresy, and more, an old heresy, for here blasphemous ghosts long believed dead appear to celebrate their wretched resurrection. That this could happen to a theologian who once associated with Karl Barth and who participated in the struggle of the Confessional Church (and therefore did not emerge from the camp of Emanuel Hirsch and colleagues) only

[7] As if such an inscription could not give equal support to the Jewish claim that Jesus' corpse was stolen by his disciples—if, indeed, there is any connection between this inscription and the Easter event. Cf. Stauffer, "Entmythologisierung oder Realtheologie?" in *Kerygma und Mythos,* ed. Hans-Werner Bartsch, II (Hamburg-Volksdorf: Herbert Reich Evangelischer Verlag, 1952).

[8] Bultmann, "New Testament and Mythology," p. 43.

made the situation more confusing. Not a few, therefore, have raised the cry against Bultmann as a David Friedrich Strauss *redivivus*, just as Herod raised it against the allegedly resurrected Baptist: "John I beheaded; but who is this about whom I hear such things?" The discussion is still in full swing. Karl Barth has said no; Friedrich Gogarten has said yes; Hans-Werner Bartsch has prepared the second volume of *Kerygma und Mythos;* pastoral conferences and briefs have attached themselves to Ethelbert Stauffer as the most powerful voice in the struggle; in many places demythologizing is the convention theme; students are continually pleading for a treatment of the question in lectures and seminars; protests are raised in abundance from congregations; synods are appealing for binding pronouncements on the part of ecclesiastical leaders, as well as for proceeding with disciplinary action; the daily press has already discussed the problem in a host of ways. That is the external situation.

In the following we will discuss a series of characteristic objections to Bultmann's program. In view of the plethora of statements available in written form or frequently recurring in oral debates, we can only make a selection and in particular a selection of arguments of very different weight. It will be shown that with all they may correctly contain, they do not really suffice.

1. The first objection is as frequent as it is dangerous. It attempts, by biblicistic argument, to drive the problem from the field, so to speak, in one fell swoop. The argument proceeds somewhat as follows: The Scripture is normative for all theological thought, but the Scripture itself inveighs passionately against all myths as useless fables (I Tim. 1:4; II Tim. 4:4; II Pet. 1:16). From the very outset, therefore, it is absurd to assert that there are mythical elements in the gospel.

Even in cases where the argument is not so formally biblicistic, but where the opposition of gospel to myth is seen in terms of the gospel's historical basis which gives evidence of its unmythical antimythical character such a summary dismissal of the entire problem is not any more convincing. Thus as it is said by Hermann Sasse, among others, "The New Testament does not need to be demythologized, because it contains no myth." [9] The thesis of Edmund Schlink, as once formulated, has considerably more weight: "Whoever would demythologize

---

[9] *Flucht vor dem Dogma,* Luthertum (1942), pp. 161 ff.

the Bible overlooks the fact that its witness is totally and altogether demythologized, since God's word, penetrating men's language in the revelation, broke through the myths of men." [10] Actually, the New Testament message itself can be and is understood as a kind of demythologizing, but the problem remaining for us is obviously rooted in the fact that not even the demythologizing carried out in the New Testament encounters us apart from a mythological mode of conception. Where this fact is overlooked, it is difficult to see how one can avoid the danger of changing the sphere of the biblical revelation into a kind of shelter and quarantine which must be a priori set off limits and which no longer allows critical observation. In that case, our quest for truth, as the destiny and task of thought, can no longer be seriously undertaken, and the believer or the one called to faith would also have to become a kind of museum visitor who upon entry would have to doff everything which otherwise belonged to his ordinary equipment of life lest the objects of his observation suffer harm.[11]

2. The argument preferred by some theologians, namely, that it is of the very nature of the gospel as scandal that it encounter us in the form of an alien world view, I can only describe as a poorly veiled, theologically tainted capitulation before the problem. To such a point of view, demythologizing would be tantamount to eliminating or attenuating the Christian scandal. It is not difficult to note in this objection a frivolous juggling with the concept of scandal, for, in truth, the *scandalon* of the Christian message can never consist in the strangeness of a world view, in the unintelligibility of a mythological language. If that were so, then we would be in a remarkably different situation as regards this message than were those who lived in the New Testament age for whom the world view was not an alien one and for whom mythological language was not at all unintelligible. Moreover, it is not at all in my power to appropriate an alien world view. Actually, however, the gospel, and precisely in its character as scandal, does not aim at such appropriation, but rather at my decision of faith. It must therefore be presented to me in a language which I

[10] *Studium Generale* (Berlin: Springer, 1948) , p. 203.

[11] Please pardon this comparison which may appear a bit in poor taste. However its intention is to refer to a very serious question. Is it so surprising that for many inquisitive people whose questions are usually ignored or discredited by theologians the Christian message seems to retain a peculiarly museumlike odor?

understand very well. Only in this way does it give me room to make the decision of faith or of unbelief. Hence, it is not a question of presenting the gospel to man today in a language which comes to him from the outside, but rather in a language which is native to him.

3. For many others the mythical does not at all belong to the gospel's character as scandal, but actually belongs to that which can prepare for the entrance of the gospel today in a special way. It is part of that in which the man of today again puts his faith, indeed, to an extreme. In contrast to earlier generations, ours has once again experienced the reality of the mythical, has "seen the demons." However a professorial, musty rationalism might react to it, the task now is to see a problem here where the myth has again become such a power for modern man's thought, where the myth of resurrection was only recently celebrated at the Feldherrnhalle or is celebrated at the sarcophagus of Lenin, where again the daily press seriously occupies itself with Lourdes and erects sanatoria at Gröning. Once again the theologians arrive too late upon the scene (e.g., Stauffer).

We shall omit from our discussion whether in this and in the above cases myth can be spoken of in the same sense (certainly not!). The theological objection to this line of argument is that we are prohibited from it by the New Testament kerygma itself. The heretics of the Colossian epistle already attempted to gain access to the gospel by way of myth. Respect for mythical powers, for the "elements of the world," was regarded by them as a prerequisite and essential part of Christian faith. To pay positive respect to the alleged mythical thought of modern man (as a rule we should rather refer to this as his "superstition") means nothing else than to exalt the devil to God's advocate. Christ himself disenchanted the world and put an end to its mythical nimbus. Our preaching can no longer retreat behind this radical coming of age, however a man may misunderstand it rationalistically and may have lost his freedom in secularism or may even have tired of that freedom.

4. For that reason, also, no further contribution is made by that argument which appeals to the questionable and changeable nature of the modern understanding of the world and of the self, an argument which is often quite clumsy and primitive, but which also results from quite weighty reflection. Certainly, the picture of the world has been subject to changes, actually to revolutions, and man can understand

181

himself in this world of his in very different ways. How differently Schiller viewed man, standing at the "decline of the century": "Free through reason, strong through laws, great through gentleness and rich through treasures which your bosom long kept hid from you, lord of nature which loves your fetters, expends your power in a thousand battles and shining rose beneath you from the wildness." And Spengler, who occasionally likens man to a victorious warrior in a chariot race who is ground to death by his own vehicle. It may be a rewarding and urgent task, not merely to accept as axiomatic modern man's understanding of the world and of himself, together with his science and technology, but rather to discover in the Enlightenment, in the world picture grounded in it and in the culture springing from it the atheistic tendency, the tendency to self-assertiveness.[12] But however modern man understands himself in his picture of the world and from whatever sources this picture has arisen for him, in no case is a return to the world picture of antiquity open to him, and our preaching cannot be sufficiently on its guard against making a virtue of a mythical concept of the world out of the necessity of the modern picture of the world.

5. Werner Georg Kümmel has expressed himself on this question in still another way.[13] He proceeds from a criticism of Bultmann's unauthorized enlargement of the concept of myth (it is "the use of imagery to express the other-worldly in terms of this world and the divine in terms of human life, the other side in terms of this side")[14] and, in terms of a definition given earlier by Martin Dibelius, understands myth as a history which somehow narrates divine actions replete with implications for man. Though Bultmann's concept of myth may in many respects be problematic, our objection to Kümmel's use of the concept is that he does not take into slightest consideration the problematic of the "mode of conception" as seen by Bultmann, and thus he minimizes the question involved. With his concept of myth, Kümmel of course need not be afraid of speaking of mythological features in the kerygma. "The mythological mode of speech is a

[12] In this regard, cf. G. Krüger, "Philosophisches Denken und christlicher Glaube" in *Studium Generale,* and W. Kamlah, *Der Mensch in der Profanität,* 1949.

[13] W. G. Kümmel, "Mythische Rede und Heilsgeschehen im Neuen Testament," *Kerygma und Mythos,* II, 153 ff.

[14] Bultmann, "New Testament and Mythology," p. 10, n. 2.

necessary form of expression for the assertion of faith regarding the divine activity in the history of Christ." [15] It is necessary, however, to distinguish between such mythical features as are essentially and inalienably peculiar to the kerygma and those which were added subsequently and which are to be described as accessories from the standpoint of the kerygma itself. Among the former he reckons the ideas of a futuristic eschatology, without which the New Testament message would lose its event-full, temporal significance and the understanding of the resurrection as an event in time. Among the latter he reckons all sorts of individual features, such as the legend of the empty grave, the ascension, the virgin birth, and the descent into hell. No doubt, Kümmel is correct when he attributes a varying weight and meaning to the individual "mythical" expressions of the Christian message. Our theological objection to his argument is that he does not really face up to the problem as principally seen by Bultmann and hence, when exposition is required, can only describe the New Testament findings. He thereby falls prey to the error which can be frequently observed in the discussion with Bultmann, i.e., of contenting himself with establishing New Testament utterances (which no one will seriously contest) instead of giving a real interpretation.

6. From the great number of voices which have been raised against Bultmann, we mention, finally, the attempt to clarify the problem of the mythical on the basis of the nature of religious language in general. Ernst Lohmeyer, among others,[16] has represented the attempt most impressively. Myth is here regarded as the language of all religion. According to Lohmeyer the secret and ultimate basis of all religion is that "human conceptions, while they remain human, are nevertheless capable of apprehending the divine and so surpass all human conception." [17] Lohmeyer thus assigns to interpretation a twofold task: First, "to appreciate that myth is the mode in which God reveals himself, and that the apparently empty and worn-out husk is the symbol of the historicity of that eschatological revelation of God in which the Word became flesh." [18] In this sense he rejects the at-

[15] Kümmel, *op. cit.*, p. 156.
[16] Ernst Lohmeyer, "The Right Interpretation of the Mythological," *Kerygma and Myth*, pp. 124 ff.
[17] *Ibid.*, p. 126.
[18] *Ibid.*, p. 130.

tempt at demythologizing: "To demythologize a religious proclamation of whatever kind is to condemn every religion to silence and
therefore to destroy it." [19] At the same time he can speak positively
of demythologizing and assign to interpretation the task of "the
translation of the New Testament material from the language of myth
into that of science," "to ascertain the abiding truth it (the myth)
enshrines and accept its mythical expression as a symbol of the unique
character of its historicity." [20]

Theology, therefore, must give the myth its due. All mythical speech
has its nature and character in the fact that every religious object
totally yields to thought and yet transcends all thought. Mythical
speech ventures to speak and is able to speak of God's being in himself (his aseity). Theology advances as far as this principle and from
thence conceives human being and world order and the existence of
man within the world. Theology thus becomes a system.

It is clear that God is not really understood here from the viewpoint
of the revelation as One who historically encounters man, but rather
as the *arche* in the Greek sense. Strictly speaking, theology no longer
has to do with revelation, with saving event, but rather with its
possibility. Its possibility is the abiding truth which lies hidden and
concealed in the myth and which is elevated by theology to a system.

Lohmeyer's ideas appear to me to renew the old dialectic between
myth and *logos* ingeniously developed by Plato and mediated in
various ways since his time. According to it, myth is a form of speech
which is not suitable to the truth and which must continually be overcome by the *logos*, but the myth is at the same time always superior
in character to the *logos*, in so far as it conceals a truth which is un-
attainable for the *logos*, a truth which continually compels us to search
and question.[21] By means of this platonic reflection, emphasis can at
times be put on the appropriateness of mythological speech in relation
to its intended truth, transcending what the *logos* can grasp, and at
times on the inappropriateness of this speech, since the myth forever
remains a mere expedient and expression of an ultimate *aporia*. Thus,
for example, Friedrich Karl Schumann in his discussion with Bult-

[19] *Ibid.*, p. 126.
[20] *Ibid.*, p. 132.
[21] Cf. G. Krüger, *Einsicht und Leidenschaft* (Frankfurt: Klostermann, 1939), pp.
29 ff., 56 ff.

mann can say that mythological language is "the best available medium" for expressing events which signify an ultimate decision regarding existence and the world.[22]

As illuminating as these theses appear to be and as applicable as this hermeneutical key may be for numerous texts, we still cannot admit that they provide a real solution. Can theology be content with this attenuation of its specific problematic into a general ontological one? Can it rest easy with this vague relationship between *est* and *significat?*

III

THEOLOGICAL CONSIDERATIONS

Our report on this discussion is far from being complete. It merely intended to give critical expression to a selection of typical arguments which have been of influence in the debate. We now proceed to develop a few theological questions and considerations in which ideas already expressed by others will be mentioned now and again.[23]

A. THE HERMENEUTICAL QUESTION

At the outset we raise the question concerning the hermeneutical principle guiding Bultmann in his interpretation. I believe that Bultmann has correctly made the message of justification and therefore the doctrine of law and gospel the guide for his exposition of the saving event. But he is obviously not intent thereby with forcing all of New Testament theology into the Procrustean bed of Pauline thought. Pauline theology for him is merely the supreme example of

[22] Friedrich Schumann, "Can the Event of Jesus Christ be Demythologised?" *Kerygma and Myth,* p. 189.

[23] Up to this point, the reader will perhaps have missed a more precise treatment of Schniewind's great article in *Kerygma and Myth* (pp. 45 ff.), an article which also appears to me to be one of the most significant. However, I believe that it requires a separate, critical translation from the kerygmatic into the theological, in order that its concerns may come to the fore and that Bultmann's insistence on an interpretation, which he has constantly reiterated to Schniewind, may not go unanswered. Among the more recent statements on the problem not mentioned above, I mention Karl Barth, *Kirchliche Dogmatik,* III/2 (Zollikon-Zürich: Evangelischer Verlag, 1948), 531 ff., and the work of his pupil W. Klaas, *Der moderne Mensch in der Theologie Rudolf Bultmanns, Theologische Studien,* ed. Karl Barth, XXIV (Zollikon-Zürich: Evangelischer Verlag, 1947), and finally, E. Brunner, *Dogmatik,* II (1950), 311 ff. (also 221 ff.).

185

a relevant exposition of the primitive Christian kerygma. Of course, this connection with the doctrine of justification leads Bultmann to reduce the entire New Testament message of salvation to the realm of a possible human understanding of existence and the world. For that reason he is repeatedly suspected of dissolving theology into Christian anthropology, and the ghost of Feuerbach in whom we can find astounding parallels to individual propositions of Bultmann is continually hovering about. The case is not that simple, however. There can be no doubt that Bultmann tries with all his might to cling to the saving event *extra nos*. The insistence on the meaning of the saving event is unquestionably with him the one factor which prevents a transmutation of theology into anthropology, a dissolution of the Christian message into a mere illumination of existence (cf. his debate with philosophy!). The saving event for him is reduced to the *brutum factum*, however, the bare, completely inaccessible fact that in Jesus Christ the revelation of God took place and God acted for our redemption, a fact which precisely in its unprovableness requires the submission of faith. Jesus Christ has become a mere saving fact and ceases to be a person. He himself has no longer any history; he himself is no longer really the One who speaks in his word. In other words, he is no longer the One who personally addresses me, who in speaking personally encounters me face to face; the word in which he encounters me, as naturally Bultmann can also emphatically say, has merely the "thatness" of the revelation for its content. Hence the pre-eminence of John's Gospel in Bultmann's theology, a Gospel, actually, in which the mere *ego eimi* (I am . . .) of the Revealer is witnessed to with a concentrated force. Hence it is typical for Bultmann that the synoptic kerygma is weakened and relegated to the background, a fact which Schniewind has correctly and repeatedly noted. Jesus Christ has become a mere saving fact. Everything which goes beyond this *brutum factum*, one might almost say this periodic "thatness" of the saving fact, is for Bultmann either past history or mythology which can no longer be elucidated anthropologically (or better, existentially). It is therefore only figurative speech. Whatever in the New Testament message is said regarding, e.g., God's saving decree from eternity, the sending of the Son when the time was fulfilled, the relation of the Father to the Son, the obedience of Jesus demonstrated in his life and suffering, his resurrection and exaltation, his intercession for us at the right hand of God, et cetera, all that is only an expression for the fact that Jesus Christ is and remains the One in whom God has acted decisively upon the world.

The retention of the saving event, of the saving action of God in Christ, thus preserves Bultmann's theology from becoming a mere Christian philosophy of existence, but his insistence upon the understanding of existence as a hermeneutical principle makes it impossible for him to understand the speech of the New Testament about the person and history of Christ as authentic speech. It is changed into a network of significant ideas; it is dissolved into a mere *significat* and has lost the force of the *est*.

With what we have just said no solution has yet been given to the question as viewed by Bultmann; rather, the question now is just put in a new way. It is the question concerning the being, concerning the reality of that which the kerygma proclaims and which faith apprehends. The theological elaboration of the concept of reality implied by the gospel message and faith is a task which still has to be performed. There can be no doubt that Bultmann, and more, that most of his opponents are led and determined by a disastrously positivistic concept of reality. Bultmann's concept of myth, his persistent differentiation between nature and existence, world and man, are burdened by such a concept. Even the majority of his opponents are in no better position, however, for they either totally deny him the right to his concern, or at least snatch this and that from his grasp—the virgin birth, the miracles, the story of the empty grave, or whatever it may be—and once more attempt to secure them "historically." [24] Thus the question of faith is always fatally captive to the alternative whether this or that event has occurred in such a way or not, and faith suffers confusion when it must admit that many occurrences (for example in the Passion and Easter narratives) can no longer be historically verified and have obviously been formed under the in-

[24] To their number Emil Brunner also belongs. In spite of a thankful recognition of Bultmann's attempt, Brunner reproaches him for having fatally orientated himself toward the irrelevant modern world view of science and toward the thoroughly unauthorized self-understanding of the modern man, and thus for having extended his demythologizing sketch in an unfortunate manner. World view and self-understanding, however, must be distinguished and differently judged. Bultmann's answer to Brunner would be, and correctly, that an inner connection exists between the two which cannot be surrendered.

fluence of scriptural argument and legend. If the latter alternative is taken, then in the opinion of some, the pastor should honestly explain from the pulpit that everything naturally did not happen as it is related; it is pious legend or a temporally conditioned myth; but we know better today. And, in the opinion of others, we must believe that it happened in just that way. "The resurrection of Christ is the best attested fact of world history." Is not the one type of preaching as dreadful as the other. What makes them so? Clearly the fact that by an acceptance of those alternatives the reality which the, e.g., Easter message proclaims, is not seen at all.

It is of the nature of this reality of which the kerygma speaks, that it encounters man only in the word and that the knowledge which corresponds to it is faith or nothing at all. I cannot, as it were, a priori isolate that reality as a realm of mysterious things totally beyond the realm of our scholarship,[25] a realm, then, in which everything and anything could be possible. Whoever makes into an a priori of knowledge the proposition that with God all things are possible and raises it to a general principle before faith, so to speak, concretely begins to believe, must of necessity face up to the childish question whether or not the dear Lord can make worms fly through the air. ("Naturally!" will come the answer, but what would be gained by it?) The sphere

[25] At this point it seems important to me to mention Karl Barth's objections to Bultmann (*Kirchliche Dogmatik*, III/2, 531 ff.). The objections are directed at five axioms by which Bultmann, in Barth's opinion, is guided: (1) Only that theological proposition is valid which can be demonstrated to be a component part of the Christian understanding of human existence. (2) Only that may be described as having occurred in time which can be demonstrated to be a historical *factum*. (3) The assertion that an event narrated with sagalike or legendary features really occurred is possible only on the basis of an irresponsible *sacrificium intellectus*. (4) The modern world view is absolutely binding for us. (5) We are prohibited from any eclectic procedure in matters of a world view. It is obvious that Barth's "No" to Bultmann's sketch would have to be more comprehensively discussed and more thoroughly considered than is possible in this context. Nevertheless, I cannot suppress the question as to whether or not Barth's criticism of Bultmann's "axioms" does not also have a priori as its aim making room for the revelatory event. I hope I have misunderstood Barth at this point, for there ought not to be any possible disagreement about this, that with all this readiness to adopt a genuine distance over against the world (a distance, moreover, which provides a foundation for humor) and thus also over against science and a world picture, the persistent earnestness of Bultmann's question cannot be dismissed with the careless counter question: "Really, why not?" (i.e. why could not an event such as the resurrection have occurred?).

188

of revelation cannot a priori be isolated and marked off in advance by an orthodox concept of Scripture and the canon, so that as a result the miracle stories of the New Testament, for example, could be subjected to a different evaluation than that which is narrated in an apocryphal tradition. I must rather recognize that the reality with which the message and faith are concerned encounters me within the completely ambiguous context of the relation between history and mythology. There is nothing which would not be historically derived or integrated and which would not, in principle, be open to observation from the standpoint of the history of religions.

It is also of the nature of faith to break through the realm of mere significances and to affirm the *est* instead of the mere *significat*. (How, and in what sense, remains the primary and still unsolved question). It is of the nature of faith to reply to the revelation of Jesus Christ: "Ah, now you are speaking plainly, not in any figure" (John 16:29). Faith thereby makes known that the reality which encounters it in the word is the transcendent reality of the risen Lord which touches me together with my world, but now in such a way that it transcends, abolishes and at the same time renews my own understanding of the world and myself.

B. THE CHRISTOLOGICAL QUESTION

Now we have reached an area of discussion in which our previous statements must be demonstrated and made more clear.

How are the christological expressions of the New Testament to be correctly understood? Perhaps, we might first tell how, in our opinion, the New Testament Christology may not be understood and developed. Our answer: In the mere sketch and description of a drama of redemptive history as recently appears, *e.g.,* in Oscar Cullmann's book *Christ and Time* and in Ethelbert Stauffer's *New Testament Theology.* I believe the general objection to be raised against Cullmann's clever and instructive book is that it allows the description of New Testament ideas of time to displace a genuine interpretation of the understanding of time in the New Testament. The mathematical clarity with which the saving event is here developed within the scheme of linear time and with which Christ likewise is set at the mid-point of a co-ordinate system of eons is deceptive. The eschatological "now" and "today" of the primitive Christian proclamation cannot be grasped *more geometrico*. And, for the New Testament, Christ is not the mid-point but the end of history.[26]

However, Stauffer's *New Testament Theology*, to a greater degree, offers a most instructive example of this type of treatment. With all respect for the achievement of this book, I can still only regard it as a thoroughgoing mythologizing of the New Testament. It is symptomatic that in this comprehensive work only one half page is given to the doctrine of justification. In lieu of this doctrine the triumphal portrait of *Christus Imperator* is pieced together from a mass of scattered mosaics which are often nothing more than splinters and fragments in the New Testament itself, but which are gleaned by Stauffer predominantly from late Jewish apocalypticism. Only in this way does Stauffer gain the great drama of the world and redemptive event, with all its acts and scenes, all its divine and demonic actors—all the way from God's primeval prescience; beyond the creation, fall, and redemption; up to the restoration of the All—a drama which, it must be said, he "produces." Seen as a whole, therefore, what Stauffer offers in his theology can indeed be read with excitement, but cannot be preached (hopefully not!). In saying this, however, I do not espouse the cause of those "practical theologians," all of whom measure theological work according to the degree to which it can immediately be changed into homiletical and catechetical currency, but I intend rather to touch on a statement of fact, namely, that the real kerygmatic character of the New Testament statements regarding salvation is completely absorbed by a great and uniform myth.

As to the way in which the New Testament message of Christ should be interpreted, what is most significant is to be learned from the New Testament itself and especially from the theology of Paul. How does he interpret the Christian tradition handed down to him? He neither narrates merely a story of Jesus, nor develops a Christ myth, as essential to him as the historical once-for-allness of the incarnation, crucifixion and resurrection is,[27] and as strongly as he shows his dependence, above all, on the ideas of the Gnostic redemption and

[26] Cf. E. Fuchs, *Evangelische Theologie* (1949), pp. 447 ff.

[27] This situation is not simply to be explained by the fact that he did not know our Gospel tradition in its entirety. II Cor. 5:16 expresses the real reason for Paul's unconcern.

anthropos myth, even in his Christology. He rather interprets the tradition according to the canon of the doctrine of law and gospel (Romans, Galatians) or, and still quite appropriately, according to the canon of the antithesis of the wisdom of the world and the word of the cross (I Corinthians). That means that the story of Christ for Paul is not a self-contained drama of salvation from which consequences of saving significance for man and the world can subsequently be drawn, but rather that the story of Christ can only be understood when the question about man, his lostness, and his redemption is always included in it. The penetration of mythical thought in Paul does not, as is occasionally heard, occur in the application of the ideas, e.g., of the *anthropos* myth to the historical figure of Jesus, but rather in the union of the message of Christ and the doctrine of justification, of Christology and anthropology. In that union Paul has understood the character of the saving revelation as kerygma and has given it its validity.[28]

No one has so thoroughly grasped and demonstrated this situation as Bultmann. But should we follow him in interpreting the christological utterances merely as an expression of the Christian self-understanding? It seems to me that such a procedure is opposed by the fact that Paul does not merely develop Christology as the doctrine of law and gospel, but also develops the doctrine of justification as Christology. This seems to involve us in a *circulus vitiosus*. It is based upon the very nature of the case, however.

We may visualize that in what Paul says about redemption in Romans 8. How does he develop the proposition that "the law of the Spirit of life in Christ Jesus has set me free from the law of sin and death" (8:2) ? By speaking of the history, the mission, the way, and the work of Jesus Christ. This history begins with God and stands wholly and totally under the sign of sin (8:3) . In contrast to the law, it does not capitulate to the self-assertiveness which sin and death have raised against God, but rather it leads to the conquest of sin and to the establishment of a new existence of the believer. Of course,

---

[28] That can be shown in a corresponding manner in the Gospel of John, in which the tradition of Jesus Christ is grasped and expounded in such an astonishingly new way. In John, the kerygmatic character of the revelation becomes visible in the peculiar style of the narratives which often, without terminating, change into speeches and are attached to the revelatory speeches as "signs."

191

however, Paul does not speak of faith here (not in the entire eighth chapter!), but of a new "being in" of the redeemed. "There is therefore now no condemnation for those who are in Christ Jesus" (8:1). They are in him, as he himself, the Spirit of God, the Spirit of Christ, is in them (8:9 ff.). The incarnation of Christ in our reality (in the same form of sinful flesh) means that he, or rather his Spirit has now made his dwelling where sin once made its home (note the recurrence of the verb *oikein* in 7:17, 18, 20–8:9). The redeemed therefore are now redemptively embraced by Christ. By his incarnation, his obedience (Rom. 5:18 ff.), his death, and his resurrection he has become the saving basis of a new existence. He not only makes possible for me the decision of faith, which I have to make, but prior to that he is the reality of a decision which God in his saving grace has made about me.[29] He not only gives me the possibility of understanding myself anew in my existence and my history, but he opens and discloses to me a new history and a new existence by taking me up into his history. Here, Bultmann's interpretations are, in my opinion, no longer sufficient, for they do not enable us to grasp the reality of the new being in Christ. They are orientated to the question: How do I understand myself? But for Paul the question is more urgent: Where am I? This question—just as in the story of the fall—has priority over and alone makes possible an answer to the question of man's self-understanding. The believer's new existence has its nature in the fact that my "I" is dissolved and is taken into Christ (Gal. 2:20), of course, not in the sense of an enthusiastic rapture, but in the sense of God's having surrendered his Son up to the real curse and death of my life. Thus, God is for us, thus he makes us righteous before him (Rom. 8:31 ff.). Hence it is by no means sufficient to describe redemption in such a way that it means nothing more than a new qualification of my own history. Paul means in fact a new history which is no longer mine. This is the purpose of the characteristically "local" expressions of Romans 8, which are of course exposed to mythological abuse (Gnosis provides sufficient examples of this!), but must not be surrendered as being mythological and replaced by definitions of being which are gleaned from existence as such. The new history of

---

[29] Also the detailed statements of Eduard Schweizer, *Zur Interpretation des Kreuzes bei R. Bultmann, Aux Sources de la Tradition Chretienne,* Festschrift für M. Goguel (Paris: Delachaux et Niestle, 1950), pp. 228 ff., correctly allude to this.

Christ into which I am incorporated begins and ends in heaven; in its basis and goal it radically surpasses my history and the understanding of my existence. Like all history, it has its past, its present, and its future. Its past, the "whence" from which as a believer I come, means now: God sent his only Son; God has given him up for us all. Its present, its "wherein," means: Christ dwells within you, God is for us . . . , Christ is with us. . . . Its future, its "whither," means: How will he not give us all things with him, who will separate us from the love of God? [30]

C. THE ESCHATOLOGICAL QUESTION

The question of eschatology is most intimately connected with the problem of Christology. No one will seriously be able to deny that primitive Christian eschatology and apocalyptic are bound up with ideas of a world picture which are simply not recoverable for us. But is the actual concern of this eschatology to be grasped on the basis of Bultmann's hermeneutics? I do not believe so and will clarify this by means of Paul's statements in Phil. 3:7 ff. Paul speaks here of abandoning what was once gain to him but which now appears to him as loss and refuse for the sake of Christ (vs. 7), for the sake of the surpassing knowledge of Jesus Christ (vs. 8). It is very characteristic of Paul to speak of Christ as "gain." Not in such a way that he says: "For his sake I have suffered the loss of all things because I have gained Christ," but rather, "in order that I may gain Christ." This gain, therefore, is not yet attained. This goal is still in the distance. The future of this final, saving gain puts an end to his own righteousness. He is already apprehended; he already has the righteousness of faith, but precisely for that reason he is only on the way toward the goal of being found in Christ and of sharing in the resurrection of the dead. Now he is only taken up into the death of Christ; life lies before him.

There are few statements in Paul which so forcefully oppose transmuting the new existence in Christ into a demonstrable, accessible world reality as this: "Not that I have already attained this or am already perfect." As much use as Paul makes of the terms of the Gnostic mysteries here, the Gnostic understanding of salvation is nevertheless radically broken through, and precisely at this point:

---

[30] Instead of giving many examples, we merely refer to the tenses of the verbs in Rom. 8:31 ff.

For Paul the "knowledge" of Jesus Christ does not mean perfection and deification. For that reason the believer's present can only be characterized by the concept of a righteousness from God on the ground of faith.

Why then is not Paul content with it? Justification is indeed still an eschatological event ("where there is forgiveness of sins, there is also life and salvation"). Why does he continue: "that if possible I may attain the resurrection from the dead" (3:11)? Obviously, because God's acquittal which has become his in Christ means precisely the obtaining of a new future. Bultmann is used to stating it similarly, but he gathers from it only that faith implies the possibility of authentic existence, a being open to the future. Once again, that means nothing else than that Christ signifies the possibility and disclosure of a new self-understanding, a new qualification of my history. Then, however, there would be no need for mythological speech about a resurrection from the dead. Now, what the New Testament age and Paul, in dependence upon late Jewish apocalypticism, have "conceived" by the resurrection of the dead is not our concern here. What is of importance is that by that concept Paul certainly had more in mind than merely a new self-understanding in my history (for which the concept of the resurrection from the dead would certainly be the worst imaginable). Again, he is concerned with a new history into which believers are taken up. It has its sign in the fact that in a radical reversal of what may otherwise be called history it does not lead from life to death, but rather originates in death—Christ's death, that is— and has life, namely, life with Christ, before it. Into this new history, which is the history of Christ, his incarnation, his cross, his resurrection and his future, the believer is personally and historically taken up. It has its end beyond the possibilities of my self, just as its beginning radically surpasses my own capacity and understanding. Paul, of course, does not speak in descriptive terms of the future of this new history—the resurrection of the dead—[31] but rather in an indirect way by explaining once more what it is which now constitutes being in faith. It has its nature in the not-yet, in forgetting what lies behind, in straining forward toward the heavenly goal. The believer is only

[31] Where he does so, as in I Cor. 15:35 ff., he is, in all certainty, to be interpreted critically. Cf. Bultmann, "Karl Barth, 'Die Auferstehung der Toten,'" *Glauben und Verstehen*, 1, 58 ff.

apprehended by Christ in order to apprehend him. By the power of the life of Christ he is first drawn into his death (3:12-21).

Therefore, speech about the resurrection from the dead must in no way involve an uncritical repetition of certain objectifying ideas. However, the interpretation may never surrender what the message of the resurrection from the dead intends to express—namely, that the destiny and realization of my existence lies beyond the possibilities of my self. They signify the disruption and the end of my history and thus the disclosure of a new history in Christ.

We conclude with a reference which clarifies what was said from another point of view. It is the uniqueness of the primitive Christian *Confessio* that in a most characteristic contrast to the, e.g., confessions of the Psalms, it no longer describes the history of an I, but only the history of Jesus Christ: He, who was in the form of God (Phil. 2:6 ff.), he is the image of the invisible God (Col. 1:15 ff.), he was manifested in the flesh (I Tim. 3:16). The third person is the mark of the primitive Christian confession. Wherever it speaks of the being of Christ as Lord and Son of God, it always embraces his history, and this history of Christ, whether or not it is unfolded, always embraces the end of our history as those imprisoned in sin and death and the disclosure of a new history which incorporates us. But the *Confessio* always merges into a proclamation which acclaims his dignity and his history. Thereby this confession corresponds to the gospel which first and finally proclaims the great deeds of God and narrates the history of Jesus Christ.

There is no question that the appropriation of this kerygma and this *Confessio* can only take place within a critical interpretation, not simply in a mere recitation. Whoever leaps over this critical interpretation betrays theology and makes the kerygma into a myth. But the interpretation, originating in kerygma and *Confessio* and leading back to kerygma and *Confessio,* will always express the fact that it is not the interpretation but the word prior to it which is the actual and suitable speech of God. That is true not although, but because the interpretation knows that this word does not encounter it directly, but always in a definite, historical presentation.[32] The nature of this

---

[32] On this point cf. Bultmann, *Das Problem des Verhältnisses von Theologie und Verkündigung im Neuen Testament, Aux Sources de la Tradition Chretienne,* pp. 32 ff.

Confessio will always be that it no longer speaks of man, but rather of God and of his activity in Christ. More precisely, it speaks of man because it is silent about him. In just such a way it demonstrates itself to be the answer of faith which surrenders its own existence to the deed of God. The simplicity of this speech in kerygma and *Confessio* must, of course, be understood. It does not stand at the beginning, but at the end.

EIGHT

HERMANN DIEM

The Earthly Jesus and
the Christ of Faith

Ever since the penetration of historical-critical thought into theology there has been inquiry into the relationship between the historical Jesus and the Christ of faith. If I feel compelled to break with this usual formulation of the question and inquire into the *earthly* rather than the historical Jesus, it is because that is the more relevant and comprehensive way of putting the question. It is only within this formulation of the question that the subordinate question regarding the historical Jesus can be properly put and answered.

The question of the relation of faith to the earthly Jesus is thus the prior question because it existed even before there was a New Testament, and hence even before there was a historical criticism of the New Testament. This question was already addressed to the eyewitnesses of Jesus' life. In any case it will always be the decisive question, no matter how we answer the subordinate question concerning the historical Jesus.

Even this subordinate question existed before the advent of historical science. Ever since the time of those first Christians who were no longer themselves eyewitnesses of Jesus' life, it was addressed to all who lived later as the question of the possibility of bridging the gap between the earthly Jesus' actual history and a present encounter with that history. We call it the "historical" question, according to the original meaning of the word *historein,* i.e., the coming to know and the bringing into experience of an event, as well as the report of that experience. Hence, what is really involved is the question as to what, in lieu of the *historein* of eyewitnesses, leads those who live subsequently to an encounter with the earthly Jesus.

The Roman Church answers this historical question by means of historically demonstrable criteria which guarantee the uninterrupted continuity of the earthly Jesus with the Christ who is presently active through the organs of the Church. Thereby, however, the historically demonstrable tradition itself does not have to bear the burden of proof. That burden is rather borne by the dogmatic decisions of the Church which legitimize this tradition in its continuity and which, conversely, are themselves legitimized by the tradition. Since in this instance the historical is not required to bear the burden of proof, no serious difficulties were inflicted on the Roman Church when it had to subject its tradition to historical criticism.

In the Church of the Reformation that gap was not bridged by a historically demonstrable continuity of tradition, but rather by the fact that the earthly Jesus encounters us in the proclamation of the Church. It could obviously be presupposed that the *Christus praedicatus* as the Exalted One is identical with the earthly Jesus, since preaching occurs on the basis of the scriptural witness to him. That Scripture witnesses to him is conversely corroborated by the fact that it can be preached and that this preaching encounters faith in him. In this way all those Catholic guarantees of continuity were abandoned and attempt was made to establish the *solus Christus* in the *sola scriptura* upon a faith in the self-evidence of Holy Scripture in the event of its being proclaimed.

Thus, for the Reformation solution everything depends on the fact that the identity of the earthly Jesus with the *Christus praedicatus* is only conceivable and demonstrable in the event of proclaiming, hearing, and believing and, of course, by virtue of the earthly Jesus' demonstrating himself to be the present Christ in this event. Apart from and without regard to this event, every question concerning the *historein* of the history of the earthly Jesus is falsely put and thus can only be falsely answered.

Soon after the Reformation, however, the question was actually put in this false way. This by no means first occurred with the penetration of modern historical science into theology as is customarily supposed, but prior to that time with the development of the doctrine of Holy Scripture in Protestant Orthodoxy. In the Council of

Trent the Roman Church had secured itself against the Reformation use of Scripture in preaching by propounding a doctrine of Scripture and tradition. The Protestants allowed themselves to be misled into taking the same ground and, with their doctrine of verbal inspiration, into creating an authority for Scripture which could also exist outside the event of proclaiming, hearing, and believing. It was not their intent thereby to surrender the Reformation *solus Christus* in the *sola scriptura*, but, on the contrary, to safeguard it. But even while they furnished this security for making contemporary the earthly Jesus in the *Christus praedicatus,* they rendered the entire solution of the Reformation untrustworthy. As soon as it was deemed possible and necessary to guarantee in some way that the Christ preached in Scripture is actually identical with the earthly Jesus, historical criticism was challenged to test the validity of this guarantee.

For a time it was possible to conceal the consequences conjured up by the assumption that the dogmatic doctrine of Scripture had answered the historical-critical question. Sooner or later this would have to be shown to be an error. We must be clear about the fact that when it finally uncovered this error historical-critical research on the Bible did not cause the injury, but only made evident what had long been present.

It did so only with great hesitation and with means which were totally inadequate theologically. It could no longer orientate itself to the Reformation conception, since Orthodoxy had concealed this conception from it as well as an understanding of its own authentic concern in this whole affair. Thus, it was unable to take into account the sense in which the historical question of truth regarding the story of Jesus should be put so as to be theologically legitimate. So, it simply did what was most obvious. First of all, it exposed the error that the Bible contains an uncontradictory historical report of the story of Jesus. In this way it was not difficult to show, by means of the facts, the absurdity of that dogmatic elimination of the historical-critical question. But what now? Since it was not possible to remain with this chaotic situation, it now became desirable to free the true picture of Jesus from its dogmatic embellishment. The Gospels were treated as other historical documents, as sources from which, by means of historical-critical science, the attempt was made to reconstruct the story of the life of Jesus and thus to discover what is called the "historical Jesus." At the same time, however, pains were again taken to harmonize those contradictions in Scripture, partly in a rationalistic and partly in a supernaturalistic fashion. At all events, pains were taken to prevent the discrepancy between the historical Jesus and the Christ of faith from becoming too great. David Friedrich Strauss should have earned great merit for himself with his discovery of this incompleteness in his first *Leben Jesu* of 1835, since he demanded a thoroughgoing application of general historical criteria to the Bible and opened the otherwise painfully avoided question as to whether in that case there could still be talk of the identity of the historical Jesus with the Christ of faith. That should finally have given the theologians occasion for reckoning with the theological problematic of their historical criticism of the Bible. But they did not listen to David Friedrich Strauss. They merely declared him a heretic because of his troublesome questions. Strauss himself obviously did not overlook the significance of what he had written. Later on, however, he was led to resume historical research into the life of Jesus, the inner impossibility of which he himself had so excellently established. And so it continued. When Albert Schweitzer finally wrote his history of the Life-of-Jesus research as a history of failure, not even this could have a telling effect, because it was still not seen from what theological bases this actual failure is to be explained.

Yet, this actual failure of historical research into the life of Jesus produced an extremely interesting shift of fronts in theology. If I may express it in terms of the old distinction between "positive" and "liberal"—a distinction which today, of course (whether rightly or wrongly shall remain undecided), is regarded as in some measure overcome—then it is at present the theological left wing which regards the attempt at historical research into the life of Jesus as having failed, that school, therefore, which once began with the protest against the obscuring of the historical question of truth on the part of dogmatics. On the other hand, it is at present the theological right wing, the erstwhile "positives" who now in their own way resume that abortive attempt of the liberals in order to establish historically the dogmatic picture of Christ. That this curious exchange of roles was actually possible shows, perhaps, more than anything else to what degree we are theologically at sea on this question, and that even today we scarcely have firm ground beneath our feet.

200

It was no doubt a significant step forward when, by the application of form critical method to the Gospels, their character as proclamation was discovered. If the Gospels, according to their own self-understanding, intend further to proclaim or to attest the proclamation of the earthly Jesus, it is an error to regard them as historical sources from which the story of Jesus behind them could be extracted. At last it could be theologically explained why the historical research into the life of Jesus *had* to fail. Now it could also be demonstrated in a purely historical way that the Reformation position corresponded to the self-understanding of the New Testament. But no one has ventured to draw the conclusion that we could simply overleap all historical criticism and return to the position of the Reformation, and rightly so. If there should actually be a way back to that point, then the modern problem of historical knowledge regarding the earthly Jesus must be thought out to its conclusion.

In addition, however, we must now gain final clarity concerning what historical question of truth is actually to be put to the Gospels, for without an answer to this question the relationship of the historical to the theological question of truth cannot be determined.

Before the historical question of truth can be posed, however, we must first determine what is the object of historical-critical research when we inquire into the story of the earthly Jesus. In pursuit of the discovery of the kerygmatic character of the Gospels an alternative question has been raised, i.e., whether this object is the life or the preaching of Jesus. No one, of course, has quite succeeded with this alternative, but that theology which regards historical research into the life of Jesus as a failure inquires first into the kerygma of Jesus. Hence, in what follows we will designate this school in abbreviated fashion as the "kerygma-theology." Those theologians who are of the opinion that they can carry on the Life-of-Jesus research by using new and especially Jewish sources, and whom we call the "theological right wing" as to their origin, do not intend and indeed cannot disregard the kerygmatic character of the Gospels. They are afraid, however, this proclamation will become merely a general truth when loosed from history, or at least when the historical knowledge of this history is declared to be theologically irrelevant. For that reason they are interested in the historically ascertainable event-character of this history and concentrate their work upon it. Since, by the very nature of the case, neither of these two tendencies may be exclusively held, there are many variations between them. I do not intend to mention any names here, in order not to evoke any of those sympathies or antipathies which are in the theological air today and which can only divert us from the matter at hand.

We come nearer the question regarding the real object of our historical work when we make clear why we cannot embrace one of the two above-mentioned possibilities. The entire content of the New Testament proclamation can be summarized as *the proclamation of Jesus Christ who proclaims himself.* Further, Jesus Christ is the *Initiator* as *Object* as well as the *acting Subject* of this proclamation. This proclamation develops within a history which begins with the earthly Jesus and continues beyond the cross and resurrection in the apostolic preaching. In this kerygmatic history the preaching of Jesus is further declared in the form of proclaiming, transmitting, and teaching. These three elements cannot be separated from each other, for the proclamation presupposes the reception of something handed down and further transmitted, not in a historical reporting, but rather in the act of proclamation. This transmission in preaching always includes teaching as a vital element, since what is transmitted must be critically examined as to its identity with the proclamation of Jesus Christ who proclaims himself, and it must be interpreted for its recipients. *This kerygmatic history is the object sought by us and, according to the self-understanding of the New Testament, is the sole legitimate object of historical research into the New Testament.* To this kerygmatic history also belongs the history of the community within which it develops, and, of course, in the sense that the community is not only the place but also the object of proclamation. This may never be forgotten, though we limit ourselves here to the kerygmatic history according to its three elements of proclaiming, transmitting, and teaching.

Before we proceed to the historical question of truth to be put to this kerygmatic history, we will first give a definition of what we mean by *Geschichte* and *Historie.* By *Geschichte* we understand simply history as event—in this instance, the event of this kerygmatic history. In this kerygmatic history, by its own statement, revelation occurs as the history of Jesus Christ who proclaims himself. By *Historie* we do not understand the event of history itself, but rather its *historein* in the already mentioned sense of a coming to know and a bringing into experience, as well as a reporting of what has been experienced. Every *Geschichte*, in so far as it occurs among men, contains in principle the possibility of its being understood as *Historie*—that is, it contains the possibility of its historical apprehension and transmission. But this proposition may not be reversed to read that only that can really have occurred which can be established historically. Such an historical concept of reality we must reject because it is impossible to see how it could be substantiated generally, to say nothing of its application to the New Testament. For, if access to *Geschichte* is only possible by means of *Historie*, then we can only establish concerning history what was historically visible in it. It is not possible, however, for us to determine whether that visible aspect is the entire history, or whether in its having occurred factors have been at work which escape historical comprehension. Indeed, in the light of that which cannot be accounted for historically and which always and everywhere encounters us in this activity of the *historein*, we have every reason for assuming that such factors do exist. Hence we must say that *Geschichte enters into Historie, but it does not become identical with it.* Of course that must hold true for all *Geschichte*, though in varying proportion.

If we apply these definitions to the New Testament kerygmatic history, then this too must have a kind of *Historie* appropriate to it. It must also be true of this *Geschichte*, that access to it is possible only by way of the *Historie* in which it encounters us. But now the particular difficulty confronting us is that *in this kerygmatic history itself Geschichte and Historie coincide in a peculiar way.* They coincide in so far as there are two phases in this *Geschichte*. These phases are to be strictly differentiated and yet may not be historically separated. They are: (1) the activity and the preaching of the earthly Jesus himself and (2) the proclamation about his activity and his preaching. Both, according to the self-understanding of this kerygmatic history, are to be strictly *differentiated*, since the first phase in its contingent uniqueness, in its *ephapax*, is the basis for the reality and knowledge of the second, the history of the proclamation about Jesus' activity and preaching. For that reason, however, both are *not to be historically separated*, because the same Jesus Christ is also the acting Subject in the second phase, the history of the proclamation about him. Thus, on the one hand, this history of the proclamation about Jesus is the historical witness to Jesus' own preaching, and on the other it is also and as such its continuation. The preaching about Jesus is therefore something new, and yet identical with Jesus' own preaching. Now Jesus' own preaching encounters us only through the preaching about him, or, more precisely, in the historical witness to him—that is, in the New Testament Scriptures which are the historical deposit of this whole kerygmatic history. The human bearers of this kerygmatic history, however, either unconsciously or intentionally omit distinguishing one phase of this history from the other, so that we can no longer recognize the limits between them. They do so obviously because they believe in the identity of the one kerygmatic history—that is, because they are conscious that even in their proclaiming *historein* the earthly Jesus proclaims himself as the Christ.

This is the peculiar and thoroughly complex phenomenon in which this kerygmatic history encounters us through its *Historie.* Now we must inquire of this *Historie* concerning that event which actually occurred. Moreover, we will not be able to proceed in any other way than to pursue the course by which this *Geschichte* became *Historie,* but now in reverse direction, i.e., to inquire into the *Geschichte* of this *Historie* by means of traditio-historical research. Of course, in so doing we must never forget that this kerygmatic history is not establishable as fact behind its *Historie,* because it occurs *in, with, and under* the *Historie* which proclaims it.

Now, what is the historical question of truth to be put to this kerygmatic history? It can consist in nothing else than in the question concerning the continuity of this history. This continuity in turn can consist in nothing else than in the identity of Jesus Christ who proclaims himself in it—that is, in the fact that he weathers variation in the proclamation brought about by the vicissitudes of time, of the persons proclaiming it, as well as of the situations in which it is proclaimed.

The critical point in this question concerning the continuity of the kerygmatic history will be the transition from the proclamation of Jesus to the post-Easter proclamation about him. Hence, we cannot begin with the kerygma of the primitive community, but must inquire into that first phase of the kerygmatic history, into the proclamation of the earthly Jesus himself. It is precisely at this point, however, that the greatest difficulties arise for the historical question of truth, since our single source for the proclamation of the earthly

Jesus, the Gospels, are already the post-Easter kerygma of the primitive community. We cannot exclude this transition from our investigation, however, because the historical question of truth to be put here concerning the continuity of the kerygmatic history is also the theological question of truth. The latter wants to know whether the earthly Jesus encounters us in the kerygmatic history as the Christ of God. This question would still not be positively answered by a historical proof of the continuity of the kerygmatic history, since it cannot possibly be answered by a historical judgment. With such a proof we would merely be in the situation of the eyewitnesses. With a *negative* reply to the historical question of truth—that is, with a historical proof of discontinuity in the kerygmatic history—the theological question would already be negatively prejudiced, since it would then at least be doubtful whether the Christ who encounters us in the kerygmatic history is the earthly Jesus or only a myth.

Can the historical question of truth regarding the continuity of the kerygmatic history be positively answered in view of the present state of New Testament research? This query cannot be answered simply with a yes or a no, because New Testament research has scarcely been carried on in terms of such a formulation of the question. It regards traditio-historical inquiries primarily as technical-literary means for separating individual layers of the tradition. Moreover, it does not evaluate the results of these inquiries with regard to their theological significance for the question concerning the continuity of the kerygmatic history, since the theological relevance of this kerygmatic history has not even been seen.

Of course, the theological right wing attempts to arrive at the oldest layer of the tradition in order to distinguish and to separate from the later tradition in as clear-cut a manner as possible the proclamation of Jesus himself as his *vox ipsissima*. That is a very difficult task, however, and its results will always be a matter of much debate. The transmitters who proclaimed this *vox ipsissima* did not make this differentiation themselves. They did not need to because they believed they were especially charismatically endowed and empowered for their kind of proclamation, and they actually could not do it, because the transmission of the proclamation of Jesus by preaching is not possible without interpreting it, without even changing it in order to suit it to a specific situation. Secondly, the question arises—and this is even more important—what theological basis can this *vox ipsissima* really provide even if it could be sporadically established? To this question, if it is put at all and if such historical technique is not merely carried on as art for art's sake, a satisfactory reply can scarcely be given. Will not some wish to conclude that only the *vox ipsissima* should be preached, however, or that the rest of the New Testament is to be regarded merely as a preaching text of lesser quality? To be sure, the question here is concerning the meaning which this proclamation of Jesus must have for the continuity and identity of that further kerygmatic history, but the mere establishment of the *vox ipsissima* itself does not in the least contribute to it. Of course, there are also a few bold theological constructions which regard not only the entire New Testament kerygmatic history, but also the whole history of Church dogma as having been "preformed" as to content in the *vox ipsissima*, or actually, e.g., merely in Jesus' self-designation as "Son of Man." These constructions, however, aside from their historically dubious nature, are also theologically suspect, since this kind of "continuity" is in complete contradiction to the essence of the New Testament kerygmatic history according to its three elements, as well as to the evangelical understanding of dogma as the free answer to the proclamation.

Partly because the theological right wing does not know how to begin theologically with the results of its traditio-historical research and partly because it makes improper use of them, it is relatively easy for the other side, the kerygma-theology, to reject its results. The latter fears above all that these results could be used to establish a mere *fides historica* which believes in "saving facts" which are historically guaranteed. This anxiety to a great extent determines not only its theological use of the results of its own traditio-historical work, but also its very emergence, for when the ascertaining of authentic words of Jesus is regarded not only as theologically irrelevant, but is actually viewed as perilous to faith, it is obvious that only a few such words will be found. Here too, of course, the oldest utterances, e.g., regarding the coming of the Son of Man, are regarded in part as authentic words of Jesus, but then a comparison with the utterances of later layers of the tradition yields the conclusion that Jesus did not have himself in mind by this coming Son of Man, but rather someone else, and that he was first identified with the Son of

Man by the post-Easter community. Hence, in this instance, historical work on the history of the tradition is done primarily to point out the change which the preaching of Jesus underwent in the post-Easter proclamation. It is of no relevance for faith that the result is a historically demonstrable discontinuity in the New Testament kerygmatic history, since faith should be concerned merely with the kerygma of the primitive community and should have its essence in the resolve to believe this kerygma in spite of its historical nondemonstrability. Of course, it is clear in all of this that the Christ of faith is on the point of being mythologized, since there is no longer any connection with the earthly Jesus beyond the mere facticity of his existence, nor is there any need for it. It would seem then, in view of the *aporia* into which kerygma-theology has obviously fallen, that this theology by that fact recognized the theological relevance of the kerygmatic history and thus also the significance of the question concerning its continuity.

In light of this situation in present-day research, therefore, it is difficult to say, on the strength of its results, whether the historical question concerning the continuity of the kerygmatic history can be answered positively or negatively. So I must limit myself to indicating what is of consequence in the reply to this question. I can do that most easily by way of the example of a new, yet unpublished, Heidelberg dissertation on the Son-of-Man sayings in the Synoptic Gospels. Free of all theological postulates and in purely historical fashion, the author attempts to answer the old question concerning the relationship of the various groups of Son-of-Man sayings within the synoptic tradition. In doing so, he arrives at the following conclusion (without going into all his arguments I will briefly refer to it, so far as it concerns our question) : Jesus himself introduced the Son-of-Man concept into his preaching without appropriating more from its complex meaning in Jewish apocalyptic than the idea of majesty inherent in it. The oldest group of Son-of-Man sayings, in which it is said that the coming Son of Man will confess those who have confessed Jesus and have followed him, contains authentic words of Jesus. Because of this *conc*ealing rather than *re*vealing usage to which Jesus puts the title Son of Man, the historical question as to whether, as Bringer of salvation, he identified himself with the coming Son of Man must be left open. It is clear, however, that he connected the blessing of salvation, fellowship in the kingdom of God, with the attitude toward himself and thus made a claim to majesty. On the basis of the Easter-event, the Church expressed this connection between the blessing of salvation and the Bringer of salvation by putting into the mouth of the earthly Jesus the self-designation Son of Man. This first of all took place in the second group of Son-of-Man sayings which concern the earthly Jesus' exercise of his authority, but which are not authentic words of Jesus. These sayings have no other purpose than to take up the proclamation of the earthly Jesus and to proclaim it further. That is indicated, among other things, by the fact that they still retain the wording of those authentic words of Jesus with their differentiation between the coming Son of Man and Jesus himself. Their authors, however, already effected the identification of the two, which, conversely, again speaks for the authenticity of the Son-of-Man sayings in the first group. In the third group of sayings on the suffering, dying, and rising Son of Man, also put into the mouth of Jesus by the Church, the latter attempts to solve the riddle of how he who encountered it as the earthly One with his divine claim to majesty could be delivered up by God into the hands of men and how he went this way willingly. This was then further elaborated in the passion kerygma which originated in another line of the tradition, along with the aid of the Old Testament witness, as God's saving will to which Jesus voluntarily submitted.

That which is of prime importance for our question regarding the continuity of the kerygmatic history is that the fixing of authentic words of Jesus is not an isolated concern, nor is it irrelevant to an understanding of the further kerygmatic history. Rather, it is established upon the kerygmatic history, and conversely again, it establishes the fact that and the degree to which the earthly Jesus is its Initiator and Object. Thus it follows that the decision of faith does not concern a kerygma whose historical Initiator could also become a myth. It concerns rather the relation to the earthly Jesus as a person. Any reduction to the mere fact of the encounter is out of the question here. Everything depends on who encounters us. Moreover, the person cannot be separated from his work, for through the preaching of the blessing of salvation, we meet the Bringer of salvation. From what he does we see who he is: In view of the kingdom of God which is coming and already breaking in, he grants that table fellowship with him which will have its confirmation in that kingdom. He exercises his authority to forgive sins as well as his power over the demons and calls to discipleship of his proclamation and suffering, and thereby also of his glory. This blessing of salvation is granted him who believes in the salvation-Bringer. Thereby the disciple's faith cannot merely accept Christ's work and ignore his identity. Obviously, the eternal validity of the blessing of salvation depends on the validity of that authority which the earthly Jesus claimed for himself as the Bringer of the blessing of salvation. The validity of his authority, however, was radically questioned when he was delivered up to men. Thus, their faith and confession in the Bringer of salvation and their participation in the blessing of salvation depends wholly on God's own witness to Jesus by his raising Jesus from the dead. That oldest tradition expresses this divine event of legitimation by having put into the mouth of the earthly Jesus during the exercise of the authority of his earthly ministry the title Son of Man, a title used by him to designate the coming One.

Thereby the historical question of truth concerning the continuity of the kerygmatic history is positively answered at this one, really decisive point. In this example we observe the formulation of the question in terms of which work on the history of the New Testament tradition must be carried on. I can only briefly indicate here what significance the results of such New Testament research have for *dogmatics:* It follows that the dogmatic-christological consciousness already has its beginning in the oldest layer of the synoptic tradition. To be sure, even in this oldest "Son-of-Man Christology" the name Christ is not used at all, but neither is it a mere "Jesusology"—that is, a doctrine of the earthly Jesus which would regard him merely as an earthly man and would thereby ignore what then was later expressed by designations of majesty, such as, Christ, Son of God, Kyrios, et cetera. Rather, in this first christological attempt, account is already given of how the earthly Jesus' claim to divine majesty relates to his entrance upon the limitations of human life. Thereby the fundamental problem of all later Christology is already posed—namely, the *vere Deus* and *vere homo*. Most signicant of all, this problem originates in encounter with the concrete history of the earthly Jesus, in which the revelatory activity of God was recognized.

Thus the history of the formation of dogma does not begin with the

Hellenization of Christianity, as has been curiously supposed, but in the *logia*-source of the Synoptics. It already undergoes its initial development within the New Testament kerygmatic history and as an integrating element of the latter. That alleged gulf between the New Testament and subsequent history of dogma does not exist; consequently, historians of dogma will have to commence their work with the earliest beginnings of the history of the New Testament tradition.

The dogmatician also can and must again make use of this historical work in answering the *questio facti* of Christology as well as in its detailed interpretation. Then he will no longer be permitted to proceed according to that narrow rule which uses single christological utterances of the Scripture biblicistically as *dicta probantia,* which harmonizes and systematizes them without regard to their historical place in the kerygmatic history and thus attempts to produce a *doctrinal unity* out of them, a kind of unity which never was nor will be. Rather, he will have to achieve complete freedom for the historical study of the history of the New Testament proclamation, and since he places himself in encounter with this history in all its concreteness, he will have to give account in his own Christology of what has encountered him in this history of Jesus Christ who proclaims himself.

Then, at least, an end would be put to that plaintive cry about the "burden and distress" which history furnishes the theologian, but then the dogmatician would no longer be permitted to refer the theologian, oppressed by the results of his historical research, to the totally inappropriate "nevertheless" of faith. He would rather have to admonish him to search further in the Scripture "whether it be so" and would also have to search along with him. Perhaps then the gulf between dogmatics and New Testament research, still oppressing us today, would fast become legend.

Before concluding, I must point out a few of the links between the historical and the theological question of truth. We defined the historical question of truth as the question concerning the *continuity* of the kerygmatic history. We saw that this continuity consists ultimately in the *identity* of Jesus Christ who proclaims himself in it and who sustains variation in the proclamation as its Initiator and Object, as well as the Subject acting in it. The degree to which the fixing of this identity can be of any concern to the historian may be debated, since, at least, the identity of the Subject acting in this kerygmatic history may never be established historically. Here the historical question of truth passes over into the theological, which we may define as the question *whether the Jesus Christ who acts as Subject in this kerygmatic history and who therefore encounters us in and through this history is identical with the earthly Jesus of Nazareth.* We have seen that a negative answer to the historical question of truth would necessarily have negative consequences for the answer to the theological question, but that cannot be reversed to read that the theological question would be positively answered with a positive answer to the historical question of truth. In this instance, only the historical interval which separates us from the preaching of the earthly Jesus would be removed and the way opened up on which the earthly Jesus will encounter us in the *Christus praedicatus.* But not even the most positive results of historical research concerning that continuity could guarantee to us that he really will or actually must encounter us here, just as little as those dogmatic certifications of the tradition on the part of the Roman Church could do it for the Reformers. This encounter can only come about when the Church simply dares to *preach* the Christ of the Scriptures in order that he may demonstrate himself to be the living and present Christ.

Now we have arrived at the Reformation position from which we set out. Our question was whether a return to that position is still possible after the problem of historical knowledge, not yet existing in such form for the Reformers, had explicitly arisen and required solution. That this is possible, after having maintained our position against all the fire of historical criticism, was precisely what I wanted to show.

NINE

Roy Harrisville

Bultmann's Concept of the
Transition from Inauthentic to
Authentic Existence

INTRODUCTION

It is the intention of this essay to concentrate upon a theme in Bultmann's theology which best illustrates his presuppositions and his method, namely, his concept of the transition from inauthentic to authentic existence. Although this theme of Bultmann has often been treated, till now the discussion has centered almost exclusively about his idea of the grace-event which effects the transition rather than upon that transition itself—that is, little notice has been taken of Bultmann's concept of the "new birth." That the discussion should have taken this turn is not surprising, inasmuch as the more provocative aspects of Bultmann's theology appear in his description of the grace-event, out of which the whole debate regarding the relation between the objective-historical (*historisch*) and existential-historical (*geschichtlich*) character of that event has resulted. It is our contention, however, that a study of Bultmann's concept of the transition from its anthropological side provides us with a most suitable key for understanding and appraising his hermeneutical method and for assigning him his place in the history of theology.

Bultmann's work is essentially apologetic in nature, that is, it is carried out under the presupposition that a relationship exists between theology and philosophy. The theology of Bultmann is dialectic, i.e., it is a theology which insists on the strict revelatory claim of the New Testament. His philosophy is existentialist, i.e., it is an analysis of human existence according to its general, formal (ontological)

212

structures. In the maintenance of the relationship between these two disciplines, Bultmann contends, his theology is prevented from degenerating into obscurantism, into a scholastic or dogmatic theology which has completely cut itself off from human nature and reason and thus falls under the sign of a *theologia contra rationem,* and his philosophy is prevented from degenerating into a humanism which construes possibilities of existence which arise only out of revelation as possibilities which are immanent in man. In other words, Bultmann attempts to overcome the embarrassment of a dialectical purism by reopening the question concerning natural theology. If, asserts Bultmann, revelation is the judgment of all that exists, the judgment of all that which a man can be and know of himself, it must, at the same time, be intelligible to man as such. As revelation, it obviously cannot annihilate its addressee—in that case it would not be recognizable as revelation—but it must address man as a real alternative in the midst of the other possibilities of existence confronting him. In other words, there must be *continuity* between the possibility of existence offered in the revelation and the old, worthless possibilities of existence of which it stands in judgment. And, Bultmann asserts, since the description of the broad structures of human existence falls within the province of philosophy, more particularly, of the existential analytic, and since revelation is concerned only with possibilities of which those structures are the condition, that analytic is best suited for making intelligible the revelation of God to man without endangering the nature of revelation as such. Bultmann thus employs the existential analysis of *Dasein* [1] in his interpretation of existence before or apart from faith, of existence in faith, and of the transition between these two possibilities.

I

INAUTHENTIC EXISTENCE

We proceed first of all to the description of inauthentic existence as conceived by Bultmann. For this description we may rely in large part upon his discussion of "Man Prior to the Revelation of Faith" in

[1] This term, which according to existentialist analysis denotes emergence, facticity (*Da-sein*="being there"), is for all practical purposes synonymous with "human being" and is used in contrast to the term *Sein* which denotes pure being, being as such. In this essay, both these terms will at times appear without translation, for purposes of differentiation.

chapter four of the first volume of his *Theology of the New Testament*.[2] According to Bultmann, inauthentic existence is characterized by a perversion in man's relationship to himself. Man is at odds with, estranged from, himself. Moreover, he is tempted to let the separation between himself and himself become a divorce, to misunderstand his relation to himself as a relation between his self and a totally foreign being (as in Gnosticism with its dualism of soul and body). He is alienated from his own true nature and from what he at heart is after —life. In his inauthenticity, however, he undertakes to seek life in the disposable or created world. He lives, in Pauline terms, a life "in the flesh," in all that is outward and visible, in that which has its nature in external appearances. Presuming to have life at his disposal, presuming to be able to procure life by his own power rather than by receiving it as a gift, he lives from his own self rather than from God. He has thus decided in favor of perishable creation which has become a destructive power; he has decided for evil. This self-powered striving to undergird his own existence in forgetfulness of his creatureliness, to procure life for and by himself, manifests itself either in a life of unthinking recklessness and desire, in the pursuit of which he believes he is performing the good when actually he is committing the evil, or it manifests itself in a zeal for the law and a striving after wisdom. In either case the result is "boasting," taking confidence in the flesh—the supposed security he achieves out of what is worldly and apparent and which he can control. This life, says Bultmann, lurks in care, in pro-vison, in foresight which self-reliantly strives to forestall the future, but whose hidden side is anxiety and fear—i.e. the hidden feeling that everything, even his own life, is escaping him. Thus, making himself dependent on that which he supposes he can control, man falls victim to the world; that which is constituted by what he does and upon which he bestows his care gains the upper hand. He falls under the spell of the antigodly power (a power which Bultmann describes as growing out of man himself) which masters him and makes the estrangement, the division in him determinative and which destroys him by wresting him out of his own hands. His guilt has become his fate; led into sinning and a prey to sin's power, he is enslaved and in bondage to death.

[2] Bultmann, *Theology of the New Testament*, tr. Kendrick Grobel, I (London: S.C.M. Press, 1952), 190 ff.

II

AUTHENTIC EXISTENCE

For Bultmann's description of authentic existence we may also rely on his *Theology of the New Testament*, particularly on chapter five of volume one, "Man Under Faith," and on chapter four of volume two, "Faith." Authentic existence is there characterized as freedom—man is "free from himself"; that is, his relationship to himself is appropriate. He is at one with himself, hence his existence has lost its enigmatic quality; he has laid hold of his true existence in a new existential understanding of self; he is freed for his authentic self. This authenticity is further a freedom from the world, a desecularization (he participates in the tumult of the world but does so with an inner aloofness, "as if he did it not"), a surrendering of all seeming security and every pretense, a smashing of all human standards and evaluations. This freedom is the willingness to live by the strength of the invisible and uncontrollable, the acceptance of a life which to the world's point of view cannot even be proved to exist; it is an understanding of existence no longer from the point of view of the world but from the point of view of God. Moreover, authentic existence is freedom from the past, forgiveness, righteousness—man's sin is not counted against him; he is absolved from sin by God's verdict; he is free for obedience. It is also freedom from the law, freedom from its demand and obligation to it nonetheless in sheer existence for the neighbor, in surrender to the other, in waiving "authorization" as a personal right when consideration for a brother demands it, in love. Bultmann further describes such existence as "eschatological"—i.e., as an existence which cannot be unequivocally described by the indicative but which is characterized by a continually being on the way between the "not yet" and the "yet already," by a continual proceeding toward a goal, by a constant appropriation of grace by faith. Since for Paul, writes Bultmann, free, ethical obedience can have its origin only in miracle, the apostle describes such authenticity in terms of the reception of the Spirit. This is only another way of expressing the factual possibility of the new life disclosed in faith, for such a "possibility" cannot be construed in terms of a natural process but must be actualized in the concrete deed from moment to moment. In a word, authentic existence for Bultmann is that state of being completely determined by the salvation occurrence, the state in which a man permits the resurrection of Christ, like his cross, to become the power which henceforth determines his life.

III

THE TRANSITION

That act which for Bultmann effects the transition from the one existence to the other is the "single," "eschatological" deed of God's grace whereby man is freed from his perverse striving to achieve self-hood by his own efforts and receives it as a gift. This salvation occur-rence (*Heilsgeschehen*) is directed at man, reaches him, and happens to him in the "word of the cross"—i.e., in the proclamation of a historical person, Jesus, and his fate. Since the salvation occurrence is nowhere present except in the proclaiming, accosting, demanding, and promising word of preaching, the "word" itself shares in, indeed *is* the occurrence. This "word" confronts man as a decisive summons to repentance—it throws him into question by rendering his self-under-standing problematical and demands from him the decision as to whether or not he is willing to "take up his cross," to be "crucified with Christ" by surrendering his previous understanding of himself and by understanding himself anew as receiving his life from the hand of God. The movement of man's will involved in such surrender, characterized by the term "faith," is not primarily a subjective despair of remorse, but above all an obedience by which man waives his right in favor of God's. Only through the fact that in the proclamation God appears to man as the One who is revealed in Jesus is this deci-sion possible, with the result that he who makes it can only understand it as God's gift.

IV

THE TRANSITION ACCORDING TO ITS ANTHROPOLOGICAL ASPECT

In chapter four, volume one of his *Theology* Bultmann asserts the unity of man's existence in the movement from the situation under law to that under grace, adding that in this movement no break takes place, no magical or mysterious transformation of man's substance, and that the new existence enjoys historical continuity with the old.[3] However, in his essay on "Das Problem der natürlichen Theologie" in

[3] *Ibid.*, pp. 268-69.

Glauben und Verstehen, Bultmann provides us with his clearest exposition of the anthropological aspect of the transition:

The structures of Dasein outlined by philosophy are valid also for believing Dasein. Not merely the factual situation makes that clear, a situation which indeed could be occasioned by a theological error, but also the assertion of faith itself, that it is unbelieving Dasein which comes to faith, that faith does not change human nature, that the justified does not have new, demonstrable qualities; rather, that the sinner is the justified one. . . . Faith indeed understands itself as concrete resolve, as concrete decision in a concrete situation constituted by the word of proclamation and the neighbor. Faith's assertion that such concrete resolve constitutes the basic condition of the Dasein anew, so that now, in addition to unbelieving Dasein there is also believing Dasein, is its specific, its offence. For this assertion is not only not demonstrable—obviously Dasein persists and even believing Dasein can be made ontologically intelligible—but even for faith it *may not* be demonstrated. And for the reason that faith understands itself as eschatological event. But that implies two things: 1) Faith in its proper sense is not perceptible as a renovation of Dasein; as the seizure of God and as *justifying faith it is no phenomenon of the Dasein.* Justification by faith is not demonstrable in the Dasein; for the justified is righteous only with God and always only with God and is a sinner on earth. The believer as well is in Dasein from birth and does not receive new structures of Dasein. His faith as historical act is always the concrete decision in the moment; that is, faith consists always and only in the conquest of unbelief. . . . 2) As eschatological event . . . *faith leads back to the original creation,* i.e. that lost, non-sensible possibility of faith as original obedience, a possibility of which philosophy is cognizant, is realized in Christian faith.[4]

It is immediately clear from these utterances that Bultmann's emphasis is upon the continuity between inauthentic and authentic existence. The transition or new birth does not disturb or change the structures of existence—they remain the same whether in or apart from faith. Herein lies the continuity. To be sure, over against the Greek, idealistic notion, the new self-understanding does indeed involve a "break," a discontinuity, but again, not in terms of a renovation of the structures of being. In support of this contention, Bultmann appeals to what he believes to be the nature of faith, as well as to the purely formal character of the philosophical analysis of *Dasein.* Faith is historical act, "concrete resolve," "concrete decision in a concrete situation," contingent upon the revelation. Moreover, the asser-

[4] Tübingen: J. C. B. Mohr, 1954, I, 308-9; 310-11.

tion of faith that "the sinner is the justified one," or, that the "basic condition of the Dasein" [5] is constituted "anew" is not demonstrable. This concreteness, contingency, and nondemonstrability give to faith its "ontical" character—that is, its character as one among many natural-historical possibilities confronting man, a possibility distinguishable from others only by the claim which it raises. Philosophy, on the other hand, speaks formally and "ontologically" of existence— i.e., it undertakes to describe only the broad, general conditions of being as such. The concreteness, contingency, and nondemonstrability of faith are thus not the proper theme of philosophy. Of course, faith must satisfy the formal, ontological structures of being, but only to that extent does philosophy take note of the theological concern. Neither the content nor the claim of faith is the object of a philosophical analysis which deals properly with the "empty" structures of being. Bultmann elsewhere points up the difference between the philosophical-ontological and theological-ontical concerns by stating that since faith and unbelief are answers to a concrete and contingent proclamation, any reflection upon faith and unbelief from the side of philosophy would be as absurd as its reflection upon a specific proposal of marriage. Bultmann adds that although the philosophical analysis of *Dasein* is obliged to exhibit the conditions of such a possibility, only to this extent does it take such a proposal into account.[6]

In view of this purely ontical character of faith, and in view of the fact that the existential analytic does not concern itself with *what* possibilities and *what* decisions confront a specific historical being, but rather only with the forms or conditions which those factual possibilities must satisfy, Bultmann concludes that the structures of being exhibited by this analytic are valid for unbelief as well as for faith. Thus, for Bultmann, whatever contrast may exist between the life apart from and in faith is a contrast between a merely being cognizant of and an actually laying hold of an original, lost possibility. The movement of faith itself does not involve an ontological change— the structures of being remain the same.

Out from this understanding of the continuity between inauthentic and authentic existence, Bultmann proceeds to demythologize those

[5] For a discussion of this phrase, cf. p., 223 *supra*.
[6] Bultmann, "Die Geschichtlichkeit des Daseins und der Glaube. Antwort an Gerhardt Kuhlmann," *Zeitschrift für Theologie und Kirche,* 27. Jahrgang (1930), Heft 5, 340.

New Testament utterances in which the Spirit is described as a miraculous, divine power conferred on the believer at baptism and endowing him with a new nature. Inasmuch as for Bultmann the transition or new birth does not involve the basic structures of existence, such utterances obviously confuse the ontical movement of faith with an ontological change. Such a confusion, Bultmann states, originates in the Gnostic redemption myth, according to which man is construed as matter, as substance. In defence of Paul, who often used animistic and dynamistic terminology "promiscuously" in reference to the Spirit (i.e. described it now as an independent, personal power which falls upon a man and takes possession of him, and now as an impersonal force which fills a man like a fluid), Bultmann writes that such a material notion of the Spirit was not really determinative for him,[7] and that "everything indicates that by the term 'Spirit' he means the eschatological existence into which the believer is placed by having appropriated the salvation deed that occurred in Christ." [8] In other words, Paul actually understood the concept of the Spirit in ontic rather than in ontological fashion. With the rest of primitive Christianity, however, he appropriated the Gnostic terminology because it offered a means of expression by which the redemption effected in Jesus could be made intelligible as a present reality.[9]

Scarcely does Bultmann's "apologetic" become more explicit than in this discussion of the transition from inauthentic to authentic existence. The aspect of continuity lies at the heart of his concern—it is the chief component of his natural theology. It furnishes the explanation for his philosophical presuppositions as well as for his hermeneutical method. It is the point at which his sharp disagreement with Karl Barth is most patent. Over against the latter who describes sin as ontological impossibility and the sinner as no real man, as "Unnatur" [10] requiring an annihilation and a being made alive in the revelation, Bultmann insists that the salvation occurrence must be recognizable to man as such, to man in his inauthenticity. More than this, it must address him as a word which gives him "the right to

---

[7] Bultmann, *Theology of the New Testament*, I, 334.

[8] *Ibid.*, p. 335.

[9] Bultmann, *Primitive Christianity*, tr. R. H. Fuller (New York: Meridian Books, 1958), p. 198.

[10] Karl Barth, *Die Kirchliche Dogmatik*, 111/2 (Zollikon-Zürich: Evangelischer Verlag, 1948), pp. 36, 41.

believe in the God in whom he would fain believe." [11] Indeed, all the results of Bultmann's demythologizing program correspond with, if they do not actually derive from, his idea of continuity. Those New Testament utterances which, according to him, describe ontical possibilities in ontological fashion and thus construe man as nature and redemption as a natural process (e.g., demon possession, the influence of angelic spiritual powers and the miracles which presuppose them, the Spirit as miraculous, divine power, general resurrection, et cetera) violate the aspect of continuity and require correction through interpretation. Or, which amounts to the same thing, those utterances which are in any way calculated to remove from faith its nondemonstrable and hence purely ontical character (e.g., facts reported of the pre-existent Son of God) offend against that aspect and require similar reinterpretation. To be sure, the Bultmann whose essay delivered to the *Gesellschaft für Evangelische Theologie* at Alpirsbach appeared and still appears to many to be nothing but an obituary on the gospel after the manner of David Friedrich Strauss seemed ruled by no other principle than the unpalatability of the tenets of orthodox Christianity for the modern man. However, that there was indeed a ruling, controlling principle was made amply clear in the debate which followed that essay, as well as in those statements which have since come from Bultmann's pen. The ruling principle was and always has been his concern for a natural theology which yielded the revelation recognizable and intelligible to man as such, a recognizability and intelligibility preserved in the aspect of continuity.

V

CRITICISM

It is important for our discussion, first of all, to note the growing suspicion among the scholars as to the appropriateness of Bultmann's understanding of the existential analytic, and precisely at that point where he assigns to philosophy and theology their ontological and ontic concerns. Such early articles as that written by Kurt Löwith in

---

[11] Bultmann, "Die Krisis des Glaubens," *Glauben und Verstehen*, II, 10. Aside from whether or not Bultmann's application to inauthentic existence of the familiar Augustinian formula ("Thou madest us for Thyself, and our heart is restless, etc.") is correct, this application is calculated to support his contention for a continuity correlative to his natural theology.

1930 [12] have led to the suggestion that Bultmann's appropriation of the Heideggerian analysis represents an essential reduction, if not a misunderstanding of Heidegger's thought. More recently, such writers as Hellmut Houg [13] have stated that although existential analysis is indifferent to the concrete variety of ontical possibilities in face of which a man may existentially [14] win or lose himself, because that analysis finds the *Dasein* fundamentally determined by a differentiation—i.e. authentic and inauthentic existence—prior to any choice of concrete possibilities, it gives evidence that it is concerned not merely with indicating to man what his decisions are, but also with outlining what makes such decisions genuine decisions. In other words, it is concerned to show what is basically to be decided in all the concrete decisions confronting man. In terms of authentic existence, that would mean that prior to the choice of concrete possibilities there occurs a "choosing of choice," before any concrete decision there is a "choosing of the choice to be a self." [15] Houg concludes by remarking that since the existential analytic always aims at describing that area within which, e.g., the decision for authenticity must take place, and for that reason sets up the conditions under which any exposition of authentic existence must be shown to be a possible exposition, it is questionable whether Bultmann's concept of authentic or "eschatological" existence satisfies even the minimum of these conditions and thus can really be valid as a mode of existence. [16]

It is clearly Houg's contention that Bultmann has misunderstood Heidegger, inasmuch as the seizure of authentic existence in a given, historical instance (a seizure which Bultmann assigns exclusively to the sphere of the ontical) has the ontological "choosing of choice" or "deciding for decision" as its presupposition. If, as Houg, Löwith, and others have suggested, Heidegger's description of the decision for

[12] "Phänomenologische Ontologie und protestantische Theologie," *Zeitschrift für Theologie und Kirche*, 11. Jahrgang (1930), Heft 3, 365-399. The gist of this essay is that although Heidegger distinguishes the ontical from the ontological in theory, in reality his concept of the ontical is charged with ontological significance because of the ideal of authentic existence underlying all his thought.

[13] "Offenbarungstheologie und philosophische Daseins-analyse bei Rudolf Bultmann," *Zeitschrift für Theologie und Kirche*, 55. Jahrgang (1958), Heft 2, 201-253.

[14] The reader will recall the current differentiation between "existential" and "existentiell," analogous to the differentiation between "ontological" and "ontical."

[15] *Ibid.*, pp. 212-13.

[16] *Ibid.*, pp. 230-31.

authenticity is ultimately the description of an ontological decision, a decision involving the constitution of being as such, then Bultmann's concept of the movement of faith as a purely ontical possibility is at least without the philosophical support which he has assumed for it.

Of greater importance, however, is the fact that in his opposition to the revelation purism of Barth, Bultmann has emphasized the aspect of continuity in the transition to the disparagement of contrast, and with unfortunate results, for, when the structures of inauthentic existence are made regulative for authentic being, as indeed they are when any change in those structures is denied to the transition, two fundamental errors may result. The first is that the biblical idea of rebirth may be eliminated in favor of a thoroughgoing scholastic doctrine of justification. To speak of Bultmann's having fallen prey to such an error might, at first, seem preposterous. There are instances, however, in which his thought appears to have carried him dangerously close to this scholastic view. For example, he attempts to support the ontical character of the faith transition by stating that "the justified is righteous only with God and always only with God and is a sinner on earth." [17] In chapter five, volume one of his *Theology*, he describes righteousness as a "forensic-eschatological" term, a righteousness which a person "has in the verdict of the 'forum,' " "in the opinion adjudicated to him by another," a righteousness which he has when he is "acknowledged to be such," [18] a righteousness "imputed to a man." [19] Bultmann's rejection of the idea that the righteous man is a man who is "regarded as if" he were righteous, and his assertion that such a person is "really" righteous is not a modification of the forensic view, inasmuch as he describes "real righteousness" in terms of a being absolved from sin by God's verdict.[20] Without understanding righteousness in this sense, Bultmann concludes, we fall prey either to ethical idealism or to Gnosticism.[21] Abstracted from the philosophical context of Bultmann's thought, the above expressions

[17] Bultmann, "Das Problem der natürlichen Theologie," p. 311.
[18] Bultmann, *Theology of the New Testament*, I, 272.
[19] *Ibid.*, p. 274.
[20] *Ibid.*, p. 276.
[21] *Ibid.*, *pp.* 277-78.

are hardly alarming. However, viewed in connection with his concept of continuity, they become at least suggestive of the old view. Indeed, as early as 1941 Bultmann indicated that he rejected a juridical interpretation of justification according to which "man's plight would be as bad as ever," [22] and in the passage already cited he describes faith as asserting that it "constitutes the basic condition of the *Dasein* anew." [23] But what possible meaning can such statements have when Bultmann has already relegated the concrete resolve of faith purely to the sphere of the ontical and when he refuses to discuss the significance of the new constitution which faith asserts beyond the vague comment that such faith consists "always and only in the conquest of unbelief"? If the movement of faith does not enjoy any "ontological" rank; if, on the contrary, the structures of inauthentic existence are unconditionally guaranteed the status of basically constituting the *Dasein*, then how can that "assertion" of faith be anything more than a mere assertion; how has the situation of man changed? When it is contended that faith, although claiming to constitute human being anew, is nevertheless merely a resolve within the unchanged structures of inauthentic existence, then the biblical concept of rebirth has been totally eliminated and a "legal fiction" theory may lie close at hand, a theory to which Bultmann has apparently crept dangerously near. Then, perhaps, it is not altogether specious that Houg, and Bonhoeffer before him, should see in Bultmann a striking parallel to Flacius,[24] whose description of man as *imago Satanae* provided him the basis for a thoroughgoing doctrine of forensic justification.[25]

The second error which may result from an overemphasis upon continuity in the transition is that the biblical idea of rebirth is abandoned in favor of a concept of faith construed as natural possibility. Again, Bultmann rejects such an idea in principle, and we are immediately

---

[22] Bultmann, "New Testament and Mythology," *Kerygma and Myth*, ed. Hans-Werner Bartsch, tr. R. H. Fuller (London: S.P.C.K., 1954) , p. 32.

[23] Bultmann, "Das Problem der natürlichen Theologie," p. 310.

[24] Matthias Flacius (1520-75) , student of Luther, bitter opponent of Osiander, and perhaps the first to develop a full-blown theory of forensic satisfaction.

[25] Cf. Houg, *op. cit.*, p. 235; and Dietrich Bonhoeffer, *Akt und Sein*, Theologische Bücherei, V (Munich: Chr. Kaiser Verlag, 1956) , 97. In this connection, cf. also the Formula of Concord, Epitome I, Neg. 9.

reminded of the accusation he hurls at philosophy, namely, that it regards as an "actual" possibility for man as such that which in reality is only a "theoretical" possibility.[26] Indeed, his entire argument with philosophy would be nothing but sound and fury if he were not in earnest about such rejection. However, by stating that inauthentic being has a pre-understanding (*Vorverständnis*) of the eschatological possibility of faith,[27] or, that philosophical analysis is cognizant of the faith possibility as an original, lost possibility,[28] Bultmann indicates the degree to which he has been intrigued by the view he proposes to reject.

From the standpoint of the existential analytic, any differentiation of authenticity as "theoretical" and "actual" possibility is suspect. If authentic being is any kind of possibility for man as such, then it is capable of being seized by man as such. Indeed, to deny to man as such the capability of that seizure is to deny to him any cognizance or pre-understanding of it and ultimately to deny to that possibility its character as true possibility. According to the existential analytic, for which knowledge and being are identical, it is inconceivable that man could be aware of a possibility, a true possibility, without at the same time being able to seize it.[29] Bultmann, knowing full well that a concession to this axiom would eliminate the necessity of the grace-event, stubbornly differentiates a knowledge of from a mastery of authenticity, a "theoretical" from an "actual" possibility. Once having set out on his course, how else could he preserve faith from becoming an altogether human, natural phenomenon?

Not only is such a differentiation philosophically suspect—but for Scripture as well, knowing and believing are identical. Bultmann, however, readily admits this.[30] Does he then conceive two types of knowing, one of unbelief and the other of faith? His answer is that the knowledge of inauthentic being is a knowledge which can initiate but

[26] Bultmann, "New Testament and Mythology," p. 29.

[27] *Ibid.*, pp. 24-29.

[28] An assertion which Bultmann qualifies only by adding that that possibility is non-sensible (*sinnlose*) to inauthentic being; cf. "Das Problem der natürlichen Theologie," p. 311.

[29] Cf. Paul Olivier, "Bultmanns Vorverständnis," *Kerygma und Mythos*, ed Hans-Werner Bartsch, I (Hamburg-Volksdorf: Herbert Reich Evangelischer Verlag, 1954), 214.

[30] Bultmann, *Theology of the New Testament*, I, 318.

which cannot effect the transition to authenticity.[31] It is at this point that Bultmann's theological passion raises itself most forcibly against the existential analytic, but in the raising strains his concept of continuity to the breaking point. Thus results that happy contradiction in Bultmann which justifies our regarding him as a Christian theologian and not as a philosopher of absolute finitude. But it is his initial appropriation of the categories of this specific philosophy of existence in support of his idea of continuity, despite his refusal to pursue that appropriation to the bitter end, which fundamentally characterizes his thought and which often brings down on him the reproach of the philosopher—i.e., that his theology can save nothing of its theme in the face of such an appropriation[32]—and of the theologian—i.e., that he has sacrificed the character of the revelation to the infinite claim of philosophy.[33] Because of his sympathy for a view of man and the world whose roots appear to him to lie in Paul, Luther, and Kierkegaard, Bultmann has been led to believe that the only alternative to the dialectic obscurantism for which he reproaches Barth is a concept of continuity construed in terms of immanence.

The question now is: Is there an alternative to the disparagement of continuity other than that which Bultmann proposes? Where may we turn for a concept of continuity which does not endanger the element of contrast but secures to the biblical idea of rebirth its proper place?

It is clear, first of all, that the biblical idea of authenticity or new birth is sociologically, or rather, ecclesiologically orientated. That is not to say that in the rebirth it is no longer the individual who matters, but rather that he lays hold upon his true "identity" (*Eigentlichkeit* for Bultmann) as a member of a corporate personality. In the Bible, authentic existence is never regarded as the existence of the individual man of faith, but always as an existence within that total personality of which Christ is the Head and to which all others are joined as mem-

---

[31] Cf. in this connection Bultmann's description of the cognitive function of conscience in man prior to faith in *Theology of the New Testament*, I, 216-219, and John McQuarrie's comments on his description in *An Existentialist Theology* (New York: The Macmillan Company, 1955), pp. 151-53.

[32] Cf. Fritz Buri, "Entmythologisierung oder Entkerygmatisierung der Theologie," *Kerygma und Mythos*, II, 89.

[33] Cf. Bonhoeffer, *op. cit.*, pp. 55-56.

bers to a body. Nor are that total personality and Christ regarded as identical, but inasmuch as such personality exists only through him and is ruled by his life, it inheres in him.[34] To this concept of authenticity the biblical concept of inauthenticity corresponds. Inauthentic life is characterized not in terms of individual, self-contained existence, though the individual is often described as struggling to achieve selfhood independent of the relational, but again in terms of that corporate existence of which he is a part. Inauthenticity is thus biblically characterized as existence "in Adam." Hence, the continuity between inauthentic and authentic being must not be sought in a purely individualistic context but in terms of a totality of personality which for the Bible characterizes all of human life. The relation between inauthentic being and authentic being is a relation between existence "in Adam" and existence "in Christ." In either case, man's life is characterized by its corporateness; in either case life is lived in relation, whether or not man struggles to assert himself against the other or realizes his authenticity in true community with the other. Inauthentic life may still be described as divorce in the self, as attempt to secure existence in the disposable, as anxiety, et cetera, and authentic life as new understanding of self, as desecularization, as hope, et cetera, but now within the context of corporate existence.

The transition from inauthenticity to authenticity thus involves a change from existence "in Adam" to existence "in Christ." Whether or not such New Testament terms as the "new birth," the "birth from above," et cetera, are initially derived from the Gnostic systems, it is clear that they intend to describe the transition not merely as "ontical" movement but as "ontological" change. Such an expression as the latter, however, is ill-suited to express what occurs in the transition, since it conjures up association with systems which are at base individualistically orientated and therefore inappropriate to the biblical idea.[35] It is because the biblical concept of the "I" or ego as organizing

[34] Traugott Schmidt, *Der Leib Christi.* Eine Untersuchung zum urchristlichen Gemeindegedanken (Leipzig, A. Deichert'sche Verlag, 1919), p. 154.

[35] There are instances in which Bultmann appears to have modified the philosophical view of the self according to its essential features, e.g., when he construes righteousness as a concept of relation, but because this modification is not consistently executed, it is only further evidence of the contradiction in his thought. Cf. Bultmann, *Theology of the New Testament*, I, 272; and Gunther Backhaus, *Kerygma und Mythos bei David Friedrich Strauss und Rudolf Bultmann, Theologische Forschung*, 12 (Hamburg: Herbert Reich Evangelischer Verlag, 1956), 60-61.

principle, preserving identity in the midst of the manifold flux and changes of time, is never construed as immanent in man, as organism or as metaphysical "sum" of individuals, that the continuity between inauthentic and authentic existence cannot be sought in the identity of the "I" in both instances, but rather in the fact that identity is always identity in relation, and that therefore the transition constitutes a radical change from one realm of existence to another.[36] Günther Bornkamm, former pupil of Bultmann, states the case for a qualitative change as follows:

By his incarnation, his obedience (Rom. 5:18 ff.), his death, and his resurrection he has become the saving basis of a new existence. He not only makes possible for me the decision of faith, which I have to make, but prior to that he is the reality of a decision which God in his saving grace has made about me. He not only gives me the possibility of understanding myself anew in my existence and my history, but he opens and discloses to me a new history and a new existence by taking me up into his history. Here, Bultmann's interpretations are, in my opinion, no longer sufficient, for they do not enable us to grasp the reality of the new being in Christ.[37] . . . it is by no means sufficient to describe redemption in such a way that it means nothing more than a new qualification of my own history. Paul means in fact a new history which is no longer mine. This is the purpose of the characteristically "local" expressions of Romans 8, which are of course exposed to mythological abuse (Gnosis provides sufficient examples of this!), but must not be surrendered as being mythological and replaced by definitions of being which are gleaned from existence as such.[38]

The imperatives which Paul, e.g., addresses to his congregations are predicated on such a qualitative change in the "structures of being." [39]

---

[36] This does not, of course, prevent the Bible's speaking of the reception of a "new heart" or a "new mind" in reference to the transition. Such terms, however, are clearly used to combat the error of construing the transition in purely empirical fashion.

[37] It is significant that another pupil of Bultmann, Heinrich Schlier, noted the same error in his teacher, but was led to construe corporate existence in Christ in terms of membership in an empirical institution. Cf. Heinrich Schlier, "A Brief Apologia," *We Are Now Catholics*, ed. by Karl Hardt, trans. by Norman C. Reeves (Westminster, Maryland: The Newman Press, 1959), pp. 206 ff. and 211 ff.

[38] Günther Bornkamm, "Myth and Gospel" in this volume, p. 192.

[39] It would require more space than this essay allows to treat of the relationship between Bultmann's concept of continuity and his interpretation of the biblical imperatives. Suffice it to say that because he does not construe the transition as radical change, an oscillation between a moralistic and an idealistic interpretation of those imperatives results.

It will be obvious to the reader that we have contented ourselves merely with a hint at the biblical view,[40] but this hint ought to have made clear that Bultmann's dilemma does not necessarily root in his appropriation of the existential analytic as such. Indeed, a propos of our discussion, one might well argue that at times Bultmann goes astray not because of his existential interpretation, but rather because of his violation of that interpretation.[41] Bultmann's error lies in his confidence that the existential analytic, with one great exception (the grace-event), can be appropriated uncritically, in his assumption that his epistemology does not require sociological reorientation in order to correspond with the revelation. For this reason his concept of continuity proceeds from pure immanence and deprecates contrast, thus eliminating the biblical idea of the transition as new birth, as true change, and plunges his theology into contradiction. Tenaciously asserting the primacy of the salvation occurrence, but at the same time uncritically appropriating the phenomenology of *Dasein*, Bultmann takes his place with other theologians of mediation, sentenced to the criticism of philosopher and theologian alike, and awaiting correction by his pupils. If the history of such mediation theologies can furnish us any clue to a probable future, however, the theology of Bultmann might well become the source and spring of a healthy tradition to follow.

[40] For further information cf. Roy Harrisville, *The Concept of Newness in the New Testament* (Minneapolis: Augsburg Publishing House, 1960), pp. 73 ff.

[41] An example of which we noted on pp. 222 ff. *supra*. On this point cf. also Backhaus, *op. cit.*, p. 63.

INDEX OF NAMES

INDEX OF SCRIPTURE